Ensuring Competent Performance

in

Forensic Practice

Recovery, Analysis,
Interpretation, and Reporting

Ensuring Competent Performance

in

Forensic Practice

Recovery, Analysis, Interpretation, and Reporting

Keith Hadley
Michael J. Fereday

CRC Press
Taylor & Francis Group
Boca Raton   London   New York

CRC Press is an imprint of the
Taylor & Francis Group, an **informa** business

CRC Press
Taylor & Francis Group
6000 Broken Sound Parkway NW, Suite 300
Boca Raton, FL 33487-2742

© 2008 by Taylor & Francis Group, LLC
CRC Press is an imprint of Taylor & Francis Group, an Informa business

Library of Congress Cataloging-in-Publication Data

Hadley, Keith.
    Ensuring competent performance in forensic practice : recovery, analysis,
interpretation, and reporting / Keith Hadley and Michael J. Fereday.
        p. cm.
    Includes bibliographical references and index.
    ISBN 978-0-8493-3358-3 (alk. paper)
    1. Forensic sciences--Standards. 2. Crime laboratories--Standards. 3.
Performance. I. Fereday, Michael J. II. Title.

HV8073.H217 2008
363.25--dc22   2007021259

**Visit the Taylor & Francis Web site at
http://www.taylorandfrancis.com**

**and the CRC Press Web site at
http://www.crcpress.com**

Dedication

To my wife, Jean; children, Joanne, Elizabeth, and Stuart;
and grandchildren, Jessica, Alexander, Rory, Alicia,
Arran, Maisie, Samuel, Jacob, and Solomon.
Always there for me.

Keith Hadley

To my wife, Lyn, and son, Alex.
Thanks for being there.

Mike Fereday

Contents

Foreword

If all the books written about forensic scientific techniques were to be placed end to end, they would probably span the Atlantic Ocean. If all the books written about ensuring competent performance in forensic practice were placed end to end, they would struggle to span an office desk—a small desk at that.

Forensic science, as Paul Kirk said in a series of excellent papers in the 1960s, has difficulty seeing itself as a profession. Why is this? Why does it not stand alongside medicine and the law as a profession?

The writings of Robertson and Vignaux throw some light on this. The media add to the confusion.

The Forensic Science Society in the United Kingdom is attempting to define forensic science as a profession—we wish it well and applaud it for its initiative. The American Board of Criminalistics shares the same goal. The American Academy of Forensic Sciences does sterling work in promoting all of the forensic scientific practices.

Several universities in the United Kingdom are attempting to collaborate through the newly created United Kingdom Forensic Science Education Group (UKFSEG) to support all UK universities and colleges that wish to present forensic science programs. The Forensic Science Society also offers an accreditation scheme for universities.

However, there is one overriding issue that must be settled urgently before any progress can be made, that is, "What is forensic science?" We have in Chapter 1 attempted to catalyze discussion on this point. At least one police force in the United Kingdom now has a director of criminalistics as head of the scientific support unit. Maybe we are moving forward!

We have asked again some questions posed by Kirk in the 1960s and have attempted to suggest some answers.

Keith Hadley and Mike Fereday
United Kingdom

About the Authors

Keith Hadley, MSc, CChem, MRSC, MCIPD, has been a forensic scientist for more than fifty years. He has practiced forensic science for more than thirty years with the Forensic Science Service (FSS) and in the 1980s headed, for the FSS, the first Centralised Forensic Science Training Unit in the United Kingdom.

In the 1990s he moved on within the FSS, and through a personal initiative commenced the development of a procedure to assess the workplace competence of forensic scientists and police scientific support personnel using a variety of methods culminating in the development of Professional Standards of Competence (National Occupational Standards).

He is a founding member of both the Executive Board of the Council for the Registration of Forensic Practitioners (CRFP), an independent body charged with establishing a register of competent forensic practitioners in the United Kingdom and regulating their practice) and the CRFP Science Assessment Panel, acted as UK liaison with the American Board of Criminalistics (ABC) for many years, and acts in a special advisory capacity to the Skills for Justice Forensic Science Committee, which embraces the forensic science sector in the United Kingdom, and the Association of Chief Police Officers (ACPO) Forensic Science Training Strategy Steering Group (FSTSSG). As a project leader for a variety of projects in the United Kingdom and Europe, all concerned with the assessment of the performance, training, and education of forensic scientists, he has developed an international reputation in the field.

E-mail address: Khforensic@blueyonder.co.uk; mobile: 07812 059666; telephone: 0121 550 1639.

Michael J Fereday, BSc, CChem, CSCi, FRSC, has been a forensic scientist for forty years, starting his career in South Wales before moving to the Aldermaston laboratory of the Forensic Science Service (FSS), where he was head of chemistry. He was actively involved in the investigative work which culminated in the release from prison of the "Birmingham Six"—one of several notorious cases resulting from the IRA bombing campaign of the 1970s which resulted in miscarriages of justice.

For the past ten years, he has been working in the area of professional standards, being actively involved in the development of standards for forensic scientists in the United Kingdom and Europe, and is currently based at the London laboratory of the FSS.

He is heavily involved with the Council for the Registration of Forensic Practitioners (CRFP) as secretary and as a lead assessor for the Science Sector Assessment panel. He was a member of the CRFP Executive Board until October 2006.

He is actively involved with the Sector Skills Council currently responsible for the forensic science sector (Skills for Justice) as a member of the Forensic Science Sector Committee. From 2004 to 2006, he was a member of the board of the Science,

Engineering, Manufacturing Technologies Alliance (SEMTA), which was the Sector Skills Council previously responsible for the forensic science sector.

He is very active on the Competence Assurance Project Group of the European Network of Forensic Science Institutes (ENFSI), which is developing a competence assurance scheme from European forensic practitioners, and he has presented on this subject in Australia, the United States, and much of Europe.

He has been a member of the FSS for more than thirty-five years, sat on the Academic and Education Committee of the Forensic Science Society (FSSoc) as an employer representative, and was vice chairman of the Professional Awards Committee (now the Standards Committee) of the Society and a member of council.

1 Introduction

In terms of public perception, forensic science is arguably one of the most fascinating areas of science within our society. It captures the imagination of millions through documentaries and television serials, and is mentioned virtually every day in the press or on TV. It is probably one of the highest profile applications of science known [1]. But is forensic science "science?" And what, indeed, is this much talked about and popularized subject called "forensic science?" It certainly attracts the attention of millions when a case in which it is involved is overturned when the forensic scientific evidence is shown to be unsound.

DEFINING FORENSIC SCIENCE

In his 1963 paper, Kirk [2] said that criminalistics is a profession that

> has all the responsibility of medicine, the intricacy of the law and the universality of science. In as much as it carries higher penalties for error than other professions it is a matter not to take lightly, nor to trust to luck.

What did Kirk mean by "criminalistics?" Probably he meant forensic science as defined by most, if not all, of the major forensic science service providers in the United Kingdom.

One might be forgiven for assuming that a profession carrying such responsibility should have no difficulty in recognizing its own identity—yet apparently it does.

So what is it about forensic science that makes it so difficult to define?

In its simplest terms, forensic science is science that is used in support of any legal process. It follows from this that any branch of science that is used in the resolution of legal disputes is a forensic science.

The Forensic Science Society (FSSoc) definition of forensic science supports this by stating, "Forensic science can be simply defined as the application of science to the law."

Those of us who have worked for many years with the major forensic science service providers in the United Kingdom see the profession of "forensic science" as being something more than simply "any science that is used in support of the justice system," whilst, on the other hand, not denying the assertion that "any science is potentially a forensic science." How can this apparent dilemma be reconciled?

The American Academy of Forensic Sciences (AAFS) defines forensic science as "science used in public, in a court or in the justice system. Any science, used for the purposes of the law, is a forensic science."

This is in line with the initial sweeping statement that any science has the potential to be a forensic science. It is also in line with the view of the Forensic Science Society in the United Kingdom.

The problem associated with the identity of forensic science was probably exacerbated when we, in the United Kingdom, began to use the title "forensic science" for what is apparently, in the United States, criminalistics, thereby subtly changing the meaning of forensic science provided by the elegant AAFS definition. We cannot interchange the words "forensic science" for "criminalistics" and still adhere to the AAFS definition of forensic science. By calling forensic science criminalistics, we make the assumption that the word "criminalistics" can be freely exchanged for the term "forensic science" in the AAFS definition. That clearly is not so. So what is special about criminalistics? Kirk [2] said that criminalistics is more about individualizing than identifying. For any scientist practicing pure science become a scientist supporting justice, it is likely to be through what Kirk calls identification. For example, an analytical chemist may unequivocally identify a fragment of material as paint. A forensic scientist (practicing the science as practiced in most forensic science service providers in the United Kingdom) might not only attempt to identify the material as paint, but also attempt to take it to a higher level (individualization) by stating that it is vehicle paint originating from a particular model of a particular manufacturer of motor vehicles, and in some instances go on to say it originated from a particular vehicle. Indeed, forensic science, as most in the profession understand it, could identify the paint as coming from a particular vehicle by using techniques not particularly "scientific" such as the physical fit of a fragment of paint, or of whatever, to a suspect vehicle; color and other simple physical features; and relevant data banks. (This hopefully does not give the impression that the word "scientific" is being used to give some form of credibility to something which is not credible [which is often the case in popular and incorrect use of the word "scientific"].) Although not particularly "scientific," the scientific process applies in carrying out the work.

Today, of course, the various DNA techniques bring us *almost* to the ultimate of individualization.

If criminalistics relates to the investigation of crime, the substituted term "forensic science" in the definition would also need to dedicate itself to crime investigation. Such an assumption would make the "forensic science" of the AAFS definition of forensic science relate only to criminal justice systems, and this clearly is not the case. Additionally in the United Kingdom, particularly in the 1950s and 1960s, there was a clear association of the forensic science laboratories with definite police force areas, thereby strongly suggesting that forensic science was solely in the domain of criminal investigations and, indeed, in those days allied solely with the prosecution. This discussion is clearly identifying criminalistics, as understood and used in the United States, as probably identical to forensic science as understood by most of the major providers of forensic science services in the United Kingdom.

Turning to the considerations of the AAFS when arriving at its definition that forensic science is science used in public, in a court, or in the justice system means that any science, used for the purposes of the law, is a forensic science.

The AAFS considered the following when arriving at its definition of forensic science:

> The word forensic comes from the Latin word forensis: public; to the forum or public discussion; argumentative, rhetorical, belonging to debate or discussion. From there it is a small step to the modern definition of forensic as belonging to, used in or suitable to courts of judicature, or to public discussion or debate.

The last sentence brings just about everyone who may be involved in the legal process under the definition of the word "forensic."

So is it possible to recognize such emerging terms as "head of forensics" for who is clearly the head of a forensic science laboratory? Or "director of forensic services" for who is clearly the head of police scientific support services? What are forensic police officers? And now we have forensic vehicle examiners! The last two terms are vying for popular use. These titles are at least a little bizarre when considered against the root of the word "forensic." A new verb, "to forensicate," is being increasingly used to describe examining the scene. The word "forensic," or indeed "forensics" when used alone, must surely include everyone, not only scientists, who has a part to play in the justice system.

Nevertheless, popular usage must be considered, and this seems to suggest that the word "forensic" or "forensics," when used alone, applies specifically to science that is used solely in the criminal justice system. The question must be put! Is that what the profession wants? There is clearly an urgent need for a debate on this vital subject, for if we cannot agree on our identity, what chance has forensic science of being recognized as a profession? The Forensic Science Society, as a newly emerging professional body, would do well to ponder this.

It may be that to fall in line with the AAFS definition of forensic science, we consider as separate issues forensic science and the forensic science(s), and that forensic science is a subject in its own right and is in fact one of the many forensic sciences! So we have forensic science, forensic chemistry, forensic archeology, and so on as forensic sciences. The AAFS, as an organization, rightly deals with all sciences, and therefore all scientists, that are involved in the legal process. As reflected through its title, the American Academy of Forensic Sciences includes within its remit "forensic science" as it does "criminalistics," amongst all of the other sciences that may be used in the legal process. There is an overwhelming emerging case to make forensic science (singular, as opposed to plural) a profession in its own right and criminalistics (which is a profession in its own right) a very special branch of the forensic sciences.

Chemistry, biology, archeology, odontology, and so on are all "sciences," and scientists practicing such pure science produce reports on the results of their scientific work; occasionally these scientists may be called upon to enter the arena of the justice system, whether it be civil, criminal, family, or whatever. It follows from the definition given earlier that such scientists could be viewed as forensic scientists for the short time that they may be involved with whatever branch of the justice system—and that such "occasional forensic scientists" should not always be considered forensic scientists.

Forensic scientists would recognize each other as people whose day-to-day activity (or specialism) consisted of using science for the benefit of the justice system, particularly in an evaluative mode. A good example of this emerging view of a forensic scientist comes from the financial sector. Here the term "forensic accountant" means an accountant who specializes by using accounting skills for the benefit of the justice system on a day-to-day basis. Many of the larger accountancy firms will have departments specializing in forensic accountancy, and accountants of some other specialism within accountancy would not be seen as forensic accountants just because, on the odd occasion, they gave evidence in court.

This discussion of forensic science brings us to the writings of Robertson and Vignaux [3]. In their book they describe how, in their view, a forensic scientist demonstrates differences to other scientists through discussing how scientists in other disciplines base their predictions on the results of replicable experiments whereas forensic scientists may have to come to a decision based on, in some cases, single nonreplicable items of information.

They go on to say that forensic scientists who consider themselves competent in the examination of blood, glass, etc. must also make themselves familiar with the interpretational armory of forensic science.

This does appear to place forensic science in a category apart from other sciences and indeed gives some academic meaning to the profession. It is undeniably different from other sciences, and this fact is expressed eloquently by Robertson and Vignaux.

There is a difference between a forensic medical examiner providing an opinion on causation of tissue damage in a case of malicious wounding and the Accident and Emergency (A&E) doctor (medical examiner) who provides testimony as to the extent of damage (fact) at the time the individual presented at the hospital A&E department.

Does the word "science" encompass all aspects of the work of the modern forensic science service provider? Given the range of activities now undertaken, from fire investigation to image analysis, fingerprints, metallurgical investigations, pathology, facial reconstruction, cell phone analysis, computer investigations, and more, does the word "science" adequately cover them? Most definitions of science would comfortably apply to these activities, as they would to geology, medicine, archeology, and others. It is true to say that the blanket term "forensic science" covers an expanding subgroup of specialisms. People practicing in these areas could be described as forensic scientists specializing in fire investigation, cell phone analysis, and the like. However, some individuals prefer to refer to themselves as a "document examiner" or "fire investigator" or "forensic (whatever)" because they do not consider themselves to be forensic scientists. However, all of these activities are primarily about individualization, providing that often elusive link between people and people, people and places, and people and objects. It is perhaps partly for this reason that the Council for the Registration of Forensic Practitioners (CRFP) refers to "forensic practitioners"— a cover-all term used for a police scene of crime officers, veterinarians, fingerprint experts, medical examiners, archeologists, anthropologists, pediatricians, and document examiners— rather than the term "forensic scientists." It could arguably include police officers and lawyers within the term "forensic practitioner"—a little thought will show that the list is almost endless. As a matter of discussion from earlier deliberations on the meaning of the word "forensic," does the term "forensic practitioner" include anyone associated with the legal process? Surely those playing any part in the legal process (lawyers, as an example) qualify for using the term "forensic" to describe their role.

It may be useful to consider all those who attempt the individualization of evidence in their day-to-day work as forensic scientists, whatever basic science they use to do this. These will in the main support investigations being carried out by the police or other investigating agencies, for example customs and excise and immigration. Their evidence may be used equally in the civil, criminal, or other parts of the justice systems and by either the defense or the prosecution, or their equivalent. There will be blurred borders to some extent. For example, the person within a forensic science laboratory who does no other job than to analyze material for the presence of drugs is acting purely as a highly skilled analytical chemist and simply *identifying* the material. If, however, the analyst takes the matter further and individualizes to some extent by carrying out some form of drug-profiling work to ascertain possible sources of the drug or carrying out work comparing the marks on wrappers, then that analyst becomes a forensic scientist by clearly carrying out some form of *individualization*. The analyst who does nothing more than identify the material as a particular drug is primarily acting as an analytical chemist. It is surprising and maybe a little disturbing to realize that many of those teaching forensic science in universities do not fully appreciate this.

There is a further view on a definition for forensic science expressed under the jurisprudence section on the AAFS Web site: "'forensic science' may generally be defined as the application of 'scientific, technical or other specialized knowledge' to assist courts in resolving questions of fact in civil and criminal cases." This does support what has been said in categorizing forensic science, or criminalistics, as one of a number of forensic sciences, where forensic scientists (criminalists) use many "sciences" in a very special way.

In the end, whatever we call those individuals who bring their professional skills into the legal arena—whether they be forensic scientists (criminalists), forensic chemists, forensic document examiners, forensic pathologists, or whatever—they all have one thing in common: accountability. They must all, in some way, be personally accountable for the quality of the work they carry out on a daily basis.

PERSONAL ACCOUNTABILITY

The traditional role of the trusted professional is now, more than ever, under pressure, and the end users of any professional service are demanding to be provided with proof of practitioner competence and are now less willing to defer without question to expert opinion. The users of the professional service are more likely to challenge findings and interpretations, and are also more likely to seek legal redress when the opinion is shown to be wrong, unsound, or unsafe. This is in line with the view of the CRFP.

Improvement in the quality of service provision is being sought through the adoption of a variety of quality assurance schemes. In the past, quality was seen as part and parcel of professional advice, and was considered to be beyond challenge. This is no longer acceptable, and all practitioners have to achieve measurable levels of service quality.

Kirk [2] said, when considering forensic science as a profession, that a profession

- is based on an extensive period of training at a high educational level.
- is characterized by some generally recognized and accepted code of behavior or ethics.
- requires established competence.

It is this last criterion relating to competence that is worthy of further consideration. Kirk went on to say that this may seem to be subsidiary to the extensive training, which was mentioned first. However, he rightly said that this is not so, implying that training does not guarantee competence.

There is overwhelming agreement that the end users of forensic science need to be assured of the competence of those who practice. Currently, end users being served by organizations employing more than a handful of forensic scientists tend to focus not on the competence of those who practice forensic science, but on the (often perceived) quality of the organization for which they work as demonstrated through some form of proficiency-testing programs. Indeed, great strides have been made in looking at organizational quality through quality management systems and accreditation. However, it is important to remember that accreditation of a laboratory does not of itself confirm that the staff of that laboratory is competent. This approach needs to be extended to individuals and to look at personal competence or personal accountability and the concept of common standards of performance for practitioners of forensic science.

Why is it important to have common standards and to understand what is meant by standards? It is important because the key stakeholders in the process are not the forensic scientists but the users of forensic science—the law enforcement agencies, the criminal justice system, and, of course, ultimately the public. They have the right to expect the same competent performance from forensic scientists irrespective of where or by whom that science is practiced.

COMPETENCE

Peter Barnett [5] said,

> Issues of technical competence have always been troublesome since there is no general agreement on what criminalists (forensic scientists) need to know in order to do their job. There is no uniform college or university curriculum, there [are] no universally applicable licensing or certification requirements, there are no universally accepted employment criteria, and there are no professional criteria for on the job training.

The standards referred to here are probably specific standards of performance giving details of exactly how a task should be carried out. Procedural standards are not the only important issue when monitoring workplace performance; they do, of course, have a place. Indeed, what professional would tolerate being told, "This is the only way that this task must be carried out?" Or, more bluntly, "There are two ways of carrying out this activity: the way I dictate and the wrong way." Several years ago in the United Kingdom, a program of work was started, at the instigation and support of the FSS, to develop a procedure that would in the first place be flexible enough to recognize that there may well be more than one acceptable way of carrying out a task yet rigorous enough to reject any unwanted practices.

Some progress has been made toward that goal.

Some of the methods that have been used and that are still being used to address competence are summarized here.

TRAINING

This was, and is by many still, seen as the answer to all of the questions on competence. It is not. Training is a means to an end and not an end in itself. That training does not guarantee competence was implied by Kirk [2] in his 1963 paper, "The Ontogeny of Criminalistics." Training says very little, if anything, about workplace competence, and discussions have continued for many years on how to transfer performance from the training room to the workplace without any satisfactory outcome. And what is the training curriculum anyway? Who decides it?

LABORATORY ACCREDITATION

There is no doubt that laboratory accreditation has a vital role to play in ensuring that the laboratory has acceptable procedures in place to carry out its day-to-day work. In the United Kingdom, the United Kingdom Accreditation Service (UKAS) is the sole national accreditation body recognized by government to assess, against internationally agreed standards, organizations that provide certification, testing, inspection, and calibration services. The UKAS currently assesses and accredits several of the larger providers of forensic science in the United Kingdom. The definition of "accreditation" is given in ISO Guide 2 [6] as a "procedure by which an authoritative body gives formal recognition that a body or person is competent to carry out specific tasks" It does not seem to describe competence, and neither does it describe standards. Part of the assessment process involves ensuring that an organization has acceptable procedures in place, that they are followed on a day-to-day basis, and that staff are trained to do the work for which the organization offers a service. But, does it say that staff can do that work competently? Or does it assume that training guarantees competence?

Accreditation is being embraced across Europe, and the European Network of Forensic Science Institutes (ENFSI) requires all of its members to be working toward accreditation by a relevant national or international body.

The American Society of Crime Laboratory Directors/Laboratory Accreditation Board (ASCLD/LAB) provides a program of laboratory accreditation in which any crime laboratory can participate to demonstrate that its management, personnel, operational, and technical procedures, equipment, and physical factors meet established standards. However, such accreditation schemes say little if anything about consistent personal workplace competence.

CERTIFICATION

The American Board of Criminalistics (ABC) has done sterling work in building on the groundbreaking work of the Californian Association of Criminalists (CAC) certification program. Here, knowledge-based examinations are used as the measure of the competence of practitioners. However, here again, there is little real consideration of workplace competence except through the occasional proficiency-testing program. The ABC approach is based on four principles:

1. No single examination is a total measure of an individual's ability to do the work. Examinations measure knowledge and reasoning.
2. A general understanding of a field is needed in addition to specializing.
3. Knowledge measured on an examination only reflects the understanding at that point in time. Continuing professional education is needed.
4. Practical exercises (proficiency tests) help measure one's ability to apply the knowledge.

REGISTRATION

There is little doubt that the best attempt to date to ensure that practitioners are performing competently in the workplace is the procedure now in use by the relatively newly emerged Council for the Registration of Forensic Practitioners (CRFP) of the United Kingdom. Here, ten basic criteria are used to gauge the work of forensic scientists. More will be said about the CRFP registration program later.

PROFICIENCY TESTING

Proficiency testing has been extensively used to measure the performance of forensic scientists. (See earlier mention of this under the ABC program.) It does this in one specific activity at one time. In other words, it gives a "snapshot" of performance at a point in time. However, usually, this is not true "workplace performance," that is to say, performance on "live" casework in typical casework situations. As such, far too much can be read into the apparent assurance such schemes provide. It does have its uses, however, for example, benchmarking performance against other people or organizations doing the same thing.

KNOWLEDGE-BASED EXAMINATIONS

These are just what they say: a "test" of knowledge at a particular time. There are several providers, notably the ABC (above) and the FSSoc, which currently offer diplomas for a variety of forensic scientific specialisms: crime scene examination, document examination, fire investigation, firearms examination, and forensic imaging. These involve the testing of relevant knowledge and skills.

WHAT IS COMPETENCE?

How is competence recognized? Is it about how a person dresses or looks? Is it about qualifications or experience? Is someone who has been doing something for thirty years more competent than someone who has been doing it for only five years? There are senior laboratory managers who say, "I know that the members of my staff are competent." However, when they are asked how they have made this judgment, they are unable to offer anything but a personal, subjective view of what a competent person would look like. That is a bit like asking someone to define an elephant, and getting the answer that to do so is not necessary because they will know one when they see one! It is impossible to define, and hence recognize, competence in any objective manner in the absence of some form of agreed standards against which to measure performance.

Just what is competence, and what is it not? Competence is about performing the role—for example, of a forensic scientist or forensic pathologist—competently. It is about demonstrating competent performance in the workplace for critical activities, and sometimes in the training environment for noncritical issues. It is not directly about qualifications and training. A "highly qualified" person need not be an occupationally competent person, and, unfortunately, we see far too many examples of this today. Ultimately, competence is the ability to work to the standards set by the profession.

Again, competence is *the ability to work to standards set by the profession.*

Is it possible for different individuals and organizations to have different standards of competence? Well, yes it is, or at least there exists the likelihood for different approaches. For example, it is possible to have individuals working to different standards in the same country. Moreover, even if every practitioner worked to the same standard in one country, that standard may be different from those of neighboring countries. It is probably better to approach the situation from a global standpoint and reduce the variation that inevitably exists when individual organizations or indeed individuals go their own way.

Competence is a mix of knowledge, skills, and the application of knowledge (working to standards) and behavior and attitudes. All of these are essential to defining competence.

What about knowledge? Relevant scientific knowledge is essential but alone is not enough. It is important to know about forensic science itself and the forensic scientific process, and how to apply scientific knowledge to the solution of forensic problems.

As to skills, there are the application of technical skills and the application of "forensic scientific" skills; by this is meant the following:

- Assessment of the requirements of a case
- Interpretation of forensic scientific data
- Report writing

It is the "forensic scientific" skills which are key to this; the modern forensic scientist is a forensic science data processor with the accent on data processing and not data generation.

To complete the competence equation, we have to consider behavior and attitudes. It is possible to be skilled and knowledgeable, but if the right behavior and attitudes are not portrayed, the practitioner cannot be classed as competent.

All of this is about individuals involved in the forensic process. Within this is the forensic scientific process, which may be described as a series of discrete steps between the apprehension of a suspect or investigation of a crime and the conclusion of an investigation at a court of law or tribunal.

What is the connection between the forensic scientific process as described here and competence? All individuals must demonstrate competence at all points in the process in which they will be involved; the chain of competence is built on the weakest link. The competence of the forensic scientist can be compromised if individuals working in other parts of the forensic process are not themselves peritus. We need to be able to determine if such a compromise has taken place.

Incompetent evidence collection or incompetent laboratory work leads to the wrong results being delivered to the judicial system. An example of this could be a crime scene investigator not correctly collecting and packaging material for laboratory examination leading in some instances to contaminated material being submitted for laboratory examination.

KEY ROLES IN THE FORENSIC PROCESS

There are many key roles in the forensic process, and in the forensic scientific process alone we can readily identify discrete steps:

- Scene investigation
- Laboratory examination
- Interpretation
- Reporting

In some forensic science organizations a single individual may perform all of these roles, whereas in others the individuals involved may be required to perform only one or two of the roles. No matter who does what, they will need to demonstrate in some acceptable way that they can work competently in that role. In developing standards, the task being carried out is considered, and not the person carrying out the task. That comes later.

STANDARDS

What is the importance of standards in all of this? Standards are the key to everything associated with ensuring competent performance. How do we define them so that they are meaningful? Should they be defined tightly? There are dangers in making standards too specific. Standards, expressed in terms of outcomes, are preferable for reasons which will become clearer later. Nowhere in this work will the standards define *how* a job must be done; there are numerous sources of this information. Again, the standard will not dictate *how* a job is to be done, a feature which is often found confusing.

Effective standards should define *what* has to be achieved or demonstrated by a competent person when carrying out an activity. Once again, they should not define *how* the desired outcome is achieved—many expect the standard to spell out exactly what must be done, but that is not the case at this point.

Two simple examples may aid the reader in understanding this vital and often misunderstood feature of standards that are to be used to ensure competent workplace performance. For the first example, there could be a standard governing a departure from London's Heathrow Airport. One part of the standard could be "You will arrive at London's Heathrow Airport in sufficient time to catch your flight." Note that the standard does not describe how that is done. "Sufficient" time may vary depending on the carrier. Arriving safely could be done by taxi, car, bus, or the like. The second example is a standard that could relate to the identification of drugs. The standard may state that the drug must be identified unequivocally. However, it does not say which technique must be used to achieve that standard. There may be more than one acceptable way of achieving the standard. Thus, through the use of outcome-based standards, practitioners can use different approaches to achieve the same result. The acceptability or not of these different approaches is addressed in a strategy for assessing workplace performance against the standards.

What is required is a set of principles that will guide us, both nationally and maybe internationally, in our quest for uniform standards that will form the basis of methods to monitor the performance of an individual and also to provide the basis of many other important activities all supporting competent performance. In view of this, there needs to be in place a procedure that will not monitor how a task is carried out but that will simply and unambiguously detect the agreed outcomes of carrying out a task. In other words, the standards define the expected outcome of carrying out any task. The method to be used to ensure that the standards are being achieved must support effective peer review and third-party scrutiny of that review and assessment process; therefore, the methods used for documenting all activities associated with assessing workplace competence must support review and scrutiny.

All of this seems a lot to ask of already overburdened practitioners but maybe not when the enormity of getting things "not quite right" is considered. The earlier reference to Kirk is worthy of repeat here:

> Criminalistics has all the responsibility of medicine, the intricacy of the law and the universality of science. In as much as it carries higher penalties for error than other professions it is a matter not to take lightly, nor to trust to luck.

There are those who say that they are the only "expert" in a particular field and that there is no one person, anywhere, who is capable of carrying out third-party scrutiny or review of their work. We must ask the question "Should such people be practicing in the justice system?" If the information they give to investigating teams is nothing more than guidance for the direction of the investigation, then the answer may well be "yes." However, all methods and techniques used in the judicial arena must be vigorously validated before information from them is brought before the courts as primary evidence, and all work carried out must be capable of withstanding robust, independent, third-party review. In other words, is the evidence to evidential standards?

It is this opportunity for third-party scrutiny and review that has guided and inspired the work to develop a procedure that should go some way to ensuring that practitioners are achieving and maintaining workplace competence in forensic science.

We appear to have entered the very popular arena of attempting to define forensic science. The work to be described in this book, with some minor modifications, is equally applicable to all whose work impinges on the justice system (and indeed elsewhere). It will apply equally to those investigating accidents, those investigating suspicious fires, document examiners, those utilizing the science of archaeology, those using the skills of the pathologist, and, topically, those involved in the investigation of e-crime—indeed, everyone practicing one or another of the "forensic sciences."

REFERENCES

1. Forensic Science: Implications for Higher Education, Science, Engineering, Manufacturing Technologies Alliance (SEMTA) (2004).
2. P L Kirk, Journal of Criminal Law, Criminology and Police Science 54, 235 (1963).
3. Bernard Robertson and A G Vignaux, Interpreting Evidence, Wiley, Chichester, UK (1995).
4. P L Kirk, Science 40, 367 (1963).
5. Peter D Barnett, Ethics in Forensic Science: Professional Standards for the Practice of Criminalistics, CRC Press, Boca Raton, FL (2001).
6. ISO/IEC Guide 2: 2004 Standardization and Related Activities — International Organization for Standardization.

2 Standards

Standards provide the key to procedures that will support forensic scientists to achieve and maintain occupational competence and provide evidence they have done just that. They also provide a basis for developing meaningful training and education programs. Although this use of standards may, to most, be as obvious as night following day, it is interesting to discover that this is a view that is not held by all. To some, the fact that they see themselves as professionals or "experts" and are highly academically or professionally qualified means that standards are unnecessary. This is a strange and totally unacceptable view.

What are standards?

There is certainly a lot of confusion over what constitutes a standard.

DEFINING STANDARDS

It is, perhaps, interesting to consider the meaning of the very word "standard," a word that can elicit slightly different interpretations by different people. The *Concise Oxford Dictionary of Current English* has a definition of the noun "standard" as a "[w]eight or measure to which others conform or by which the accuracy or quality of others is judged."

Many people have a very fixed view of what a standard is, particularly when the word is used as an adjective, as in "standard method," and invariably believe a standard is in some way set in tablets of stone that describe in great detail the only way a task can be carried out. The terms "gold standard," "silver standard," and even "minimum standard" are often used by people, sometimes inappropriately. A standard is a standard—no more and no less. Some people use the term "minimum standard" in an almost derogatory way.

One way to consider this is to look at something remote from forensic science, such as qualifying to be a member of a national squad for some event in the Olympic Games. The qualifying time may be three minutes. That is the "standard" that must be achieved to qualify as a team member. Some people may run a race in three minutes exactly, whereas others may run their race in a lesser (quicker) time. It matters not. All potential team members achieving three minutes or less will have achieved the "standard." Some people like to refer to this as a "minimum standard." It is not. There is no "minimum standard" or any other standard; there is simply the "standard."

The terms "gold standard" and "silver standard" date back to describing the proportion of precious metal in an item. The "standard" for jewelry and other gold items is another example of the use of the word "standard." To meet the nine-carat "standard" means an item has to contain a certain proportion of gold. It is not a "minimum standard," and it is acceptable for an item to contain more than the specified amount. It has simply met the "nine-carat standard."

There are of course examples where a particular standard is an "absolute standard," an exact and very accurate measure (e.g., time, weight, or length) against which all other items (clocks, weights, rulers, etc.) are compared.

The "professional standards" described by Peter Barnett [1] are actually ethics and are concerned among other things with rules of profession conduct and the activities of committees that judge alleged cases of misconduct.

The standards for forensic practice to be discussed here are different from the standards that have been discussed thus far in that they will describe the outcome of carrying out any of the many tasks in the extensive repertoire of a forensic practitioner. Because of this, they are often called "outcome-based" standards and are ideally placed to underpin procedures to assure the workplace competence of forensic practitioners.

Standards are broadly classified into three types: procedural, professional, and occupational.

Procedural Standards

Procedural standards are concerned with the procedures used within organizations or by individuals, that is, the way a task is carried out. They are often accredited by recognized bodies such as the United Kingdom Accreditation Services (UKAS).

It is often, mistakenly, thought that these standards are all that is needed. They are not, for one very vital reason. Procedural standards say very little if anything about personal competence or how effectively the accredited procedures are used by individuals.

Professional Standards

Professional standards cover such vital issues as ethics and codes of practice [1].

Occupational Standards

These are the outcome-based standards already briefly mentioned. They do not say how a task is carried out; that is the purpose of procedural standards. They provide a framework for ensuring procedural standards are used in the correct way. Therefore, together procedural and occupational standards are vital for ensuring personal competence in forensic practice—or in any other profession, for that matter.

It would be a major advance if, when standards are referred to, they could be classified.

SOME HISTORY

To understand how the current proposals have evolved, it may be useful to review some of the early work.

The development and agreement of outcome-based standards for the many forensic scientific activities and associated police scientific support activities were traditionally catered for by the Forensic Science Lead Body Consortium, which represented employers of forensic scientists and police scientific support personnel in the United Kingdom. The consortium was supported by the then UK government body, the Department for Education and Employment (DfEE). Under this body, the sector developed nationally agreed standards known as National Occupational Standards for a number of forensic scientific activities and police scientific support work [2].

These National Occupational Standards are:

- Investigating scenes of incident
- Managing and coordinating scenes of incident
- Recovering materials of evidential value—laboratory based
- Document examination
- Blood and body fluids
- Marks and impressions
- Fingerprint operations
- Accident investigations
- Firearms
- Trace evidence

National Occupational Standards describe what individuals must do in order for them to be considered competent to carry out a particular task. Although they require the demonstration of conceptual and factual knowledge, they are concerned primarily with the ability of individuals to apply this knowledge in the workplace wherever that may be—in other words, the ability of practitioners to use the various accredited procedural standards.

The profession used National Occupational Standards as a basis for the development of National and Scottish Vocational Qualifications (N/SVQs); however, these qualifications were never accepted, being perceived as far too bureaucratic to implement. But the principles on which N/SVQs are based were fully embraced by the Forensic Science Sector Committee (formerly the Forensic Science Lead Body) as the employer representative body, and National Occupational Standards were accepted as a basis for the assessment of workplace competence and as a focus for the development of training and education programs. The sector was now working with the support of the Science Technology and Mathematics Council (ST&MC), the National Training Organisation (NTO) for forensic science.

The standards are represented as a number of individual units, each unit dealing with a particular activity of an individual's job. All such units are laid out in a similar way, providing an easy reference to the content of the standard.

The units for the activity "Recovering Material of Evidential Value—Laboratory Based" are:

1. Prepare to carry out laboratory-based recovery.
2. Carry out laboratory-based recovery of materials.
3. Contribute to the operational effectiveness of the working environment.
4. Provide information and documentation.
5. Establish and maintain effective working relationships.
6. Contribute to the maintenance of health and safety in the workplace.
7. Carry out primary analysis of recovered material.

The standards describe what an individual must do to be recognized as occupationally competent.

Following the rejection of N/SVQs, a new direction was sought, and very soon a set of outcome-based generic occupational standards was seen as the way forward and was developed by the sector with the support of the ST&MC. These standards are called "Professional Standards of Competence" or "National Occupational Standards." To complement this work, an assessment strategy was developed and accepted. The standards and assessment strategy remain in place and are beginning to be taken up by the profession. To bring the history up-to-date, the government has now created a number of Sector Skills Councils (SSCs), the NTO for forensic science no longer exists, and the profession, under this new scheme, was supported initially by the Science, Engineering, Manufacturing Technologies Alliance (SEMTA) SSC, which on the demise of the NTOs took over the responsibilities of the ST&MC. The Forensic Science Sector Committee was then known as the Forensic Science Sector Strategy Group (FSSSG), and with the support of SEMTA the generic Professional Standards of Competence and the Assessment Strategy were completed and a major report on higher education in forensic science delivered [3].

Another change took place in September 2006, and the forensic science profession has now migrated to the Sector Skills Council for the Justice Sector—Skills for Justice, which amongst its activities caters to the police sector for which it has developed a suite of National Occupational Standards. Skills for Justice (SfJ) has also developed National Occupational Standards for Crime Scene Investigation and fingerprint operations. The FSSSG is now known as the Skills for Justice Forensic Science Committee and is called the Forensic Science Occupational Committee.

NATIONAL AND SCOTTISH VOCATIONAL QUALIFICATIONS

The National and Scottish Vocational Qualification (N/SVQ) program offers a set of qualifications based on units at a range of levels which are underpinned by nationally defined and agreed standards of competence—National Occupational Standards. They hallmark performance in the workplace.

To understand N/SVQs [2], it is necessary to consider how they have been developed—a lot of the hostility aimed at N/SVQs was undoubtedly through a lack of understanding of what they offered, and this needs remedying.

The first task of the Lead Body was to establish small working groups of practitioners to develop the standards on which the qualifications were to be based. These practitioners were identified by employers, through the Lead Body, as best practitioners in their particular fields, and they carried out their standards development work under the guidance of a specialist consultant. To start the qualification development process, an occupational and functional mapping exercise of the profession, which was an attempt to define the extent of the sector and the roles and types of work identified (see Appendix 1 and Appendix 6 at the end of the book). The outcome of this exercise identified the many tasks associated with forensic science and for which National Occupational Standards needed to be developed. Note at this time, August 2007, work is being initiated through Skills for Justice to carry out a new Occupational and Functional map.

To aid an explanation of what N/SVQs stand for, "The N/SVQ for Recovering Material of Evidential Value—Laboratory Based" will serve.

THE N/SVQ FOR RECOVERING MATERIAL OF EVIDENTIAL VALUE— LABORATORY BASED

This N/SVQ, like all others, is described in terms of high-level activities called "units," where a unit is essentially an activity associated with the act of recovering material of evidential value.

As stated above, the full suite of units for "Recovering Material of Evidential Value—Laboratory Based" identified by the specialist practitioner working group is:

1. Prepare to carry out laboratory-based recovery.
2. Carry out laboratory-based recovery of materials.
3. Contribute to the operational effectiveness of the working environment.
4. Provide information and documentation.
5. Establish and maintain effective working relationships.
6. Contribute to the maintenance of health and safety in the workplace.
7. Carry out primary analysis of recovered material.

Units 3, 5, 6, and 7 do not strictly apply to carrying out the task of recovering evidential material; those units that do are 1, 2, and 4. Why do units not strictly applicable to the task need to be included? The "other" units (i.e., 3, 5, 6, and 7) are included because the N/SVQ looks at a job holistically and says that for an individual to be effective, as well as competent, there may be other qualities needed in addition to those solely concerned with the task in hand. One of these, Unit 5 ("Establish and maintain effective working relationships"), is an example of intersector collaboration where another sector (profession) may have developed a unit which is suitable to some other sector; this may then be imported with prior permission into that sector's standards development program. This particular unit was imported from the Management Charter Initiative where standards were being developed for all managerial roles.

N/SVQs are developed at a number of different levels depending on the responsibilities associated with the job.

NATIONAL AND SCOTTISH
VOCATIONAL QUALIFICATIONS: LEVELS

Level 1: Competence that involves the application of knowledge in the performance of a range of varied work activities, most of which are routine and predictable.

Level 2: Competence that involves the application of knowledge in a significant range of varied work activities, performed in a variety of contexts. Some of these activities are complex or nonroutine, and there is some individual responsibility or autonomy. Collaboration with others, perhaps through membership of a work group or team, is often a requirement.

Level 3: Competence that involves the application of knowledge in a broad range of varied work activities performed in a wide variety of contexts, most of which are complex and nonroutine. There is considerable responsibility and autonomy, and control or guidance of others is often required.

Level 4: Competence that involves the application of knowledge in a broad range of complex, technical, or professional work activities performed in a variety of contexts and with a substantial degree of personal responsibility and autonomy. Responsibility for the work of others and the allocation of resources is often present.

Level 5: Competence that involves the application of a range of fundamental principles across a wide and often unpredictable variety of contexts. Very substantial personal autonomy and often significant responsibility for the work of others and for the allocation of substantial resources feature strongly, as do personal accountabilities for analysis, diagnosis, design, planning, execution, and evaluation.

"The N/SVQ for Recovering Material of Evidential Value—Laboratory Based" is set at Level 3. The units are divided into elements (subactivities); for "Recovering Evidential Material—Laboratory Based," the unit and element titles are:

Unit 1. Prepare to carry out laboratory-based recovery.
    Element 1.1. Obtain and confirm instructions.
    Element 1.2. Prepare equipment and work area.
    Element 1.3. Obtain and confirm items for examination.
Unit 2. Carry out laboratory-based recovery of materials.
    Element 2.1. Inspect items submitted for recovery.
    Element 2.2. Recover materials.
    Element 2.3. Prepare recovered materials for analysis and comparison.
    Element 2.4. Complete the recovery process.
Unit 3. Contribute to the operational effectiveness of the working environment.
    Element 3.1. Monitor and maintain operational effectiveness of the working area.
    Element 3.2. Monitor and maintain functional effectiveness of equipment, instruments, and reagents.
    Element 3.3. Maintain a working knowledge of trends and developments within the area of responsibility.
Unit 4. Provide information and documentation.
    Element 4.1. Provide examination records and summaries.
    Element 4.2. Provide administrative records.
Unit 5. Establish and maintain effective working relationships.
    Element 5.1. Maintain and enhance working relationships with colleagues.
    Element 5.2. Establish and maintain working relationships with one's immediate manager.

Unit 6. Contribute to the maintenance of health and safety in the workplace.
  Element 6.1. Contribute to the safety of the workplace.
  Element 6.2. Contribute to the health and safety of personnel.
Unit 7. Carry out primary analysis of recovered material.
  Element 7.1. Prepare to analyze recovered material.
  Element 7.2. Perform primary analysis of recovered material.

For a more detailed examination of the standard, Unit 2 will be taken as an example.

Recovery of Material (RM2): Carry Out Laboratory-Based Recovery of Materials

The associated elements are as follows:

Element 2.1. Inspect items submitted for recovery.
Element 2.2. Recover materials.
Element 2.3. Prepare recovered materials for analysis and comparison.
Element 2.4. Complete the recovery process.

The full N/SVQ for recovery is given in Appendix 2.

Each of the elements is further described in terms of performance criteria, and these give the performance standard which any candidate for the N/SVQ must achieve in order to demonstrate the competent use of procedures. These performance criteria are clearly written in terms of an outcome, and nowhere does the standard dictate how a job will be carried out; it simply states the result or the outcome expected when the job is carried out competently. The "how" is given by procedural standards. In this "evidence recovery" qualification, the units are described as mandatory and additional. Why is this necessary? During the development work, it became clear that some organizations allowed their staff to do some basic analytical work on the recovered material, whilst others did not. If the qualification depended upon each candidate doing analytical work, some would never achieve the N/SVQ; and in such cases the unit of competence in question is described as an additional unit, thereby allowing those who do analytical work to achieve the additional unit if they so wished. Others who did no further work on the recovered material also achieved the qualification through the mandatory units. In other words, the qualification is about recovery, and the additional unit plays no part in achieving the N/SVQ in recovering material of evidential value; but for added value to individuals and organizations, it gives those who do that additional work the hallmark of competence in that activity. The breakdown of the qualification into units and elements is given at Table 2.6.

The performance criteria for Unit RM2 and its associated elements of competence are:

Recovery of Material (RM2): Carry Out Laboratory-Based Recovery of Materials

Element 2.1: Inspect Items Submitted for Recovery

Performance Criteria
1. Identities of submitted items are confirmed against documentation, and any problems are reported to the relevant personnel.
2. Removal of items from packaging and subsequent handling are safe, avoid contamination and cross contamination, and minimize loss of potential evidential material.
3. Recovery plan is confirmed against agreed prioritization and sequence of laboratory work, and is adjusted as necessary in light of observations made.
4. Appropriate location techniques are employed to detect potential evidential material, and located material of potential significance is reported to relevant personnel before continuing with the process.
5. Existence and location of evidential material, where detected, are recorded accurately in accordance with organizational requirements.
6. Continuity and integrity of items are maintained throughout the inspection process.
7. Inspection process is carried out safely and with due attention to minimizing hazards to self and others in accordance with statutory requirements.

Element 2.2: Recover Materials

Performance Criteria
1. Examination is carried out in the agreed sequence to ensure detection and optimum recovery.
2. Methods selected and employed optimize recovery, minimize loss, and avoid contamination.
3. Samples of materials are handled safely and securely in a manner commensurate with their size and nature.
4. Relevant information is accurately, comprehensively, and contemporaneously recorded onto appropriate documentation.
5. Continuity and integrity are maintained throughout the recovery process.
6. Samples of materials, records, and (where appropriate) items are carried forward for further examination and analysis in accordance with investigation requirements.
7. Recovery process is carried out safely and with due attention to minimizing hazards to self and others in accordance with statutory requirements.
8. Nonrepeatable tests are carried out in the presence of relevant personnel.

Element 2.3: Prepare Recovered Material for Analysis and Comparison

Performance Criteria
1. Analytical requirements and instructions are obtained; difficulties in carrying out the instructions are clarified with the relevant personnel.
2. Selection and preparation of recovered material for analysis and comparison are carried out in the agreed sequence, and optimum recovery is achieved.

3. Methods selected and employed avoid contamination, minimize loss, and present materials and samples in a manner appropriate to their size, their nature, and the type of analysis to be carried out.
4. Materials and samples selected and prepared are of the appropriate size and condition, representative, and suitable for analysis and comparison.
5. Relevant information is accurately, comprehensively, and contemporaneously recoded onto appropriate documentation.
6. Continuity and integrity are maintained throughout the process.
7. Preparation process is carried out safely and with due attention to minimizing hazards to self and others in accordance with statutory regulations.
8. Nonrepeatable tests are carried out in the presence of relevant personnel.

Element 2.4: Complete the Recovery Process

Performance Criteria
1. Items and samples are handled, packaged, and stored in a way which prevents contamination, cross contamination, and loss of evidence.
2. Items and samples are uniquely labeled and accurately recorded.
3. The continuity of items and samples is maintained.
4. Items and samples are stored in safe, secure conditions and are accessible to relevant personnel.
5. Relevant information is accurately, comprehensively, and contemporaneously recoded onto appropriate documentation.
6. Packaging and storage of items and samples are carried out with due regard to safety considerations in accordance with statutory requirements.

There is one other feature of N/SVQ units that has not yet been described: the possibility of having optional units in addition to mandatory and additional units—optional units which offer a choice to the candidate of selecting one or more units from a number of optional units. This may be seen in the N/SVQ for marks and impressions, at level 5, which is shown here.

Note: The qualification (NVQ) structure has been summarized and modified as an aid to explanation (Table 2.1).

MARKS AND IMPRESSIONS: TEN MANDATORY UNITS (ALL TO BE TAKEN)

Unit 1. Prepare to carry out comparisons and provide advice.
Unit 2. Assess and advise on the assessment of examination items.
Unit 3. Examine and advise on the examination of items.
Unit 4. Interpret and advise on the interpretation of finding.
Unit 5. Report findings (NVQ).
Unit 6. Contribute to advances in the body of professional knowledge and practice.
Unit 7. Provide information to support decision making (MCI D4).
Unit 8. Chair and participate in meetings (MCI D3).
Unit 9. Contribute to establishing and maintaining quality services.
Unit 10. Provide consultancy, advice, and guidance.

TABLE 2.1
Unit and Element Titles

Units	Elements
1. Prepare to carry out examinations and provide advice.	1.1. Determine case requirements and provide advice on the investigation.
	1.2. Prepare and advise on the preparation of equipment and the work area.
	1.3. Advise on the integrity of items and samples.
2. Assess and advise on the assessment of examination items.	2.1. Inspect and advise on the inspection of items submitted for examination.
	2.2. Monitor and maintain the integrity of items and samples.
	2.3. Identify and advise on the identification of potential evidence.
3. Examine and advise on the examination of items and samples.	3.1. Advise on the determination of examinations and comparisons.
	3.2. Carry out examinations and comparisons, and provide advice.
4. Interpret and advise on the interpretation of findings.	4.1. Summarize results, and advise on the summary of results of examinations and comparisons.
	4.2. Interpret and advise on the interpretation of results of examinations and comparisons.
5. Report findings.	5.1. Produce report.
	5.2. Participate in pretrial consultation.
	5.3. Present oral evidence to courts and inquiries.
6. Contribute to advances in the body of professional knowledge and practice.	6.1. Contribute to advances in knowledge and theory which underpin forensic science.
	6.2. Contribute to advances in forensic science practice.
	6.3. Contribute to advances in technology related to forensic science.
	6.4. Enable others to learn and benefit from one's experience.
7. Provide information to support decision making (MCI D4).	7.1. Obtain information for decision making.
	7.2. Record and store information for decision making.
	7.3. Analyze in formation to support decision making.
	7.4. Advise and inform others.
8. Chair and participate in meetings (MCI D3).	8.1. Chair meetings.
	8.2. Participate in meetings.
9. Contribute to establishing and maintaining quality services.	9.1. Introduce and evaluate quality assurance systems.
	9.2. Maintain and improve operations for quality and functional specifications.
10. Provide consultancy, advice, and guidance.	10.1. Exchange information, and provide advice on scientific matters.
	10.2. Develop solutions to unique scientific problems.
11. Create and develop effective working relationships.	11.1. Establish and maintain effective working relationships with colleagues.
	11.2. Establish and maintain working relationships with contacts external to the organization.

TABLE 2.1 (CONTINUED)
Unit and Element Titles

Units	Elements
12. Determine the work of teams and individuals to achieve objectives (MCI C13).	12.1. Allocate work to teams and individuals.
	12.2. Agree on objectives and work plans with teams and individuals.
	12.3. Evaluate the performance of teams and individuals.
	12.4. Provide feedback on performance to teams and individuals.
13. Undertake and advise on specialist scene examinations.	13.1. Establish and advise on the requirements for the investigation.
	13.2. Prepare to examine and advise on the examination of the scene of the incident.
	13.3. Examine and advise on the examination of the scene of the incident.
	13.4. Arrange packaging, storage, and transportation of items.
14. Determine the effective use of resources (MCI B4).	14.1. Make proposals for expenditures on programs of work.
	14.2. Agree on budgets for programs of work.
	14.3. Control activities against budgets.

Four Optional Units (one to be taken from the following)

Unit 11. Create and develop effective working relationships.
Unit 12. Determine the work of teams and individuals to achieve objectives.
Unit 13. Undertake and advise on specialist scene examination.
Unit 14. Determine the effective use of resources (MCI B4).

There are four optional units described, from which the candidate is invited to select one. It is clear how much more rigorous this qualification is compared to level 3 for recovery—at level 5, the highest attainable, there is much more emphasis on consultancy and advice than there is at level 3.

There are other features included within this NVQ, and these are shown below in Table 2.2 from the qualification dealing with laboratory-based recovery, which shows by way of an example the full layout of this unit.

UNIT 2: CARRY OUT LABORATORY-BASED RECOVERY OF MATERIALS

Element 2.4: Complete the Recovery Process

Performance criteria describe the performance standard to be achieved, so why is there any need for other features to be included? Why not simply ensure that every

TABLE 2.2
Performance Criteria and Evidence Requirements

The Standard

Performance Criteria

1. Items and samples are handled, packaged, and stored in a way which prevents contamination, cross contamination, and loss of evidence.
2. Items and samples are uniquely labeled and accurately recorded.
3. The continuity of items and samples is maintained.
4. Items and samples are stored in safe, secure conditions and are accessible to relevant personnel.
5. Relevant information is accurately, comprehensively, and contemporaneously recorded onto appropriate documentation.
6. Packaging and storage of items and samples are carried out with due regard to safety considerations in accordance with statutory requirements.

Evidence Requirements

The candidate should be able to demonstrate competence over a period of time across all the performance criteria and range statements. Competence is to be demonstrated in real work situations. Where opportunities for work-based assessments are not readily available, realistic simulations of the work activity may be used, although these should be set up and assessed in the normal working environment. The candidate should be able to explain the reasons for all of his or her actions and cover "what if" scenarios. The candidate should be able to answer oral or written questions covering items specified in the "Knowledge and Understanding" specification.

Range Statements

1. Items and samples include different types of items which will have different packaging, handling, labeling, safety, and storage requirements.
2. Health and safety considerations: item type, condition of item, personal safety, and safety of others.
3. Relevant personnel: line manager, case supervisor, and other specialists.
4. Recording information: written, drawn, and photographic.
5. Common evidence types: chemical, biological, and physical.

Principles, Methods, and Techniques Relating to Knowledge and Understanding Specification

- Establishing and maintaining continuity and security (a–f) (range 4)
- Avoiding and minimizing potential hazards (f) (range 1, 2, and 5) Selection of packaging materials (a) (range 1, 2, and 5)
- Packaging items (a) (range 1 and 5) Storing items (a) (range 1 and 5)
- Preservation of items and samples (a, d, and f) (range 1 and 5)
- Contamination dangers and how they can be avoided (a and d) (range 1, 2, and 5)
- Recording information (e) (range 4)
- Health and safety considerations (f) (range 2)

TABLE 2.2 (CONTINUED)
Performance Criteria and Evidence Requirements

The Standard	Evidence Requirements
	Information and Data About
	• Continuity and security requirements (a–f) (range 4)
	• Statutory requirements and Health and Safety at Work and COSHH Regulations (f) (range 2)
	• Types of packaging materials (a) (range 1)
	• Evidence types (a) (range 1, 2, and 5)
	• Storage requirements and facilities (a, d, and f) (range 1 and 5)
	• Contamination dangers (a and d) (range 1, 2, and 5)
	• Personnel who have access to items and samples (d) (range 3)
	Assessment Guidance
	Competence will be demonstrated across a range of different cases by a combination of observation in the work environment, oral and written questioning, and a review of a portfolio of evidence of competence.

successful candidate for the qualification can meet the performance criteria? These "other" features are significant and are:

Range Statements
Range statements define the context in which the job is carried out. The range statements for element 2.4 are:

1. *Items and samples*: to include different types of items which will have different packaging, handling, labeling, safety, and storage requirements.
2. *Health and safety considerations*: item type, condition of item, personal safety, and safety of others.
3. *Relevant personnel*: line manager, case supervisor, and other specialists.
4. *Recording information*: written, drawn, and photographic.
5. *Common evidence types*: chemical, biological, and physical.

Wherever the range statement appears in the standard, the range of options to be covered during assessment is given.

Knowledge and Understanding Specification
The "Knowledge and Understanding" specification will give the essential knowledge to underpin competent performance. For element 2.4, this is:

Principles, Methods, and Techniques Relating To …
   • Establishing and maintaining continuity and security (a–f) (range 4)
   • Avoiding and minimizing potential hazards (f) (range 1, 2, and 5)

- Selection of packaging materials (a) (range 1, 2, and 5)
- Packaging items (a) (range 1 and 5)
- Storing items (a) (range 1 and 5)
- Preservation of items and samples (a, d, and f) (range 1 and 5)
- Contamination dangers and how they can be avoided (a and d) (range 1, 2, and 5)
- Recording information (e) (range 4)
- Health and safety considerations (f) (range 2)

Information and Data About …
- Continuity and security requirements (a–f) (range 4)
- Statutory requirements and Health and Safety at Work and COSHH Regulations (f) (range 2)
- Types of packaging materials (a) (range 1)
- Evidence types (a) (range 1, 2, and 5)
- Storage requirements and facilities (a, d, and f) (range 1 and 5)
- Contamination dangers (a and d) (range 1, 2, and 5)
- Personnel who have access to items and samples (d) (range 3)

The statements also describe the relevant performance criteria and the range to be covered. For example, taking "Selection of Packaging Materials (a) (range 1, 2, and 5)" from the Knowledge and Understanding statements indicates that for performance criterion (a), "Items and samples are handled, packaged, and stored in a manner which prevents contamination, cross contamination, and loss of evidence." The range statement indicates that range 1, 2, and 5 must be considered here.

Evidence Requirements

The evidence requirements spell out to a candidate how and in what circumstances competence must be demonstrated. Competence had to be demonstrated in real work situations. Where opportunities for work-based assessments are not readily available, realistic simulations of the work activity may be used, although these should be set up and assessed in the normal working environment. The candidate should be able to explain the reasons for all his or her actions and cover "what if" scenarios. They should be able to answer oral or written questions covering items specified in the Knowledge and Understanding specification.

The evidence requirements tell the candidate what has to be done to demonstrate competence.

Assessment Guidance

We need to be careful with this definition in the forensic science profession, for here, in the qualification structure, we are concerned with the evidence of competent performance, not the "evidence" that forensic scientists are more familiar with. This section defines what evidence the successful candidate for the qualification must collect. Interestingly, it emphasizes that the competence must be demonstrated in real work situations.

Outcome-Based Standards

To demonstrate the outcome-based nature of the standards, performance criterion (e) from element of competence 2.4 tells us, "Relevant information is accurately, comprehensively, and contemporaneously recorded onto appropriate documentation."

This performance criterion says nothing about how the information is to be recorded in order for it to be recorded accurately, comprehensively, and contemporaneously, or what the appropriate documentation is. In other words, it describes the desired outcome when carrying out the task. It does not dictate how that outcome is achieved.

Assessing Workplace Competence

Probably the most significant use of N/SVQs is for assessing the workplace performance of forensic scientists.

Barnett [1] says, "Professional work may be done in a very competent manner but lead to a result that is less than optimum." And also, "The judgment of whether a professional service was competently rendered can only realistically be made by other members of the professional community."

It is this last statement that forms the basis of an assessment procedure where professionals (peers) judge, with controls, the competence of individuals—however, there must be no room for personal views of competence, and there are major checks and balances in the procedure to avoid this.

It is this process of assessment of competent workplace performance within the N/SVQ program, which, whilst essential, was perceived as too bureaucratic and time-consuming. However, it may be informative to present a brief summary of the N/SVQ assessment procedure. We must always keep in mind the fact that, according to Kirk [4], forensic science

> has all the responsibility of medicine, the intricacy of the law and the universality of science. In as much as it carries higher penalties for error than other professions it is a matter not to take lightly, nor to trust to luck.

So maybe a little effort in ensuring we do not trust luck to get it right should be incorporated into our already healthy quality assurance programs.

Competence simply means working to the standards set by the profession. The standards, on which the N/SVQs are based, have been determined by working groups and then exposed to sector-wide consultation. Any relevant feedback from the sector is considered by the working groups, and the standards modified where necessary. The standards have therefore been agreed by the profession. What we need now is some means of ensuring that agreed standards are being worked to. This brings us to the assessment procedure.

ASSESSMENT OF WORKPLACE PERFORMANCE AGAINST THE STANDARDS

The assessment strategy is based on the following principles [5].

There must be an agreed set of standards as the basis for assessment. We have seen that the national occupational standards on which N/SVQs are based have been developed by the best practitioners under guidance and then agreed by the profession through consultation; they will provide a framework for ensuring that practitioners work to acceptable procedural standards. The national occupational standards are outcome based, which means they define the expected outcome resulting from carrying out a task using procedural standards.

Assessment must be based on both performance on real casework in the working environment and some agreed instances in the training environment—supported by essential knowledge. It must be kept firmly in mind that the final assessment will be aimed at practitioners who carry out their normal day-to-day duties working on real cases in a real working environment. The workplace assessment program on operationally critical activities is assessed on real casework and is not for trainees; there are, however, some noncritical operational activities which may be assessed in training or other nonoperational environments. The assessment procedure is for those scientists who have already, in some way, been assessed as competent by their organizations according to their organization's methods of assessment and now seek national (or maybe international) hallmarking.

The assessment process must be consistent across different sites and organizations. To achieve this, the following must be in place:

1. The procedure for carrying out and recording the outcomes of assessment must be such as to facilitate review and third-party scrutiny.
2. The assessment process should respect that there may be more than one acceptable way of carrying out a task, yet be robust enough to reject any unacceptable activities.
3. The evidence of competence, collected by the candidate and reviewed by assessment, must be:

Sufficient: covering all the knowledge and performance requirements of the defined standards
Current: not too "old" to be of value
Valid: relevant to the standard being addressed
Authentic: demonstrably produced by the practitioner
Consistent: "proving" that competent performance is the norm

The whole thrust of the process is to ensure fair and equal rigor for assessment practices wherever the assessments are carried out and, indeed, by whoever they are carried out. This is ensured through the rigor of the procedure.

There are a number of fundamental principles relating to the assessment of workplace competence of forensic scientists within the N/SVQ program. These are:

- National Occupational Standards (the standards on which N/SVQs are based) establish the forensic science profession's benchmark of competent performance.
- National Occupational Standards, together with clear evidence of competence requirements and guidance to assessors on certain aspects of the standards, provide the basis for consistent assessment practices.

- The assessment of a practitioner's competence should be fair, rigorous, efficient, and cost-effective, using approaches that have the support of employers, awarding bodies, and other sector interest groups.
- The assessment must be conducted by suitably qualified individuals who demonstrably maintain their occupational competence.
- The assessment should be carried out over a period of time.
- Assessments should be carried out in the workplace wherever practical. This can include the use of simulations to increase access to assessment in certain defined areas.
- The assessment process should be tailored to meet individual needs, taking account, where relevant, of prior learning and achievement and special needs.
- There should be open access to assessment to all who can provide evidence of the ability to perform to the National Occupational Standards.

NATIONAL OCCUPATIONAL STANDARDS

The standards on which the N/SVQs are based (the National Occupational Standards, or NOS) set out the workplace activities in which forensic (science) practitioners are involved. They identify the performance criteria (what practitioners must be able to do) and the essential underpinning knowledge and understanding (what practitioners must know). National Occupational Standards are useful to many different people and organizations (Appendix 3). They must form the basis of vocational qualifications; they should inform the development of training courses and training materials as well as education programs.

Awarding Body

There must be some central oversight of the assessment process; this is provided by an awarding body. The Open University Validation Services (OUVS) acted as an awarding body in the early days of the proposed N/SVQ implementation in forensic science.

The awarding body will control and monitor the entire procedure for assessments and therefore control the award of an N/SVQ. The awarding body is independent of the forensic science profession. The profession, through employers, has said that any awarding body for forensic science qualifications must demonstrate that they will:

- Assist employers in the development and refinement of technical and occupational criteria for the appointment of verifiers and assessors.
- Involve employers in the selection and appointment of the external verifiers.
- Deploy external verifiers according to their technical expertise.
- Provide the opportunity for external verifiers to participate in sector-specific reviews and awarding body-specific training events for continuous professional development on a regular basis.
- Consult employers on the acceptability of any qualifications submitted by assessors as proof of their occupational competence other than any qualifications that can be approved at the launch of the qualification.

It is expected that the awarding body will ensure

- that assessment instruments do not directly or indirectly discriminate against any particular group of people.
- that arrangements are put in place for assessments to be carried out at a time to meet individual needs and rate of progress.
- that, where necessary, suitable arrangements are in place for reassessment of those areas where candidates have been shown to be "not yet competent."
- that the qualifications and occupational expertise requirements of all involved in the assessment and verification process will be regularly monitored and recorded.
- cross-center consistency of interpretation and assessment against the National Occupational Standards through the establishment of effective systems such as national external verifier meetings and regional assessor and internal verifier meetings. It is at such meetings where all of those involved in the assessment process are able to discuss concerns about acceptable methods and the like. It is this practice that may well play a role in advancing the effectiveness of any profession.

Expertise of Assessors

- Assessors, for the qualifications, must be occupationally competent in the area in which they are carrying out assessments. (It is recognized that initially assessors will be chosen through agreement within the sector of "best practitioner" status supported by proof that they possess the required knowledge. In time, however, they will themselves prove their competence against the standards, including proof that their knowledge of the occupational area is adequate through, in some cases, the completion of a knowledge-based examination. This will ensure that they are up-to-date with the principles and practices specified in the standards they are assessing.)
- Assessors must not assess any candidates that they have had a principal role in training. This is to avoid the temptation of saying, "I trained this person; therefore, he or she must be competent."
- Assessors must have a full understanding of the National Occupational Standards and requirements of any qualification being assessed; they must also have an understanding of the awarding body policies and procedures.
- Assessors must only assess in their acknowledged area of occupational competence.
- Assessors must be registered with the awarding body by the approved center, and must be appropriately qualified for the role of assessor and be accountable to that organization for their assessment practice. It is not acceptable for the assessor role to be given to anyone with the "time to spare."

- Assessors must provide evidence of maintaining their occupational competence; they must not have been out of the job role in which they are assessing for more than twelve months in order to start, or to continue, working as an assessor. Assessors must be able to demonstrate to their awarding body that they engage in appropriate continuing professional development activities on an annual basis.

Internal Verifiers

The prime role of internal verifiers is to ensure that the evidence of competent performance being used by the assessor is acceptable evidence and is meaningful for its use as an indicator of competent workplace performance. Internal verifiers work for the awarding body through the approved center.

Internal verifiers:

- Must be competent current practitioners in the area in which they are carrying out internal verification, or not out of the job role in which they are carrying out internal verifications for more than three years. This will ensure that they are up-to-date with the principles and practices specified in the standards. (Internal verifiers will be required to prove that they are knowledgeable in the area in which they carry out verifications through, in some cases, the successful completion of a knowledge-based examination.)
- Must be in a position to contribute to and influence an approved center's assessment policy. They should be *either*
  - employed by the same organization as the assessors, *or*
  - working in partnership with the approved center and having access to the evidence used by the assessors.
- Must have a full understanding of the National Occupational Standards and any requirements of the qualification for which they are verifying assessments. They must also have an understanding of the awarding body policies and procedures.
- Must demonstrate a commitment to uphold the integrity of the National Occupational Standards and their assessment and auditing practices. Internal verifiers will not carry out assessments in those instances where they are carrying out internal verification. They may act independently as assessors if trained and qualified for that role.
- Must provide evidence of maintaining the knowledge of the area in which they are carrying out verification; and must be able to demonstrate to their awarding body that they engage in appropriate continuing professional development activities on an annual basis.

External Verifiers

The principal role of the external verifier is to ensure that the agreed assessment protocols are adhered to. External verifiers work directly for the awarding body. External verifiers must

- be people who are familiar with the area of work in which they are carrying out external verification and must not have been unassociated with the job role in which they are externally verifying for more than five years.
- demonstrate a commitment to uphold the integrity of the National Occupational Standards and their verification practices. External verifiers will not carry out assessments.
- participate in training initiatives for their continued professional development.
- demonstrate their ability to maintain credibility within the sector and be suitably qualified for their external verification duties.

Methods of Assessment

A range of sources of evidence of competence is acceptable and includes:

- Observations of performance
- Questioning
- Witness testimony
- Personal statements
- Review of products of performance, for example case files, case notes, and other documentary evidence

Documentary evidence is a rich source of evidence of competence in a profession where there is a judicial requirement to keep complete, accurate, and contemporaneous notes of all activities that are adequate to support third-party review of the casework at a later stage. Observation should only be used where other methods are not practicable (a misunderstanding of this fact contributed to the profession rejecting N/SVQs on the grounds of bureaucracy—it was wrongly assumed that all activities must be "observed," clearly a costly activity and not necessary).

- No individual unit of competence should be assessed using only one form of assessment.
- As a principle, the evidence of competence used by assessors must be accessible for external verification.

Simulation

Simulations can only be used under exceptional circumstances, and where they are used they must replicate real work activities and the real working environment as closely as possible. Actual simulations must be preapproved by the awarding body in consultation with an employer group. Further guidance will be found in the schedule related to a specific qualification.

Realistic simulations are defined as:

- Incorporating a comprehensive range of demands, activities, and constraints relevant to those that would be met in a real working context
- Providing candidates with access to the normal facilities, support, and advice that would be available in the context and type of working situation

- Including normal working contexts and conditions
- Placing candidates under pressure of time, resources, and working demands that would normally operate in the working environment
- Being planned, developed, and documented by the center in a way that ensures that simulations correctly reflect what the standard seeks to assess (validity)

Knowledge and Understanding

- It is vital to ensure that the essential underpinning knowledge and understanding are demonstrated by candidates to support the performance criteria defined by the National Occupational Standards.
- To achieve this, the employer group will look to awarding bodies and others involved in the assessment process to develop and deliver a procedure that will effectively assess the essential knowledge and understanding in each forensic science discipline and that is relevant to each qualification. This may involve the successful completion of a knowledge-based examination.

It will be seen that the lengths taken to ensure all the conditions of assessment are met leave little to chance and even less to personal subjective views of competence. Interestingly, although the undeniably rigorous N/SVQ assessment process has led to not too warm a reception in the profession, many other professions in the United Kingdom are successfully using it in their field. It is planned that shortly the N/SVQ procedure will be in place for policing activities, including scientific support and fingerprinting practices.

The collection of the evidence of competence and recording is vital to the procedure, and we will say a little about that now.

Assessment of Competence

Through the achievement of an N/SVQ, a practitioner will have successfully demonstrated the ability to work to standards developed and nationally agreed by the profession. Working to standards set by the profession hallmarks competent performance. It is, as mentioned above, this process of assessment of competent workplace performance which was perceived as far too bureaucratic and time-consuming. However, it may be informative to expose readers to a brief résumé of the N/SVQ assessment procedure.

The essential requirement of an effective assessment procedure is to ensure that all of the evidence used to demonstrate competent performance is recorded and preserved in a way that makes it readily retrievable for third-party scrutiny. A tick-box approach is not acceptable.

Effective recording of performance during the assessment process is therefore vital and is carried out through the compilation of a portfolio of evidence of competence. A portfolio should relate each piece of evidence of competence to the relevant performance criterion.

Preparing the Portfolio

The first stage in the assessment process is for individuals to decide, with their assessor, the activities which are to be tackled first. This will require a detailed understanding of the standards. The standards should be carefully read and understood before proceeding with assessment.

In the major forensic science service providers in the United Kingdom, nearly all of the tasks associated with the standards will be carried out by individuals on a regular basis; this will make it relatively easy to collect effective evidence of competence. If the standards have been designed correctly, there should be no need to "search around" for evidence of competence; it should be available over time as a consequence of carrying out day-to-day work.

An assessment plan should be developed in collaboration with the assessor (Table 2.3 gives a sample of an assessment plan). Copies of assessment plans should be included in the portfolio and provide a useful way to record progress through the assessment procedure. It is at this point that careful consideration needs to be given to any opportunities for integration of assessment. What is integration of assessment? On reading the standards, it is clear that many of the performance criteria are repeated under different elements; this is deliberate and may be explained by considering that many candidates will not need to obtain a complete vocational qualification for a variety of reasons. In such situations, it is perfectly acceptable to demonstrate competence in single units; a unit of competence is, however, the smallest assessable part of a qualification—it is

---

TABLE 2.3

Activity Assessment Plan, Unit 2: Carry Out Laboratory-Based Recovery of Material

Typical Evidence	Estimated Complete Date	Limit to Other Activities or Subactivities
Element 1: Inspect Items Submitted for Recovery		
Check exhibit labels' details against submission form; reporting officer (RO) informed of any problems regarding time delays. Ensure that any discrepancies are recorded in case notes.		
Scene marks handled with care to avoid damage or loss of detail, and packaged appropriately for submission to photography. Handle footwear with care to avoid any further damage.		
Ensure original file instruction followed; and if any further or alternative instructions need to be observed, ensure that RO is consulted regarding amended instructions.		
Element 2		

not possible to request assessment in single elements. If, when the standards are written, those performance criteria that are repeated across different elements are omitted and a candidate opts to be assessed in a unit that comprises an element from which performance criteria have been omitted, that candidate will not be assessed in what could be vital performance criteria. In integration of assessment of those candidates who take the full qualification and have demonstrated their competence in a performance criterion that is repeated elsewhere, an assessor is able to accept that performance criterion as part of an element of competence under other units of competence.

The progress of an individual through the assessment procedure should be maintained, and a suggestion of a form for doing this is given in Table 2.4.

The portfolio is important: it is an individual's record of achievement which will be used in the verification process and must therefore be presented logically so that the verifiers are able to scrutinize the assessment procedure. To achieve this, the following suggestions are made on the layout of the portfolio.

1. A title page
2. Contents list
3. A personal profile
4. A summary of the units comprising the standards
5. A detailed listing of the units (with any assessment plans)
6. Glossary of terms used
7. An indexed list of the evidence of competence
8. Evidence collected—which could include an audit trail

All of the evidence of competence that is presented must be relevant to demonstrating that the occupational standard has been achieved. All of this evidence should be obtainable from current work, and to do this the following methods are used.

Observation: In certain circumstances, an assessor may wish to observe some part of the activity being carried out by the individual (Table 2.5).

Personal statement: A personal statement, by the individual, may be used to explain how a situation arising as part of the job was handled and should contain not only a description of what was done but also, equally important, why it was done (Table 2.6).

Witness testimony: In some instances, a person other than an assessor may have witnessed something which a person undergoing assessment did. In such cases, it is possible to call upon them to give a witness testimony to the actions. A sample form is given in Table 2.7. Witness evidence will never be accepted as prime evidence of competence but may be taken as supporting evidence. Witness testimony should:
   - Comment on performance which relates to the standards.
   - Identify clearly the witness.
   - The witness should be in a position to make meaningful comments on an individual's performance.

Personal views: Personal views of competence are not acceptable as evidence.

TABLE 2.4

Recovering material of evidential value

Name: A N Individual

To achieve the standard in recovering material of evidential value – laboratory based (forensic science) individuals must demonstrate consistent competent performance in each of the following Units

Unit Ref. No.	Title	Assessor's Signature	Date
1.	Prepare to carry out laboratory based recovery.		
2.	Carry out laboratory based recovery.	A N Assessor	8-6-05
3.	Contribute to the operational effectiveness of the working environment		
4.	Provide information and documentation	A N Assessor	8-6-05
5	Establish and maintain effective working relationships		
6	Contribute to the maintenance of Health and Safety in the workplace		
		Assessor to sign each time an activity is satisfactory achieved	

Questions and answers: Questions, both written and oral, may be used by assessors to establish that the individual possesses the right level of knowledge and understanding. The question and answers must be recorded by the assessor (Table 2.8).

The evidence of competence must be presented clearly and be legible. The assessor will then be able to establish whether it is appropriate for making judgments on currency, quality, and quantity of the evidence of competence.

TABLE 2.5
Record of Observation

Unit/element: _____

Candidate: _____ Date of observation: _____

Evidence index: _____

Skills/Activities Observed	Measures of Performance and Range Covered

Knowledge and understanding apparent from this observation:

Other units and/or elements apparent from this observation:

Assessor comments and feedback to individual:

I can confirm the individual's performance was satisfactory.

Assessor's signature: _____ Date: _____

Individual's signature: _____ Date: _____

In major forensic science service providers, evidence of performance will originate from the real day-to-day work of the individual and the evidence can be kept in its normal location, for example case files. There will need to be in the portfolio, however, a clear audit trail for such casework evidence. Any evidence of competence which has been collected primarily to show that individuals have met the occupational standards (e.g., witness statement or personal statement) must be located in the portfolio. It is vital that assessors and verifiers can locate the "evidence" at all times, and this is a responsibility of the individual undergoing assessment. In a profession where, as mentioned above, there is a judicial requirement to keep full, complete, and detailed records of all casework activities, retrieving "evidence" of competence should not present a problem.

To help the assessor and those involved in the verification process to access a portfolio, it is suggested that each item of evidence is given a reference number; and where integration of assessment has been used, all the units and elements of competence

TABLE 2.6
Personal Statement

Date	Evidence Index	Details of Statement	Links to Other Evidence of Competence	Units and/or Elements and Range Addressed
10-6-05	3	I met with PD (reporting officer).		
		We discussed and agreed the following: −Sequence of examination −Best systems		

Individual's signature: _____ Date: _____

TABLE 2.7
Witness Evidence

Standards Title	Recovery of Evidential Material—Laboratory Based
Name	A N Individual
Evidence index	8
Element	RM 1.3
Range	
Date evidence of competence obtained	19-5-05
Name of witness	A Witness
Relationship to person being assessed	

Evidence Details:

I can confirm that the individual met with me to discuss the quality of packaging for item X/Y/OO. I can confirm the individual evidence is authentic.

Signed witness: _____ Date: _____

Name: _____

Please confirm that you are familiar with the standards to which the individual is working.

Signed witness: _____ Date: _____

which are associated with a specific item of evidence should be made very clear. Any connections which are identified in the integration of assessment should also be noted on the relevant items of evidence—in other words, effective cross referencing is advised.

The evidence of competence is given a reference number which is recorded on a form (Table 2.9). Associated with this reference number should be a brief description of every item of evidence of competence. It is important also to identify the location of the evidence and to reference each of the items of evidence to the appropriate activities and subactivities or performance measures.

TABLE 2.8
Questions and Answers: Record

Units	Elements
Evidence index	
Questions and answers	
Q:	
A:	
Q:	
A:	
Q:	
A:	

Signed individual: _____ Date: _____

Signed assessor: _____ Date: _____

TABLE 2.9
Index of Evidence of Competence

Evidence of Competence Number	Description	Standard Title Location of Evidence	Units and/or Element Links	Item Verifier (signature)

REFERENCES

1. Peter D Barnett, Ethics in Forensic Science: Professional Standards for the Practice of Criminalistics, CRC Press, Boca Raton, FL (2001).
2. K Hadley, Journal of the Forensic Science Society 34, 5 (1994).
3. Forensic Science: Implications for Higher Education, Science, Engineering, Manufacturing Technologies Alliance (SEMTA) (2004).
4. P L Kirk, Journal of Criminal Law, Criminology and Police Science 54, 235 (1963).
5. An Assessment Strategy for Forensic Science Practitioners, Forensic Science Sector Strategy Group (Forensic Science Sector — Skills for Justice).

3 Generic Standards

At this point, the moves to take the original National and Scottish Vocational Qualification (N/SVQ) program forward to a more acceptable procedure will be described. It may, however, be prudent at some time to revisit the vocational qualification concept. That is a matter for the profession to consider. So what is the next stage? Let us develop some proposals on this vital issue of competence in forensic practice.

The standards for the vocational qualifications that have been developed specifically for each work area are:

- Investigating scenes of incident
- Managing and coordinating scenes of incident
- Recovering materials of evidential value—laboratory based
- Document examination
- Blood and body fluids
- Marks and impressions
- Fingerprint operations
- Accident investigation
- Firearms
- Trace evidence

What very soon became apparent during the standards development work was that much of the activity in forensic practice can be represented generically in terms of five high-level activities or units; these are:

1. Preparing to carry out examinations
2. Examining items and samples
3. Undertaking specialist scene examinations
4. Interpreting findings
5. Reporting findings

It was clear that these activities were common throughout forensic practice.

These five high-level activities match closely the so-called paradigm of forensic science of Inman and Rudin [1], which is summarized as follows:

1. Classification and examination of evidence
   a. Identification
   b. Individualization
2. Interpretation
   a. Association
   b. Reconstruction

3. Reporting
   a. Written report
   b. Pretrial conferences
   c. Courts and inquiries

The five high-level activities that emerged during standards development describe what has become known as the forensic scientific process and are ideally placed to act as a focus against which forensic practitioners will be called upon to demonstrate occupational competence. These five high-level activities have been called "units of competence," thereby keeping the terminology in line with earlier work on vocational qualifications.

DEVELOPING THE GENERIC STANDARDS

The Forensic Science Sector Committee, as an employers' representative, did not accept the N/SVQ program, perceiving it as far too bureaucratic, but fully endorsed the principles on which N/SVQs are based. It was the rejection of N/SVQs by the profession that prompted the search for a procedure that was simpler but retained the essential principles of N/SVQs—ideally, a procedure that would monitor occupational competence.

At this point, the idea of a formal qualification was abandoned and efforts were made to represent the standards in a manner that would make them suitable for the attestation of occupational competence.

As with N/SVQs, the standards describe the outcome when carrying out any task that falls within the forensic scientific process. They will not tell us how the task is carried out—that is deliberate, and the reason for this will become apparent later. The ultimate goal of the standards is to continuously monitor, in some way, the occupational competence of practitioners. It will be readily apparent by the definition of "competence" given earlier as "the ability to work to the standards set by the profession" that any standards that are developed must be agreed by the profession.

The Forensic Science Sector Strategy Group (FSSSG) has the responsibility, on behalf of employers, to set standards of performance. (The FSSSG is now the Skills for Justice Forensic Science Committee.) The National Occupational Standards (NOS) development procedure employed by the FSSSG was exactly the same as that used by the lead body when it developed standards for N/SVQs—through working groups of practitioners under the guidance of a consultant. The standards are now expressed in one generic suite.

The newly developed generic standards in forensic science were exposed to the widest possible consultation throughout the profession. The feedback from the consultation process was incorporated into the draft standards, where appropriate, thereby giving a set of standards, covering all activities that were acceptable to the forensic science profession in the United Kingdom and that are therefore, by our definition of competence, the standards against which a forensic scientist will be called upon to demonstrate competent performance.

These standards are variously called National Occupational Standards or Professional Standards of Competence in forensic science. In this book, the former name for the standards will be used, although the two names are freely interchangeable.

THE STANDARDS

To understand what the generic National Occupational Standards in forensic science mean, it is necessary to appreciate the structure and form of representation of the standards. They have many similarities to the standards developed for the N/SVQs. When first encountered, they may be a little daunting to most people; because of this, a detailed explanation of them is essential. The starting point for this explanation will be the five high-level activities mentioned on page 41.

Keeping firmly in mind that the ultimate goal is the development of a procedure for assessing the personal occupational competence of forensic practitioners against universally agreed occupational standards, we can see that by using these high-level descriptors (1–5), we are approaching the vision of assessing performance against some form of "standard." As an example of the use of the high-level descriptors, we see that those practitioners who deal, for instance, with specialist scene examinations (this activity does not equate to the standards developed by Skills for Justice for crime scene investigators) may be assessed against the simple high-level descriptor for "undertaking specialized scene examinations," the descriptor serving as a rudimentary "standard." However, it is not difficult to see that the sole use of this high-level descriptor as the "standard" to be achieved would not support consistent assessment of performance, which is a vital prerequisite. Using the high-level activities alone as a standard against which to assess practitioners' performance would not only be influenced by personal views of competence—which are to be avoided at all costs—but also leave the assessment process vulnerable to unacceptable variations in rigor and consistency when carried out against such a loose "standard." To support a more rigorous assessment process, a more detailed description of the activity is needed.

To achieve this, standards are written in terms of units (the high-level activities), elements (subactivities), and performance criteria—as, indeed, are the National Occupational Standards of the N/SVQ program. The units are derived directly from the five high-level activities. They are:

Unit 1. Prepare to carry out examinations.
Unit 2. Examine items and samples.
Unit 3. Undertake specialist scene examinations.
Unit 4. Interpret findings.
Unit 5. Report findings.

These high-level activities have then been divided into elements to provide more detail and guidance for the assessment process. This division of units into elements can be shown by taking as an example "Unit 2: Examine Items and Samples" and dividing this into its elements as follows.

Unit 2: Examine Items and Samples

Element 2.1. Monitor and maintain integrity of items and samples.
Element 2.2. Identify and recover potential evidence.
Element 2.3. Determine examinations to be undertaken.
Element 2.4. Carry out examinations.
Element 2.5. Produce laboratory notes and records.

The "standard" is now becoming more detailed. However, to provide the ultimate in detail to support the achievement of acceptable rigor and fairness in assessing the performance of forensic practitioners, we take each of the elements and further divide these into a number of performance criteria. We have already seen in the description of N/SVQs that it is these performance criteria that define the standard against which performance will be measured. What makes the performance criteria attractive as a measure of performance is that each is written in terms of an outcome (hence, they are often called "outcome-based standards") and a very important evaluative statement.

Taking element 2.2, "Identify and Recover Potential Evidence," to demonstrate this, it is seen that the performance criteria for this element are to

1. carry out examinations in a sequence which will ensure detection and optimum recovery of all types of potential evidence.
2. detect the existence of and identify the location of evidential material.
3. select and use recovery methods that will optimize recovery.
4. identify the need for additional areas of expertise.
5. maintain the integrity and continuity of items and recovered material throughout the recovery process.
6. record relevant information accurately, comprehensively, and contemporaneously.

This detailed description of the element ("Identify and Recover Potential Evidence") provided by the performance criteria gives far more information for the guidance of any potential assessment process than simply stating the description of the unit or element. This method of representing the standard will support rigorous and fair assessments.

It follows from this that to be deemed to be working to the standards—hence, by definition, working competently—in one of the elements, namely, "Identify and Recover Potential Evidence" associated with the unit "Examining Items and Samples," the forensic practitioner must demonstrate competent performance in all of the performance criteria defining that element of competence.

Perusal of the full suite of standards shows that there are in total some 100 performance criteria associated with the five units and sixteen elements.

None of the performance criteria associated with this element of competence, or any other element of competence for that matter, describes precisely how tasks are to be carried out. This is in line with the N/SVQ performance criteria described earlier and is a critical, deliberate, and often misunderstood feature of the standards. It may be explained by taking performance criterion 2 from the six performance criteria associated with element 2.2, where performance criterion 2 states that forensic practitioners are required to demonstrate that they are able to "Detect the existence of and identify the location of evidential material."

This statement describes the outcome that the practitioner is expected to achieve when carrying out the task to detect the existence of evidential material and to identify its location. It says nothing about how the existence of evidential material is detected, and neither does it suggest how the location of the evidential material is identified.

It provides an example of where accepted procedures (procedural standards) may be used to achieve the outcome described by the NOS (occupational standards).

Associated with each of the five units are the essential knowledge and understanding needed to support carrying out any task competently.

The knowledge and understanding to support the "Examination of items and samples" in Unit 2 are shown in Table 3.1.

WHAT DO THE STANDARDS TELL US?

A summary of the five units which form the backbone of the NOS in forensic science will tell us a great deal about what areas of work the standards cover and the structure of the units. Here are the summaries of the units:

Summary of Unit 1: Prepare to Carry Out Examinations

This unit is about insuring that adequate preparations are made prior to the examination of items and samples.

1. Establishing the requirements of the case and the types of examinations that will meet them and the development of the examination strategy
2. Physical preparation of suitable equipment and work area(s) in order to maintain the integrity of the items and samples
3. Initial inspection of the items and samples and confirmation that the examination is appropriate

---

TABLE 3.1
Knowledge and Understanding for Examination of Items and Samples

You Must Know and Understand

1	The methods available to detect evidential material, and how to carry them out and achieve optimum recovery
2	The range, purpose, and limitations of different location and recovery methods
3	How to determine the most appropriate recovery method(s) to suit different situations and different evidence types
4	How to identify the location of evidential material
5	How the recovery methods selected optimize recovery, minimize loss, and avoid contamination
6	Why it is important to assess the effect of different location and recovery methods on different evidence types
7	The amount of time that each location and recovery method is likely to take
8	How to prepare yourself correctly to carry out the location, recovery, and examination of potential evidence
9	Current relevant health and safety legislation, and how it applies to your own work role
10	How to establish and maintain the integrity and continuity of potential evidence, and the importance of this
11	Why items and samples are uniquely identified
12	Ways in which potential evidential material may be lost, and how to avoid this
13	How to identify and prevent contamination and cross contamination
14	The range, purpose, and limitations of different examination methods

(Continued)

TABLE 3.1 (CONTINUED)
Knowledge and Understanding for Examination of Items and Samples
You Must Know and Understand

15	How to determine the most appropriate examination method to suit different situations and circumstances
16	The use and relevance of the examinations that are carried out
17	The operational and scientific factors to consider when determining the examinations to be undertaken
18	The criteria to work to in order to plan and schedule examinations
19	How to perform different examination methods effectively
20	The established scientific principles and practices to consider when carrying out different types of examinations
21	Why it is important to carry out the examinations in a particular sequence
22	Why it is important to assess the effect of different examination methods on different evidence types, and how to do this
23	The different circumstances and conditions you might be faced with when examining potential evidence
24	How to ensure that results are reliable and fit for purpose
25	How to recognize the limitations of your expertise and knowledge, and the importance of not exceeding these
26	The circumstances which might lead you to seek expert advice and/or additional expertise, and how to obtain this
27	How to recognize contamination, and the actions to take
28	How to adapt working practices and procedures to accommodate different circumstances such as size and condition of the potential evidence, location of the examination, time constraints, emergency, and risk of contamination
29	How to identify insufficient and inconclusive results from examinations, and how to rectify the problem
30	What recording systems are available, and how to use them
31	What information to record, and how it should be recorded
32	Why it is important to record information in a format suitable for further use
33	How to ensure that notes and records are fit for purpose, clear, and unambiguous
34	How to identify the need for contemporaneous records and notes, and how to make them
35	Who has the right of access to information held on record
36	How to keep records to protect the security of information
37	Who might wish to use the examination notes and records, and the ways in which they might be used
38	What the procedures and requirements are on the security and transmission of information
39	The classification systems used, and how they operate
40	How to collate and order notes and information, and the importance of this
41	How and where to record adaptations made to working practices and procedures, and why it is important to record these

These activities may be carried out at the scene of the incident, in a specialized environment such as a laboratory, or at another suitable location. Scientific principles and practices must be adopted throughout this unit.

The methods used to recover and examine the scientific evidence will depend upon the type(s) of items and samples and the evidence type. Health and safety of self and others, and the preservation, integrity, and continuity of potential evidence, are paramount throughout the unit.

This unit applies to any individual who examines items and samples that have been submitted for forensic examination. The unit consists of five elements:

2.1. Monitor and maintain the integrity of items and samples.
2.2. Identify and recover potential evidence.
2.3. Determine examinations to be undertaken.
2.4. Carry out examinations.
2.5. Produce laboratory notes and records.

Summary of Unit 2: Examine Items and Samples

The unit covers:

1. Searching items and samples
2. Recovering potential evidence, and its testing and comparison
3. Recording the details of examinations and the collation of notes, including notes made by others

These activities may be carried out at the scene of the incident, in a specialized environment such as a laboratory, or at another suitable location. Scientific principles and practices must be adopted throughout this unit.

The methods used to recover and examine the scientific evidence will depend upon the type(s) of items and samples and the evidence type. Health and safety of self and others, and the preservation, integrity, and continuity of potential evidence, are paramount throughout the unit.

This unit applies to any individual who examines items and samples that have been submitted for forensic examination. The unit consists of five elements:

2.1. Monitor and maintain the integrity of items and samples.
2.2. Identify and recover potential evidence.
2.3. Determine examinations to be undertaken.
2.4. Carry out examinations.
2.5. Produce laboratory notes and records.

Summary of Unit 3: Undertake Specialist Scene Examinations

This unit is about carrying out an in-depth scientific examination of a scene of incident. The unit covers:

1. Establishing the requirements of the case and the types of examinations that will meet them and the development of the examination strategy
2. Physical preparation of suitable equipment and work area(s) in order to maintain the integrity of the items and samples
3. Initial inspection of the items and samples and confirmation that the examination is appropriate

The purpose of a scene examination is to obtain information and to recover items and samples for subsequent examination in order to assist in determining what happened, the sequence in which it happened, and who might have been involved in the incident. This investigative phase will often be followed by an evaluation of the findings within the context of one or more hypotheses (Unit 4).

There is likely to be more than one organization represented at the scene, so good communication skills and collaborative approaches to work are therefore essential.

Locating, preserving, and gathering potential evidence are key skills within the unit. It is essential to take adequate precautions to prevent contamination and possible degradation of the evidence both at the scene and when submitting the evidence for forensic examination. Health and safety of self and others and the preservation of potential evidence are paramount throughout the unit.

This unit applies to any individual who carries out forensic examination of a scene of incident. The unit consists of three elements:

3.3. Establish the requirements of the investigation.
3.2. Prepare to examine the scene of the incident.
3.3. Examine the scene of the incident.

Summary of Unit 4: Interpret Findings

This unit is about summarizing and assessing the examinations, interpreting the results, and drawing conclusions prior to the preparation of a final report or statement. The opinions drawn by the practitioner will be informed by databases, historical data, and/or personal experience. Rigorous quality assurance checks are of paramount importance throughout this unit. The conclusions will address the case requirements as identified in Unit 1 and will:

1. Provide support for a single hypothesis.
2. Provide support for more than one hypothesis.
3. Not support any particular hypothesis.

This unit is relevant to any individual who is responsible for interpreting the findings of forensic examinations. The unit consists of two elements:

4.1. Collate the results of the examinations.
4.2. Interpret examination findings.

Summary of Unit 5: Report Findings

This unit of competence is about reporting the findings of the forensic scientific examination. The unit covers:

- Production of reports on the examinations that have been carried out
- Participation in pretrial consultations, and presentation or oral evidence to courts and inquiries

Reports will be read by a wide range of individuals, most of whom will have little forensic scientific knowledge. They will also be read aloud in courts of law. They must, therefore, be written as clearly and unambiguously as possible. In particular, care should be taken to ensure that the examinations conducted and the practices behind these examinations are described in a language that ensures that they are understandable to non-forensic scientists, such as a judge and jury.

Reports may provide factual information only. However, where an opinion is given, the report will:

- Outline the background to the incident, as understood by the forensic scientist.
- Explain the requirement of the commissioning agency or customer.
- Provide a description of the examinations conducted and their outcomes.
- Make an assessment of the likelihood of the examination results given the hypotheses tested and the circumstances as understood by the forensic scientist.

Pretrial consultation may be required in order to explain findings to the prosecution or defense barrister or solicitor. These consultations may occur well in advance of the trial or when the trial is underway. The forensic scientist will often be required to present evidence as an expert witness in court.

It is the responsibility of the forensic scientist to clearly explain the significance of the findings and to consider other hypotheses that may be proposed in pretrial consultation or in court. The forensic scientist may also have to present evidence that has been established by others working under the forensic scientist's supervision.

This unit is relevant to any individual who is responsible for reporting the findings of forensic scientific examinations. The unit of competence consists of three elements:

5.1. Produce report.
5.2. Participate in pretrial consultation.
5.3. Present oral evidence to courts and inquiries.

The full suite of NOS (or Professional Standards of Competence) in forensic science is in Appendix 4.

There are many uses apart from assessment of competence to which these NOS (Appendix 3) may be put, not least the development of training and education programs and the assessment of workplace performance.

REFERENCE

1. Keith Inman and Norah Rudin, Principles and Practice of Forensic Science: The Profession of Forensic Science, CRC Press, Boca Raton, FL (2000).

4 Use of Standards

INTRODUCTION

Often when presenting proposals for the use of the National Occupational Standards in forensic science, it is seen as being nothing more than an intrusion into how individuals and organizations practice forensic science, or any other profession for that matter. It is almost seen as suggesting, "Here is an outsider in no way connected with our organization with an agenda to tell us how we must do our job." With regard to National Occupational Standards (NOS), such a view is wrong and arises as a result of a fundamental misunderstanding of what occupational standards are and what they mean. The literature adds to the confusion: there are so many so-called standards referred to without any clear definition of what they stand for. The standards promoted here are National Occupational Standards or Professional Standards of Competence, a term not far removed, at first glance, from "Professional Standards for the Practice of Criminalistics" as promoted in Peter Barnett's excellent work discussing ethics as professional standards [1]. They are in fact very different. National Occupational Standards can be used in a flexible manner, and it is this flexibility that enables them to be used by organizations or individual practitioners without changing any of their *acceptable* methods of working. However, if the method being used to carry out any task is not acceptable to the profession, there will be a mechanism in place to reject it. A similar, agreed scheme could be used internationally, for no matter where forensic science is practiced, it has ideally to be to the same occupational standard. So, as long as the outcome described by the Professional Standards of Competence (i.e., NOS) is achieved, the procedural standard used to do that will surely be an acceptable way of performing the task.

To understand NOS, it is first necessary to understand their characteristic features, the most outstanding of which is that they do not dictate how a task must be carried out; this offers "flexibility" in the way a task is carried out. What they do state very clearly is what the outcome is of carrying out any task. This unique, outcome-based feature must be clearly understood before any progress can be made in understanding their use. The standards do not dictate any particular method of carrying out the tasks in forensic practice.

To complement this, the standards describe the essential knowledge and understanding associated with carrying out the task in a competent manner. The possession of such knowledge and understanding by the practitioner is necessary to support delivery of the performance outcome described by the standards. Another unusual feature is the use of the word "essential" in relation to knowledge, indicating there is no requirement to know everything there is to know about a subject before a task associated with that subject can be carried out competently.

It is the description of the outcome expected when carrying out any task, and not describing how that outcome is achieved, which endows the standards with the powerful potential for universal use to support competent forensic practice; this includes forensic science as well as, for example, forensic pathology.

The standards provide many clues to the ways they may be used to unify nationally, and internationally, the occupational performance of forensic practitioners. By defining generically the tasks associated specifically with forensic science, a basis of a procedure for developing education and training programs and for the assessment of the occupational competence of practitioners emerges. Any procedure to assess the workplace performance of practitioners must have sufficient flexibility to recognize that there may very well be more than one acceptable way of carrying out a task and at the same time must be rigorous enough to reject any unacceptable practices. Because of this almost defining principle of allowing for flexibility in the way in which tasks are done, a cautionary note may be in order. There are some who, in many instances, although on the outside of mainstream organizations with regard to the practice of forensic science, may be tempted to state precisely how all organizations must achieve the agreed outcome defined by the outcome-based standards. These individuals may be involved in some way with the development and implementation of occupational standards, but it is not their role to state rigidly how a task should be carried out and to present this as though it were part of the occupational standards. Such a rigid definition would undermine the very principle on which the use of the occupational standards is based. Defining how tasks should be carried out is not the concern of those involved in developing and using the occupational standards. It is the role of organizations that must rigorously research and validate methods before they are recommended for use. These then become acceptable standard operating procedures (SOPs), or procedural standards.

This complex, vital, and often controversial point must be respected, and it is the aim of this work to suggest a procedure that will support forensic practitioners to achieve, maintain, and above all demonstrate their occupational competence which is open for third-party review and scrutiny.

There are many stages on the road to the ultimate goal of workplace competence. These stages can be represented in a cycle of competence (Figure 4.1), which puts standards (National Occupational Standards) firmly at the heart of the entire process.

Occupational standards may be used as a basis of a procedure for ensuring the occupational competence of forensic practitioners. It is proving very difficult (to date, impossible) to find a published procedure for consistently assessing the occupational competence on casework against standards set and agreed by the profession. After all, it is working competently when carrying out day-to-day activities that is as crucial for all those who provide forensic science services on a daily basis as it is for the end users of those services.

In spite of the importance of occupational competence, it is a feature that has been sadly neglected for many years. The cycle of competence (Figure 4.1) shows that the first stage on the route to achieving workplace competence is effective education.

Standards are the foundations for everything that affects forensic science. They have many uses. Indeed, occupational standards in general have many uses. Skills for Justice, the Sector Skills Council for the justice sector, has suggested over seventy potential uses for occupational standards (see Appendix 3).

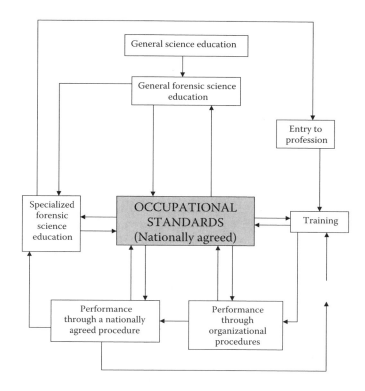

FIGURE 4.1 The route to occupational competence: The cycle of competence.

Four key uses of the National Occupational Standards for forensic science practitioners are as a basis for:

- Training and learning programs
- Qualifications
- The continual assessment of competent forensic practice
- Certification or accreditation

USING THE STANDARDS AS A BASIS FOR TRAINING AND LEARNING PROGRAMS

There is all too often a tendency to develop training packages or learning packages in isolation from the real world. The training packages themselves are usually well presented and have stated aims, learning outcomes, and, hopefully, assessment strategies to test the efficacy of the learning outcomes. However, there is often no direct correlation with the "industry standards." All training courses should be designed in the light of the outcome-based, generic occupational standards which indicate both the expected outcomes and also the knowledge and understanding required to meet the standard. It follows that all training design should start, and flow, from the standards. An excellent guide to developing training and learning programs from National Occupational Standards has been published by Skills for Justice [2].

The same argument applies to learning packages—particularly those which form part of, for example, degree- and postgraduate degree-level provision in forensic science. There is a big difference, of course, in that university students are not practitioners, and they will not be practitioners at the end of their university courses. Nevertheless, the knowledge and understanding requirements, in particular, and also the outcome statements themselves should be capable of translation by academics into a meaningful syllabus relating to any forensic specialty that it is proposed to include in the course, whether document examination, tool mark examination, or any other.

In the United Kingdom, there is an ever growing number of university degree programs associated with forensic science, some with such bizarre titles as Forensic Science and Child Care and Forensic Science and Theology [3]. Most of the universities developing and delivering forensic science programs are often supported by experienced forensic scientists or police scientific support personnel (scene examiners, etc.) who are often former practitioners. It is they, in many cases, who provide the syllabus detail for the education program, and it is partly because of this that the course content varies so widely from university to university. Many programs do not appear to address the fundamental question: what is forensic science as practiced by the major service providers in the United Kingdom? Some offer a mix of what is called by most service providers in the United Kingdom "forensic science"—probably the same as criminalistics and other forensic sciences, namely, chemistry and scene of incident examinations, the latter aimed in the main at police scientific support personnel. There is a widely held view, mainly amongst the major forensic science service providers, that it is not the role of the university to engage in producing fully performing forensic scientists. Others have similar views. Universities should accept the challenge of ensuring that the nascent forensic scientist has the necessary knowledge of the general and all embracing scientific principles that underpin much of forensic science. As a scientific discipline it has special requirements for education beyond those of other scientific disciplines, because it employs science in a unique manner. Such a strong knowledge base will equip any emerging forensic scientist to progress to competence in his or her chosen field and will also provide a useful springboard to other specialized science-based vocations. In support of this view, the report by the Science, Engineering, Manufacturing Technologies Alliance (SEMTA) [3] emphasizes that most employers of forensic scientists would prefer a no-nonsense first degree in one of the natural sciences such as chemistry or biology, with the emphasis probably being on chemistry [4]. Possession of such a good degree would provide evidence that all the essential underpinning science-based knowledge had been acquired by the potential forensic scientist. The ideal raw material for developing into a forensic scientist is an honors graduate in one of the natural sciences; the profession can then have confidence that such an individual will possess the necessary basic science demanded for a successful career in forensic science.

Once all of these features are in place, the next stage is to begin the development of a forensic scientist.

Does the university have a role in the development of a forensic scientist apart from ensuring that the essential basic scientific knowledge is possessed? Yes, it most certainly does. There are some who feel that anyone who aspires to be a forensic scientist should have been exposed to the widest possible range of forensic scientific activities prior to specializing. Dated 1957 and reprinted in 1963, a very early syllabus of laboratory work in criminology from the University of California, Berkeley (where Paul Kirk was the instructor), describes the curriculum under "outline of laboratory work in criminology":

> A flexible curriculum is provided, in which the regular student may survey the broad field of identification of evidence, and the special student can emphasize more intensively those subjects of greatest interest.

This could be the commencement of the generalist education for a potential forensic scientist at that time. The full syllabus is all embracing, student grading is rigorous, and high student commitment is demanded.

This general all-round education in forensic science is not unlike many other professions where, after undergoing initial education in the general principles of the profession, students undergo some form of specialized training. Specialized training is not the role of the university, however; specialized education may follow on from a general forensic science degree course. The important role of universities is for them to carry out general education in forensic science and, where demanded, specialized education.

The syllabus for the programs could be based on the entire repertoire of work carried out by the major forensic science organizations. There is also a need, as a precursor to such a general program of education in forensic science, to provide the essential specialist underpinning scientific knowledge on which forensic science is based and often ignored.

How would education providers identify the detailed content required for the syllabus? How would they ensure they had the correct information? This is where the National Occupational Standards in forensic science are poised to play a major role [2].

National Occupational Standards have been developed by practitioners and endorsed through rigorous consultation and feedback by the profession in the United Kingdom prior to being accepted by the profession. This makes the detail expressed by the standards acceptable to the forensic science community at large—at least in the United Kingdom. The NOS describe fully the activities within forensic science laboratories. They are expressed generically and do not refer to specific standards or to procedures for carrying out, say, tool mark examinations and comparisons, nor for DNA, nor (for that matter) anything else. They simply describe generically the outcome associated with carrying out a task. What better basis could there possibly be for degree courses on forensic science? Not only will the program be based on what the profession has identified as essential, but it will also encourage the design of a teaching program around a consistent and meaningful syllabus.

The way in which the National Occupational Standards may be used to achieve this can be explained through first considering a summary of the units and elements of competence that make up the standards; from this, it is seen that there are vast amounts of detail defining the outcome of carrying out essential tasks even in this brief summary of the units and elements of competence. For example, under the unit dedicated to "examining items and samples," it is mandated that the practitioner must:

- Monitor and maintain the integrity of items and samples.
- Identify and recover potential evidence.
- Determine examinations to be undertaken.
- Carry out examinations.
- Produce examination notes and records.

Associated with this unit are the essential knowledge and understanding required to carry out a task in a competent manner.

SUMMARY OF UNITS AND ELEMENTS OF COMPETENCE FOR THE PROFESSIONAL STANDARDS OF COMPETENCE IN FORENSIC SCIENCE

Unit 1. Prepare to carry out examinations.
    Element 1.1. Determine case requirements.
    Element 1.2. Establish the integrity of items and samples.
    Element 1.3. Inspect items and samples submitted for examination.

Knowledge and understanding

Unit 2. Examine items and samples.
    Element 2.1. Monitor and maintain the integrity of items and samples.
    Element 2.2. Identify and recover potential evidence.
    Element 2.3. Determine examinations to be undertaken.
    Element 2.4. Carry out examinations.
    Element 2.5. Produce examination notes and records.

Knowledge and understanding

Unit 3. Undertake specialist scene examinations.
    Element 3.1. Establish the requirements of the investigation.
    Element 3.2. Prepare to examine the scene of the incident.
    Element 3.3. Examine the scene of the incident.

Knowledge and understanding

Unit 4. Interpret findings.
    Element 4.1. Collate the results of the examinations.
    Element 4.2. Interpret examination findings.

Knowledge and understanding

Unit 5. Report findings.
    Element 5.1. Produce report.
    Element 5.2. Participate in pretrial consultation.
    Element 5.3. Present oral evidence to courts and inquiries.

Knowledge and understanding

The full suite of standards (Appendix 4) gives even more detail about each of the elements of competence. To demonstrate this, unit of competence 2, which deals with examining items and samples each of the elements associated with Unit 2, describes a high-level subactivity which must be carried out when examining items and samples. This subactivity or element is defined even more precisely by the performance criteria. Performance criteria describe the desired outcome when carrying out a task under an element of competence. These performance criteria are described below under the headings entitled "You Must Ensure That You ..."

UNIT 2: EXAMINE ITEMS AND SAMPLES

PERFORMANCE CRITERIA

Element 2.1: Monitor and Maintain the Integrity of Items and Samples

You must ensure that you:

1. Handle items and samples in a way that prevents contamination, cross contamination, and loss of evidence.
2. Uniquely label items and samples.
3. Maintain the continuity of items and samples throughout the examination process.
4. Record information accurately, comprehensively, and contemporaneously.

Element 2.2: Identify and Recover Potential Evidence

You must ensure that you:

1. Carry out examinations in a sequence which ensures detection and optimum recovery of all types of potential evidence.
2. Detect the existence of and identify the location of evidential material.
3. Select and use recovery methods that optimize recovery.
4. Identify the need for any additional areas of expertise.
5. Maintain the integrity and continuity of items, samples, and recovered material throughout the recovery process.
6. Record relevant information accurately, comprehensively, and contemporaneously.

Element 2.3: Determine Examinations to Be Undertaken

You must ensure that you:

1. Identify and select relevant examinations based on an accurate evaluation of the items and samples and the nature of the investigation.
2. Plan and schedule examinations to enable reliable, fit-for-purpose results to be gathered.

3. Seek expert advice in instances where additional specialist information is required relevant to the investigation.
4. Record relevant information accurately, comprehensively, and contemporaneously.

Element 2.4: Carry Out Examinations

You must ensure that you:

1. Carry out relevant examinations safely and in a manner appropriate to the items and samples being examined.
2. Adapt working procedures and practices appropriately to allow for different circumstances and conditions.
3. Identify insufficient and inconclusive results, and take remedial action.
4. Seek expert advice in instances where additional specialist information is required relevant to the examination.
5. Record examination results and any adaptations to working procedures and practices accurately, comprehensively, and contemporaneously.

Element 2.5: Produce Examination Notes and Records

You must ensure that you:

1. Make contemporaneous examination notes and records, ensuring they are fit for purpose, accurate, legible, clear, and unambiguous.
2. Order notes and record information in a way that supports validation and interrogation.
3. Uniquely classify records.
4. File records securely in a manner which facilitates retrieval.
5. Accurately collate examination notes on work carried out by others into the overall records.

Such a detailed description of the expected outcome when carrying out the task, provided by the performance criteria, describes what must be achieved; it does not tell us how the outcome is achieved. To show how this is so, consider element of competence 2.3, "Determine examinations to be undertaken."

Whereas performance criterion 4 states, "Record relevant information accurately, comprehensively, and contemporaneously," nothing is said about how the recording is to be carried out for it to be *accurate*, *comprehensive*, and *contemporaneous*. It does, however, make a clear demand on any education program to deal with this by suggesting that any education program in forensic science must address methods of recording information accurately, comprehensively, and contemporaneously in order to satisfy the performance aspects of the Professional Standards of Competence in this one small area.

There are also the defined knowledge and understanding associated with the standards to consider. The knowledge and understanding for unit of competence 2, "Examine items and samples," give a wealth of essential detail for course developers to feast upon, and there are numerous sources of this information (see Table 4.1).

TABLE 4.1
Knowledge and Understanding for Unit 2, "Examine Items and Samples"

1 The methods available to detect evidential material, and how to carry them out and achieve optimum recovery
2 The range, purpose, and limitations of different location and recovery methods
3 How to determine the most appropriate recovery method(s) to suit different situations and different evidence types
4 How to identify the location of evidential material
5 How the recovery methods selected optimize recovery, minimize loss, and avoid contamination
6 Why it is important to assess the effect of different location and recovery methods on different evidence types
7 The amount of time that each location and recovery method is likely to take
8 How to prepare yourself correctly to carry out the location, recovery, and examination of potential evidence
9 Current relevant health and safety legislation, and how it applies to your own work role
10 How to establish and maintain the integrity and continuity of potential evidence, and the importance of this
11 Why items and samples are uniquely identified
12 Ways in which potential evidential material may be lost, and how to avoid this
13 How to identify and prevent contamination and cross contamination
14 The range, purpose, and limitations of different examination methods
15 How to determine the most appropriate examination method to suit different situations and circumstances
16 The use and relevance of the examinations that are carried out
17 The operational and scientific factors to consider when determining the examinations to be undertaken
18 The criteria to work to in order to plan and schedule examinations
19 How to perform different examination methods effectively
20 The established scientific principles and practices to consider when carrying out different types of examinations
21 Why it is important to carry out the examinations in a particular sequence
22 Why it is important to assess the effect of different examination methods on different evidence types, and how to do this
23 The different circumstances and conditions you might be faced with when examining potential evidence
24 How to ensure that results are reliable and fit for purpose
25 How to recognize the limitations of your expertise and knowledge, and the importance of not exceeding these
26 The circumstances which might lead you to seek expert advice and/or additional expertise, and how to obtain this
27 How to recognize contamination, and the actions to take
28 How to adapt working practices and procedures to accommodate different circumstances such as size and condition of the potential evidence, location of the examination, time constraints, emergency, and risk of contamination
29 How to identify insufficient and inconclusive results from examinations, and how to rectify the problem
30 What recording systems are available, and how to use them
31 What information to record, and how it should be recorded
32 Why it is important to record information in a format suitable for further use
33 How to ensure that notes and records are fit for purpose, clear, and unambiguous
34 How to identify the need for contemporaneous records and notes, and how to make them
35 Who has the right of access to information held on record

(Continued)

TABLE 4.1 (CONTINUED)
Knowledge and Understanding for Unit 2, "Examine Items and Samples

36 How to keep records to protect the security of information
37 Who might wish to use the examination notes and records, and the ways in which they might be used
38 What the procedures and requirements are on the security and transmission of information
39 The classification systems used, and how they operate
40 How to collate and order notes and information, and the importance of this
41 How and where to record adaptations made to working practices and procedures, and why it is important to record these

As can be seen in Table 4.1, for this unit alone, there are forty-one items of knowledge and understanding. These knowledge and understanding statements describe what the student of forensic science needs to know, and it is clearly presented for lecturers to use in the development of forensic science degree programs. For example, there is a requirement to know and understand *methods available to detect evidential material, and how to carry them out and achieve optimum recovery.* Again, there are numerous sources of this detail, and it would be a welcome support to education if employers of forensic scientists could be persuaded to play a role here.

Occupational standards tell us what is to be achieved when carrying out a task. Under 2, "Examine items and samples," performance criterion 4 asks for relevant information to be recorded accurately, comprehensively, and contemporaneously, but (as mentioned above) gives no indication as to how such recording is to be carried out to satisfy this requirement. This demonstrates a significant feature of the standards, flexibility. This flexibility is apparent in the way they may be used and significantly recognizes that there may be more than one acceptable way of carrying out a task. This at first glance may be seen as offering a "rogues' charter," but in practice there will be a safety measure in the assessment program that will reject any unacceptable practices and that will also offer a way in which the profession can advance its performance by eliminating unacceptable practices. The ways in which these outcomes may be achieved will be the subject of education programs, the details of which can be obtained from the many textbooks and organizational SOPs. Finding out how to do something in forensic science should not present too much of a problem since there are numerous textbooks on the techniques of criminalistics, but there are very few that address competence.

The knowledge and understanding specification and the performance criteria described by the National Occupational Standards provide the ideal platform for the development of a university education program in forensic science aimed at the natural science graduate.

The design of education programs in forensic science as suggested here would ensure consistency of the syllabus content and teaching of the subject in universities. In many universities, the syllabus seems to revolve around "interesting" case studies, whereas if universities were doing their job they would be looking at the underpinning of forensic science, which has been already stated is unique, of forensic science. This is what is needed from universities. All the research effort and resources seem to go into developing new ways of doing things, but some could usefully be diverted into a program to ensure workplace competence within the profession. Using National

Occupational Standards would address what employers have agreed to as being the forensic science education requirements for a nascent forensic scientist and would go some way to developing the ideal person for conversion into a specialist forensic scientist. It would also support the move to get recognition of forensic science as a profession.

Use of occupational standards alone for the development of a forensic scientist in the "hope" that it will, through some stroke of good fortune, produce an individual equipped to go forward to achieve specialist forensic scientific "fame" will not work. Progress against the occupational standards should ideally be monitored through knowledge-based examination such as those offered by the American Board of Criminalistics (ABC) and the Forensic Science Society (FSSoc). Practical examinations based on materials similar to those provided for proficiency testing and project work should form major monitoring devices for the progress of individuals through courses on offer. The grading of the knowledge-based examinations and the assessment of any practical and project work should be against the National Occupational Standards. The alignment of any knowledge-based examinations with the occupational standards will be necessary to ensure that they reflect what is demanded by the standards and therefore what is demanded by the profession. The nearest we come to ideal knowledge-based examinations at present are those offered by the American Board of Criminalistics, where both the general (forensic science) knowledge examination and the specialty (forensic science) examinations would form a good monitoring device for the progress of education in forensic science.

It is by no means the aim of these education programs to produce the fully competent forensic scientist who can walk into any practicing organization and, when familiar with the territory, perform competently in any area of the profession. Not at all—what organizations want, certainly in the United Kingdom, is a natural science graduate (probably chemistry) who ideally has at least undergone some general education in forensic science. This type of person is the ideal product of any "university" education program in forensic science and is now ready for training by any forensic science organization to become a proficient practicing forensic scientist.

This introduces the second of the steps on the route to workplace competence—training.

TRAINING

It is strongly recommended that more emphasis and organizational support is given to training on the job.

Training is still seen by many as the answer to all of the questions surrounding competence—an assertion that needs challenging, because training is simply a means to an end and not an end in itself. That training does not guarantee competence was implied by Kirk [5] in his 1963 paper, "The Ontogeny of Criminalistics." Training says very little, if anything, about workplace competence, and discussions have continued for many years on how to transfer performance in the training room to the workplace without any satisfactory outcome. At its best, training gives a view of a person's performance during training; we will see later, however, that this, in the right context, offers an invaluable tool in supporting practitioners to achieve competent performance, but at the moment the assessment of the performance of an individual on a training course is nearly always relegated to knowledge assessment alone, which means that those emerging from the training program at best "know" how a job should be done but may have little ability to "do" the job.

Training is part of a process that will, if supported correctly, help in the development of the competent practitioner. It is a very important step on the route to workplace competence but not by a long way the only step, as a great deal of evidence suggests.

How is training carried out?

Many organizations will provide support for new entrants and will in many instances allocate them a mentor who will not only be a "best practitioner" in the field in which the emerging forensic scientist is about to work but also have been trained in a variety of training and mentoring techniques and will have the overall responsibility for supervising and training the emerging practitioner. Traditionally, training was often delivered by anyone with the time to spare, and worse still the "trainers" were free to deliver training as they saw fit to any standard—and presumably with no real measured outcome. The program content was for the "trainer" to decide upon, and often it was not necessarily relevant to the needs of the individual or the organization. It was as if it was mandated somewhere that to be a good employer, employees had to attend a training course of some sort; surprisingly, this view persists in some organizations today, where "blanket" training at set career times is viewed as a panacea for all problems with the organization. Some training organizations went as far as purchasing expensive, up-to-the-minute equipment matching that which was being used operationally but solely for use on training courses. This method of "off-the-job" training for forensic scientists soon becomes nonviable, because when new equipment is in place operationally there is the additional expense of providing similar equipment for use in the training room. There were often conditions in a well-provided-for training room that did not reflect operational conditions at all. Surprisingly, there is still an element of this in place where entrepreneurs are allowed to do their own thing. Again, as in the development of education programs, we turn to the Professional Standards of Competence to provide a sharp focus for the design of training.

From within the generic National Occupational Standards emerges a training syllabus that is meaningful with agreed standards as the source of its content. The forensic scientific process may be represented by five stages:

1. Preparing to carry out examinations
2. Examining items and samples
3. Undertaking specialist scene examinations
4. Interpreting findings
5. Reporting findings

These may be considered as the five high-level activities which are divided into a series of subactivities and performance criteria.

These high-level activities, subactivities, and performance criteria are ideally placed to form the basis for a generic training program for forensic science, and since they have derived from the Professional Standards of Competence for forensic science they have been agreed to by the profession in the United Kingdom.

A generic training syllabus for all forensic scientific activities derived from the standards may be represented as shown below.

A SUMMARY OF THE STANDARDS

Activity 1. Prepare to carry out examinations (aim of the training).

Summary

Subactivity 1.1. Determine case requirements (learning outcome).
Subactivity 1.2. Establish the integrity of items and samples (learning outcome).
Subactivity 1.3. Inspect items and samples submitted for examination (learning outcome).

Knowledge and understanding

Activity 2. Examine items and samples.

Summary

Subactivity 2.1. Monitor and maintain the integrity of items and samples.
Subactivity 2.2. Identify and recover potential evidence.
Subactivity 2.3. Determine examinations to be undertaken.
Subactivity 2.4. Carry out examinations.
Subactivity 2.5. Produce examination notes and records.

Knowledge and understanding

Activity 3. Undertake specialist scene examinations.

Summary

Subactivity 3.1. Establish the requirements of the investigation.
Subactivity 3.2. Prepare to examine the scene of the incident.
Subactivity 3.3. Examine the scene of the incident.

Knowledge and understanding

Activity 4. Interpret findings.

Summary

Subactivity 4.1. Collate the results of the examinations.
Subactivity 4.2. Interpret examination findings.

Knowledge and understanding

Activity 5. Report findings.

Summary

Subactivity 5.1. Produce report.
Subactivity 5.2. Participate in pretrial consultation.
Subactivity 5.3. Present oral evidence to courts and inquiries.

Knowledge and understanding

A GENERIC TRAINING PROGRAM FOR FORENSIC SCIENTISTS DERIVED FROM THE PROFESSIONAL STANDARDS OF COMPETENCE

ACTIVITY 1: PREPARE TO CARRY OUT EXAMINATIONS

Summary

This activity is about ensuring that adequate preparations are made prior to the examination of items and samples, originating from an incident that is subject to forensic scientific investigation.

The activity divides into three distinct parts:

1. Establishing the requirements of the case and the types of examinations that will meet them, and the development of an examination strategy
2. Physical preparation of suitable equipment and work area(s) in order to maintain the integrity of the items and samples
3. Initial inspection of the items and samples, and confirmation that the examination strategy is appropriate

The preparations that are made apply in all cases, irrespective of the environment in which the activity is conducted, for example at the scene of the incident or in a specialized environment such as a laboratory. Scientific principles and practices must be adopted throughout this activity. Health and safety of self and others and the preservation, integrity, and continuity of potential evidence are paramount throughout.

This activity applies to any individual who prepares items and samples that will be subject to forensic scientific examination. The individual may or may not go on to carry out the examinations him or herself. The activity consists of three subactivities:

1.1. Determine case requirements.
1.2. Establish the integrity of items and samples.
1.3. Inspect items and samples submitted for examination.

Training Syllabus

The training syllabus is based on the performance criteria from the Professional Standards of Competence.

Following training, the student will be able to:

Determine case requirementsrequirements by

1. Establishing the circumstances of the incident, and considering these against exhibits received and examinations requested
2. Confirming that the items submitted are appropriate for the work to be undertaken
3. Establishing the storage requirements of potential evidence, and making arrangements for safe, secure, and clean facilities
4. Agreeing and prioritizing the sequence of the various aspects of the work

5. Preparing equipment and work area(s) appropriate for the intended examinations
6. Identifying and rectifying nonconforming equipment

Establish the integrity of items and samples by

1. Receiving items safely and securely from storage facilities
2. Checking items and samples against records, and identifying any inaccuracies so that they can be rectified
3. Documenting details of storage, handling, transfer, and packaging of items and samples in a way which establishes continuity
4. Identifying details of any packaging problems, and providing a resolution
5. Storing and transferring items and samples in a way that avoids contamination, cross contamination, and loss of potential evidence

Inspect items and samples submitted for examination by

1. Safely removing items and samples from packaging in a manner that avoids contamination and cross contamination
2. Confirming the identity and identification of submitted items against documentation
3. Identifying scientific evidence that can be derived from the items and samples
4. Selecting examination methods relevant to the items and samples submitted
5. Identifying problems and potential problems, and consulting others to resolve the matter
6. Identifying and establishing a sampling protocol for items to be examined
7. Maintaining continuity of items throughout the inspection process
8. Recording information accurately, comprehensively, and contemporaneously

Knowledge and understanding: Following training, you will know and understand:

---

1   Why it is important to establish the details of the case, and how to do this
2   How to ensure that items and samples are safely and securely received
3   How to recognize relationships between the case and the items and samples received
4   Why it is important to assess the effect of potential evidence on other evidence types
5   How to select and prepare a range of equipment, consumables, and reagents that may be needed to locate, recover, and examine potential evidence
6   The extent and range of facilities available for examining items and samples
7   How to select the appropriate type of examination and work area
8   How to identify and rectify nonconforming equipment
9   The factors to consider when planning the storage and packaging of items and samples
10 How to store and transfer potential evidence, avoiding contamination, cross contamination, and loss of evidence
11 How to establish and maintain the integrity and continuity of potential evidence, and the importance of this
12 The legal requirements regarding the integrity and continuity of evidence, and the importance of satisfying them
13 What is meant by contamination and cross contamination, and how it can occur
14 How to identify and prevent contamination, cross contamination, and loss of evidence
15 How to avoid jeopardizing the integrity of potential evidence
16 Ways in which potential evidence may be lost, and how to avoid this
17 Why it is important to identify inaccuracies between items, samples, and records

18 The types of inaccuracies that might occur, and how to rectify them
19 The range, purpose, and limitations of different recovery methods
20 How to determine the most appropriate recovery and examination method(s) to suit different situations and different evidence types
21 The importance of identifying submitted items and samples
22 How to identify all relevant evidence types
23 How to sequence and prioritize the work, and the criteria to work to
24 How to assess the effect of examinations on other types of potential evidence
25 The principles of sampling
26 The problems which might occur when inspecting items and samples, and how to resolve them
27 The types of packaging problems that can occur and how to resolve them, including dealing with inappropriate labeling and packaging, inadequate seals, damaged packaging and seals, and contamination dangers
28 How to resolve problems associated with insufficient evidential material, inappropriate evidential material, additional evidence types, and contamination of evidential material
29 The type of advice to give clients, and how to provide advice
30 The importance of consultation
31 Who to contact to clarify any discrepancies concerning the items, samples, and records, and the importance of this
32 The roles and functions of the different organizations that may be involved in the forensic science process
33 What information is relevant, and how it should be recorded
34 Why it is important to record information in a format suitable for further use
35 How to identify the need for contemporaneous records and notes, and how to make them
36 What recording systems are available, and how to use them
37 Why it is important to record details of storage, handling, transfer, and packaging of items and samples

ACTIVITY 2: EXAMINE ITEMS AND SAMPLES

Summary

This activity is about identifying and recovering potential evidence from the items and samples submitted for examination. The activity covers:

1. Searching items and samples
2. Recovering potential evidence, and its testing and comparison
3. Recording the details of examinations and the collation of notes, including notes made by others

These activities may be carried out at the scene of the incident, in a specialized environment such as a laboratory, or at another suitable location. Scientific principles and practices must be adopted throughout this unit.

The methods used to recover and examine the scientific evidence will depend upon the type(s) of items and samples and the evidence type. Health and safety of self and others and the preservation, integrity, and continuity of potential evidence are paramount throughout. This activity applies to any individual who examines items and samples that have been submitted for forensic scientific examination.

The activity consists of five subactivities:

2.1. Monitor and maintain the integrity of items and samples.
2.2. Identify and recover potential evidence.

2.3. Determine examinations to be undertaken.
2.4. Carry out examinations.
2.5. Produce laboratory notes and records.

Following training, the student will be able to:

Monitor and maintain integrity of items and samples by

1. Handling items and samples in a way that prevents contamination, cross contamination, and loss of evidence
2. Uniquely labeling items and samples
3. Maintaining the continuity of items and samples throughout the examination process
4. Recording information accurately, comprehensively, and contemporaneously

Identify and recover potential evidence by

1. Carrying out examinations in a sequence which ensures detection and optimum recovery of all types of potential evidence
2. Detecting the existence of and identifying the location of evidential material
3. Selecting and using recovery methods that optimize recovery
4. Identifying any need for additional areas of expertise
5. Maintaining the integrity and continuity of items, samples, and recovered material throughout the recovery process
6. Recording relevant information accurately, comprehensively, and contemporaneously

Determine examinations to be undertaken by

1. Identifying and selecting relevant examinations based on an accurate evaluation of the items and samples and the nature of the investigation
2. Planning and scheduling examinations to enable reliable, fit-for-purpose results to be gathered
3. Seeking expert advice in instances where additional specialist information is required relevant to the investigation
4. Recording relevant information accurately, comprehensively, and contemporaneously

Carry out examinations by

1. Carrying out relevant examinations safely and in a manner appropriate to the items and samples being examined
2. Adapting working procedures and practices appropriately to allow for different circumstances and conditions
3. Identifying insufficient and inconclusive results, and taking remedial action
4. Seeking expert advice in instances where additional specialist information is required relevant to the examination

Produce examination notes and records by

1. Making contemporaneous examination notes and records, ensuring they are fit for purpose, accurate, legible, clear, and unambiguous
2. Ordering notes and record information in a way that supports validation and interrogation
3. Uniquely classifying records
4. Filing records securely in a manner which facilitates retrieval
5. Accurately collating examination notes, on work carried out by others, into the overall records

Knowledge and understanding: Following training, you will know and understand:

1	The methods available to detect evidential material, and how to carry them out and achieve optimum recovery
2	The range, purpose, and limitations of different location and recovery methods
3	How to determine the most appropriate recovery method(s) to suit different situations and different evidence types
4	How to identify the location of evidential material
5	How the recovery methods selected optimize recovery, minimize loss, and avoid contamination
6	Why it is important to assess the effect of different location and recovery methods on different evidence types
7	The amount of time that each location and recovery method is likely to take
8	How to prepare yourself correctly to carry out the location, recovery, and examination of potential evidence
9	Current relevant health and safety legislation, and how it applies to your own work role
10	How to establish and maintain the integrity and continuity of potential evidence, and the importance of this
11	Why items and samples are uniquely identified
12	Ways in which potential evidential material may be lost, and how to avoid this
13	How to identify and prevent contamination and cross contamination
14	The range, purpose, and limitations of different examination methods
15	How to determine the most appropriate examination method to suit different situations and circumstances
16	The use and relevance of the examinations that are carried out
17	The operational and scientific factors to consider when determining the examinations to be undertaken
18	The criteria to work to in order to plan and schedule examinations
19	How to perform different examination methods effectively
20	The established scientific principles and practices to consider when carrying out different types of examinations
21	Why it is important to carry out the examinations in a particular sequence
22	Why it is important to assess the effect of different examination methods on different evidence types, and how to do this
23	The different circumstances and conditions you might be faced with when examining potential evidence
24	How to ensure that results are reliable and fit for purpose
25	How to recognize the limitations of your expertise and knowledge, and the importance of not exceeding these
26	The circumstances which might lead you to seek expert advice and/or additional expertise, and how to obtain this
27	How to recognize contamination, and the actions to take

28   How to adapt working practices and procedures to accommodate different circumstances such as size and condition of the potential evidence, location of the examination, time constraints, emergency, and risk of contamination
29   How to identify insufficient and inconclusive results from examinations, and how to rectify the problem
30   What recording systems are available, and how to use them
31   What information to record, and how it should be recorded
32   Why it is important to record information in a format suitable for further use
33   How to ensure that notes and records are fit for purpose, clear, and unambiguous
34   How to identify the need for contemporaneous records and notes, and how to make them
35   Who has the right of access to information held on record
36   How to keep records to protect the security of information
37   Who might wish to use the examination notes and records, and the ways in which they might be used
38   What the procedures and requirements are on the security and transmission of information
39   The classification systems used, and how they operate
40   How to collate and order notes and information, and the importance of this
41   How and where to record adaptations made to working practices and procedures, and why it is important to record these

ACTIVITY 3: UNDERTAKE SPECIALIST SCENE EXAMINATIONS

Summary

This activity is about carrying out an in-depth scientific examination of a scene of incident. The activity covers:

1.   Establishing the purpose and requirements of the scene examination
2.   The preparations required before the scene examination
3.   The scene examination

The purpose of a scene examination is to obtain information and to recover items and samples for subsequent examination in order to assist in determining what happened, the sequence in which it happened, and who might have been involved in the incident. This investigative phase will often be followed by an evaluation of the findings within the context of one or more hypotheses (Unit 4).

There is likely to be more than one organization represented at the scene, so good communication skills and collaborative approaches to work are therefore essential.

Locating, preserving, and gathering potential evidence are key skills within the unit. It is essential to take adequate precautions to prevent contamination and possible degradation of the evidence both at the scene and when submitting the evidence for forensic scientific examination. Health and safety of self and others and the preservation of potential evidence are paramount throughout.

This activity applies to any individual who carries out forensic examination of a scene of incident. The activity consists of three subactivities:

3.1.   Establish the requirements of the investigation.
3.2.   Prepare to examine the scene of the incident.
3.3.   Examine the scene of the incident.

Following training, the student will be able to:

Establish the requirements of the investigation by

1. Ascertaining the circumstances of the incident and the scene of the investigation from the relevant personnel and other sources
2. Determining the types of examinations to be carried out in accordance with the reported circumstances
3. Giving due consideration to the possibility of linked scenes to ensure that relevant avenues of investigation are followed up
4. Determining the logistics of the operation, and resolving known problems with due regard to effectiveness, efficiency, and economy
5. Considering the safety of all personnel at the scene, and giving advice to ensure relevant safety precautions are carried out
6. Identifying equipment needed for the investigation, and making suitable arrangements to get it to the scene

Prepare to examine the scene of the incident by

1. Establishing effective working relationships with scene personnel in order to manage the scientific investigation of the scene
2. Assessing, determining, and agreeing the types and sequence of necessary examinations with the relevant personnel in accordance with the circumstances of the incident
3. Identifying the area of the scene, and delineating and protecting it to preserve the scene
4. Agreeing and establishing access to the scene, taking account of potential contamination and loss of evidence
5. Advising other personnel on the requirements for collecting data and recording notes
6. Recording relevant information accurately, comprehensively, and contemporaneously

Examine the scene of the incident by

1. Locating, identifying, collecting, and preserving potential evidential materials in a manner which ensures their integrity and reduces loss and degradation
2. Identifying the need for additional areas of expertise and facilities, and employing and coordinating relevant personnel, where required
3. Collating preliminary investigations, and formulating initial hypotheses
4. Evaluating and interpreting hypotheses, and undertaking further action as necessary
5. Accurately reporting preliminary findings
6. Handling, packaging, sealing, labeling, and recording items in a way which prevents contamination and loss of evidence
7. Establishing priority for the submission of items and samples to the laboratory
8. Making recommendations to relevant personnel to ensure that items and samples are securely packaged, stored, and transported

9. Recording relevant information accurately, comprehensively, and contemporaneously

Knowledge and understanding: Following training, you will know and understand:

---

1   How to establish the details of the case, and the importance of this
2   The principles and methods involved in the investigative process
3   How to plan the logistics of the scene investigation
4   The use and relevance of the scientific investigative work that needs to be undertaken
5   How to determine the most appropriate examination methods to use
6   Why it is important to assess the effect of potential evidence on other evidence types
7   How to establish access to the scene
8   The information needed to plan the scientific investigative work
9   The operational and scientific factors to consider when planning the preservation, recovery, packaging, and transportation of items and samples
10 How to identify and preserve the scene(s) and the potential evidence
11 The extent and range of facilities and equipment available for preserving, recovering, and examining potential evidence
12 How to sequence and prioritize the scientific investigative work, and the criteria to work to
13 Why it is important to assess the effect of scientific investigative work of potential evidence on other evidence types
14 How to select, prepare, and use a range of equipment, consumables, and reagents that may be needed to preserve, recover, and examine potential evidence
15 How to apply dynamic assessment of risk at the scene(s) of incident
16 Current relevant health and safety legislation, and how it applies to your own work role
17 The types of safety precautions that may need to be taken to ensure the safety of all personnel at the scene
18 How to prepare yourself correctly to preserve and recover potential evidence and to carry out scientific investigative techniques
19 How to perform the scientific investigative work safely
20 The roles and functions of the different organizations and personnel that may be involved in investigating the scene(s) of incident
21 How your own role relates to that of others involved in the scene investigation
22 How to develop links and relationships with other personnel at the scene, and the protocols for doing this
23 The communications systems available, and how to make best use of them
24 The principles involved in giving advice on the interpretation of scene examination results
25 How to direct others to achieve common objectives
26 How to establish and maintain the integrity and continuity of potential evidence, and the importance of this
27 The legal requirements regarding the integrity and continuity of evidence, and the importance of satisfying them
28 How to avoid jeopardizing the integrity of potential evidence
29 How to identify contamination dangers, and how to avoid them
30 The established scientific principles and practices to consider when examining the scene(s)
31 How to determine the most appropriate recovery and examination method(s) to suit different situations and different evidence types
32 The operational and scientific factors to consider when performing different types of scientific investigative work
33 How to assess the effect of scientific investigations on other types of potential evidence
34 How to identify all relevant evidence types
35 How to preserve, recover, package, and transfer potential evidence, avoiding contamination, cross contamination, and loss of evidence

36   How to perform different preservation, recovery, and examination methods effectively
37   The amount of time which each preservation, recovery, and examination method is likely to take
38   How to establish valid and reliable information about the incident and to form an initial hypothesis
39   The information which would confirm or deny an initial hypothesis, and the reasons for this in particular cases
40   The importance of recognizing and taking account of any inconsistent information gained during the scene investigation
41   The principles and factors involved to process, evaluate, and interpret the results of the scene examinations
42   How to recognize and resolve problems during the scene investigation—including problems concerned with preservation of evidence, transportation, coordination with other scene personnel, welfare, time constraints, prevailing weather conditions, security, economics, safety, and risk of contamination
43   How to adapt working practices and procedures to accommodate different situations and circumstances and different evidence types
44   How to recognize the limitations of your expertise and knowledge, and the importance of not exceeding these
45   How to identify what information to record, and how it should be recorded
46   What recording systems are available, and how to use them
47   How to make contemporaneous records and notes, and the importance of this
48   Why it is important to record information in a format suitable for further use
49   The importance of and methods used to collate notes on work carried out, and the use to which the notes will be put

ACTIVITY 4: INTERPRET FINDINGS

Summary

This activity is about summarizing and assessing the examinations, interpreting the results, and drawing conclusions prior to the preparation of a final report or statement. The opinions drawn by the practitioner will be informed by databases, historical data, and/or personal experience. Rigorous quality assurance checks are of paramount importance throughout this activity.

The conclusions will address the case requirements as identified in activity 1 and will:

1. Provide support for a single hypothesis.
2. Provide support for more than one hypothesis.
3. Not support any particular hypothesis.

This activity is relevant to any individual who is responsible for interpreting the findings of forensic scientific examinations. The activity consists of two subactivities:

4.1. Collate the results of the examinations.
4.2. Interpret examination findings.

Following training, the student will be able to:

Collate the results of the examinations by

1. Recording and collating results accurately in a clear and unambiguous format
2. Completing an accurate evaluation of the examination results
3. Using sufficient results from specified examinations

4. Summarizing results to meet the examination requirements
5. Presenting the results clearly in a structured format
6. Confirming that the evaluation, commentary, and support information is accurate and clearly presented

Interpret examination findings by

1. Confirming that examinations data are complete, comprehensive, and accurate
2. Basing interpretations on the documented results and information provided about the incident
3. Consulting relevant reliable sources of information at an appropriate time and in an appropriate way to assist the interpretation
4. Confirming results and data for accuracy, validity, and reliability
5. Drawing opinions from the results and data clearly based on agreed criteria
6. Recording relevant information accurately, comprehensively, and contemporaneously

Knowledge and understanding: Following training, you will know and understand:

1	The principles and factors involved in the examinations used
2	How to summarize results in relation to the examination requirements
3	How to collate and use results prepared by yourself and by others
4	The importance of and ways to establish the accuracy, validity, and reliability of examination methods
5	The range, purpose, and limitations of different methods available to present results
6	How to ensure that the presentation of results will meet the needs of the end user
7	How to ensure the accuracy of evaluation, commentary, and support information
8	How to present evaluation, commentary, and support information
9	The use and relevance of the different types of examinations
10	The scientific principles and practices on which interpretations are based
11	Why it is important to ensure the examination data are complete, comprehensive, and accurate
12	Why it is important to establish the accuracy, validity, and reliability of the examination results
13	The principles involved in processing, evaluating, and interpreting results
14	The criteria on which opinions are based, and how to record opinions
15	The sources of information available for consultation
16	How and when to access and consult sources of information
17	How the sources of information can be used to assist the interpretation
18	How to ensure that the sources of information are reliable, and the importance of reliability
19	What recording systems are available, and how to use them
20	What information is relevant, and when and how it should be recorded
21	Why it is important to record information in a format suitable for further use
22	How to identify the need for contemporaneous records and notes, and how to make them
23	How to keep records to protect the security of information
24	Who has the right of access to information held on record

ACTIVITY 5: REPORT FINDINGS
Summary

This activity is about reporting the findings of the forensic examinations. The activity covers:

1. Production of reports on the examinations that have been carried out
2. Participation in pretrial consultations, and presentation of oral evidence to courts and inquiries

Reports will be read by a wide range of individuals, most of whom will have little scientific knowledge. They will also be read aloud in courts of law. They must, therefore, be written as clearly and unambiguously as possible. In particular, care should be taken to ensure that the examinations conducted and the practices behind these examinations are described in language that ensures that they are understandable to nonscientists, such as a judge and jury.

Reports may provide factual information only. However, where an opinion is given, the report will:

1. Outline the background to the incident, as understood by the practitioner.
2. Explain the requirement of the commissioning agency or customer.
3. Provide a description of the examinations conducted and their outcomes.
4. Make an assessment of the likelihood of the examination results given the hypotheses tested and the circumstances as understood by the practitioner.

Pretrial consultation may be required in order to explain findings to the prosecution or defense barrister or solicitor. These consultations may occur well in advance of the trial or when the trial is underway. The practitioner will often be required to present the findings as an expert witness in court.

It is the responsibility of the practitioner to clearly explain the significance of the findings and to consider other hypotheses that may be proposed in pretrial consultations or when in court. The practitioner may also have to present evidence that has been established by others working under his or her instructions and supervision.

This activity is relevant to any individual who is responsible for reporting the findings of scientific examinations. The activity consists of three elements:

5.1. Produce report.
5.2. Participate in pretrial consultation.
5.3. Present oral evidence to courts and inquiries.

Following training, the student will be able to:

Produce report by

1. Establishing the type, scope, and purpose of the report
2. Using information in the report which is current, relevant, and accurate
3. Reporting all results accurately, and clearly expressing the limitations of any tests used
4. Presenting a report that is logical, unbiased, accurate, and relevant and that meets the needs of the end user
5. Expressing conclusions and opinions within your area of expertise firmly based on the results and available information
6. Confirming that the report conforms to legal requirements and that you make appropriate reference to case notes and related materials

7. Submitting the report for checking, and acting upon any alternative explanations suggested in accordance with established scientific principles

Participate in pretrial consultation by

1. Providing advice based on established scientific principles which is balanced and realistic within the context of the case
2. Clearly explaining your findings and their interpretation in the context of the case
3. Considering alternative explanations, testing alternative hypotheses, and providing opinions
4. Identifying, clarifying, and summarizing areas of agreement and disagreement
5. Seeking feedback to determine whether those involved understand the outcomes of the consultations
6. Recording relevant information accurately and comprehensively

Present oral evidence to courts and inquiries by

1. Conducting yourself in accordance with acceptable professional standards
2. Delivering your evidence in an audible and understandable manner
3. Giving evidence consistent with the contents of the written report
4. Dealing with questions truthfully, impartially, and flexibly in a language which is concise, unambiguous, and admissible
5. Identifying and clarifying any unclear questions before offering a response
6. Giving explanations to specific questions in a manner that facilitates understanding by nonscientists
7. Considering and evaluating any additional information and alternative hypotheses presented to you and expressing relevant opinions, taking into account the limitations on opinions which cannot be given without further examination and investigation
8. Clearly differentiating between fact and opinion
9. Expressing opinions within your area of expertise

Knowledge and understanding: Following training, you will know and understand:

---

1   The different types, scopes, and purposes of reports
2   How to ensure that the information used is current, reliable, and accurate
3   How to structure the report and to present the results
4   Who the end users of reports are, and how they use the reports
5   Techniques to use to ensure that the report meets the needs of the end user(s)
6   The importance of expressing the limitations of any tests, examinations, and comparisons
7   How to use the results and other available information to support your opinions and conclusions
8   The use to which case notes and related materials are put, and how to reference them in the report
9   How to collate and use case notes
10 How to make balanced decisions and judgments
11 The established scientific principles and practices underpinning all conclusions and opinions
12 The importance of submitting the report for checking

13   The importance of investigating any alternative explanations offered, and the established scientific principles and practices involved
14   The legal requirements relating to scientific evidence, and the production and presentation of reports
15   The purpose of pretrial consultations
16   Court procedures, and the importance of following the procedures
17   Your role in the pretrial consultation
18   How to provide advice in pretrial consultations
19   The established scientific principles and practices involved in providing advice
20   How to ensure the advice you give is balanced and realistic
21   The ways available to explain your findings and to ensure that the explanation is clear
22   How to seek feedback to ensure that those involved understand the outcomes of the consultation
23   Your role in any court and inquiry procedures
24   How to address the different people involved in court and inquiry proceedings
25   The effect that your appearance and behavior can have on others
26   The importance of ensuring that evidence is consistent with the written report, statement, or other relevant document
27   How to present technical explanations to facilitate understanding by nonscientists
28   How to respond to questions
29   Why it is important to deal with questions using unambiguous language
30   How to clarify unclear questions before responding, and the importance of so doing
31   How to ensure that your evidence is audible and understandable
32   When and how to consider alternative hypotheses
33   How to test alternative hypotheses: when producing the report, suggested in pretrial consultation, or suggested in the court or inquiry proceedings
34   The established scientific principles and practices in responding to alternative explanations and hypotheses
35   The areas of disagreement that might arise, and how to handle them
36   The importance of clarifying areas of agreement and those of disagreement
37   How to recognize the limitations of your expertise and knowledge, and the importance of not exceeding these
38   How to assimilate differing opinions and propositions in order to formulate opinions within your area of expertise
39   How to identify what information to record, and how it should be recorded
40   The classification systems used, and how they operate
41   What recording systems are available, and how to use them

TRANSLATING THE GENERIC TO THE SPECIFIC

To translate the generic training program to the specific training program, subject specialists will be needed to develop the specific subject detail.

To explain this, consider Unit 2, "Examine items and samples," where any training program must take account of all the performance criteria associated with that unit of competence.

Table 4.2 takes the examination and comparison of tool marks as a vehicle to demonstrate how the translation to the specifics of tool marks may be achieved by using the generically expressed Professional Standards of Competence.

The specific working procedures which will be incorporated by the subject specialist into the generic framework must have been rigorously researched, proved, tested, and validated. It is therefore the organization, not enthusiastic individuals,

TABLE 4.2
Element 1.1: Determine Case Requirements

You Must Ensure That You … (generic)	What This Means for Tool Marks (specific)
1 Establish details of circumstances, and consider these against exhibits received and examinations requested.	The case circumstances are important to determine because it must be clear with an instrument mark examination that there is ownership of the tool in question. In cases where ownership must be established, other examinations may be required.
2 Confirm that the items submitted are appropriate for the work to be undertaken.	Having identified what is the purpose of the examination, it is necessary to establish that the items submitted will provide a meaningful examination with the possibility of addressing the question required. This may involve consideration of whether the correct scene marks have been taken. One aspect that can lead to problems is the use of inappropriate casting material to recover the marks. There are normally a number of options open to the examiner regarding equipment. The examiner must consider whether it is possible to visualize the potential detail with the equipment available. Extremely small detail may require specialist equipment such as the use of a scanning electron microscope. Other considerations may include the size of the item. In tool marks, there may be other forensic scientific evidence that must be considered. The evidence types for consideration are mainly DNA, fingerprints, paint, and fibers. It is important that all other possible evidence is considered, as it may be lost if not treated appropriately. There is also the possibility that the evidence required by the investigation is best answered by comparison not of the tool mark but of other evidence.
3 Establish the storage requirements of potential evidence, and make arrangements for safe, secure, and clean facilities.	It must be ensured that the storage for any tool will mean that no potential evidence is lost including DNA, fingerprints, and contact trace material. It is also important to ensure that no additional damage can occur to the ends of the tool or to any area of potential interest. They should, where possible, be protected. This is also the case for any item that has marks on it, and that area must be covered and protected.
4 Agree and prioritize the sequence of the various aspects of work.	In terms of any examination, it is very important that an agreed sequence of work is identified. This is to ensure that no evidence is lost. It must also consider questions that may need to be answered quickly, or examinations that may take a long time and need to be considered early. In tool mark cases, it is possible to undertake other examinations in full or at least recover material and store it until required. The actual tool mark examination is not often affected adversely by other examinations being undertaken beforehand.
5 Record relevant information accurately, legibly, and comprehensively.	The main criteria to bear in mind in tool mark examinations are factors such as whether evidence will be lost as a result of handling and undertaking activities such as making test marks. It is also normal for fingerprints and DNA to be undertaken before any examination due to contamination issues.

(Continued)

TABLE 4.2 (CONTINUED)
Element 1.1: Determine Case Requirements

You Must Ensure That You ... (generic)	What This Means for Tool Marks (specific)
	The methods available to the examiner for recording relevant information are those that are normally available.
	What can be very useful are details that are recorded about the location and orientation of the mark. This can help to establish the likely method of attack.
6 Prepare equipment and work area appropriate to the examination.	In tool mark casework, it is important to ensure that microscopes (both bench and comparison) are working to the required standard. It may also be necessary to ensure that casting materials are available which enable casting and recasting.
	The examination of the scene material and the submitted tool, if there is any potential for particulate material to be present, should be done on separate benches, or using different pieces of examination paper after cleaning. It is always important that all steps are undertaken to ensure no loss of material or potential contamination.
	Very large items are sometimes submitted, and these must be treated carefully and may require a large movable bench microscope to be used. In any examination, all normal procedures that ensure that there is no loss of material and that no contamination occurs must be followed.
7 Identify and rectify nonconforming equipment.	In tool mark casework, it is usually easy to see when equipment is not working to the expected standard. For the comparator, it is a requirement to check the balance using agreed methods. If this is not correct, there are procedures to follow to rectify this.

that has developed the procedures and through its use is recommending the way in which the outcome, defined generically by the Professional Standards of Competence, is achievable. Anyone carrying out translation from the generic to the specific must be aware of all the acceptable methods of achieving the outcome defined by the standard. This is in line with the fundamental principle of the standards to accept that there may be more than one acceptable way of carrying out a task.

Demonstrating the translation activity of the generic to the specific unit that deals with preparing to carry out examinations can be taken as an example.

UNIT 1: PREPARE TO CARRY OUT EXAMINATIONS

This unit is about ensuring that adequate preparations are made prior to the examination of items and samples, originating from an incident that is subject to forensic scientific (criminalistics) investigation.

The preparations that are made apply in all cases, irrespective of the environment in which the unit (activity) is conducted, for example at the scene of the incident or in a specialized environment such as a laboratory. Scientific principles and practices must be adopted throughout this unit. Health and safety of self and others and the preservation, integrity, and continuity of potential evidence are paramount throughout the unit. This unit applies to any individual who prepares items and samples that will be subject to forensic examination. Individuals may, or may not, go on to carry out the examination themselves.

The detail expressed in the right-hand column of Table 4.1 is ideal for use as the basis of a specific training program, and the trainee will need to be rigorously exposed to all of these issues during training. It is worth emphasizing yet again that it is of paramount importance that subject specialists are closely involved in this process.

As an example of this, take performance criterion 6 in Table 4.1, "Prepare equipment and work area appropriate to the examination," and take the translated performance criterion: "The examination of the scene material and the submitted tool, if there is any potential for particulate material to be present, should be done on separate benches, or using different pieces of examination paper after cleaning. It is always important that all steps are undertaken to ensure no loss of material or potential contamination."

It is readily seen that this small statement, one of very many, contains a whole lot of detail which must be included in any training program. It indicates the need for training in anticontamination techniques, amongst other things.

But how will the mentor or trainer know when the trainee is approaching competent performance? What is needed is some form of assessment of performance for the individual which, at this point in training, will be carried out by representatives of the organization using the organization's own assessment techniques—whatever they may be. There will, of course, be a focus for these assessments even at this organization stage—the performance criteria and the knowledge and understanding statements detailed in the National Occupational Standards. This is represented in the cycle of competence (see Figure 4.1) by the section "Performance Scrutinized through Organizational Procedures."

Most practitioners will initially receive some training in laboratory examinations. The development of the outline training program for "Preparing to carry out examinations" demonstrates how the details of a specific activity—tool mark examinations—may be derived from the generically expressed Professional Standards of Competence.

The relevant parts of the training program will be used by the practitioner's mentor, and the progress of the trainee toward competence will be monitored against the occupational standards until the mentor is satisfied as to the trainee's performance. This point of assessment is shown in the cycle of competence (Figure 4.1) under the section "Performance through organizational procedures."

Supervision of the trainee by the mentor will be progressively relaxed as competence is approached until the practitioner is working with normal organizational or statutory supervision. Through the use of the organization's own methods and against the National Occupational Standards, the practitioner is pronounced competent—competent, that is, to the organization's requirements.

In an ideal world, it would be good to be able to say that the forensic scientist is now working to the National Occupational Standards, in whatever field, and has been assessed as doing so through a nationally monitored assessment procedure. That is the next part of the procedure leading to a competent practitioner—and, indeed, maybe to the Council for the Registration of Forensic Practitioners (CRFP) registered practitioner!

The generic training program expressed in this chapter will provide a vital tool, not only for training designers but also for universities involved in the design of forensic science education programs.

USING THE STANDARDS AS A BASIS FOR THE CONTINUAL ASSESSMENT OF COMPETENT FORENSIC PRACTICE

Elsewhere, it is stated that the National Occupational Standards for forensic science practitioners are written in terms of outcomes—that is to say, the level of performance that has to be achieved. Given that they define the level of performance that must be achieved, they are the ideal tool for use in the continual assessment of competence in forensic practice.

When the standards are used as the basis for a National Vocational Qualification, an individual has to provide evidence of meeting every performance criterion of the elements and units chosen to make up the qualification over a period of time. Someone who did in fact meet all of the performance criteria and underpinning knowledge and understanding requirements would be judged as competent in a particular area of forensic science.

However, competence is the requirement every single day that an individual is involved in practicing forensic science. The standards are the ideal, and proper, vehicle for addressing this.

In most organizations where forensic scientists practice, in any of the forensic sciences there are various mechanisms in place to "assure" that forensic science casework is carried out properly. The efficacy of these mechanisms can vary greatly. Some organizations will stipulate the qualifications required of forensic science experts.

Most organizations will have training plans and programs, and some will go so far as to have assessments at the conclusion of a training course or program. Most organizations seek accreditation with one of the recognized accrediting bodies. All members of the European Network of Forensic Science Institutes (ENFSI) now, as a requirement of membership, have to be accredited to ISO17025 or working toward that goal.

Few have satisfactory procedures for recognizing the competence of practitioners. Many will use peer review of critical findings and interpretation. Case files are often reviewed by a peer or manager. However, there is little commonality in approach or any standardized way of doing this … in other words, much effort is put in, but such reviews and checks are done without reference to national standards.

This is where the National Occupational Standards come into their own. Every case file or peer review should be carried out against the standards (or the parts of the standards that are relevant to any particular role). The person carrying out the review must be able to understand the principles of assessing against standards, and be able to translate generic parts of the standard to the area of specialism under review (assessment). For example, in their generic form the standards are applicable to all forensic disciplines, whether that is forensic pathology, DNA, criminalistics, or anything else. For use in a specific area of forensic practice, they will need some "translation" to the language and environment of the particular specialism. As a simple example, although contamination will be understood by all forensic practitioners, the actual type of contamination may well be different from one specialism to another.

In theory, therefore, evidence must be provided that a practitioner has met each of the relevant standards (detailed as "You must ensure that you ...") and all of the associated knowledge and understanding (detailed as "You need to know and understand ...").

Much of the knowledge and understanding should be self-evident from the way that casework has been carried out, but some may not be. Where the possession of such knowledge is not obvious from case file assessment, supplementary evidence may be required, particularly to address the underlying principles of forensic practice. Success in relevant examinations, such as the existing American Board of Criminalistics General Knowledge Examination or the ENFSI equivalent, currently in preparation, and the American Board of Criminalistics specialist examinations, would provide much of the required evidence.

In terms of assessing against the standards generally, the evidence of how each particular component of the standard is met must be recorded, in sufficient detail for any external scrutineer to be able to locate the evidence and agree it (or not). Such a system would require some form of assessment record sheet(s) relating to each case or group of cases.

One option would be to have an assessment form which listed every standard and every criterion listed as "You must ensure that you ...." This would result in a complete, but lengthy, assessment form. It is doubtful that this option would find acceptance amongst busy practitioners, and it could be viewed as bureaucratically "heavy." Back to the N/SVQs!

A second option would be to have an abbreviated assessment form based around the units and elements. The individual carrying out the case file review (or such other assessment as might be undertaken) would use all the "You must ensure that you ..." criteria listed in the Professional Standards of Competence but would record the evidence on an abbreviated assessment form based around the units and elements. An example of an abbreviated assessment form is shown as at Appendix 6.

This kind of assessment could be carried on every piece of casework, or it could be done at defined intervals, for example once a week, once a month, every third case, or every tenth case, depending on specific casework circumstances. Such an ongoing assessment scheme should provide assurance that an individual meeting all of the standards relevant to his or her role was competent in a particular area of work.

Continuous assessment against the National Occupational Standards must surely provide the "gold standard" of competence assurance. ENFSI is providing funds to set up examinations in forensic science.

USING THE STANDARDS AS A BASIS FOR QUALIFICATIONS

Reference has been made to National/Scottish Vocational Qualifications earlier and how occupational standards are used for this purpose. However, that is but one type of qualification. The standards could be used for a myriad of vocational qualifications, for example postgraduate or other diplomas in the various forensic specialist areas (based on occupational competence) covering as broad or narrow an area as the forensic science sector deemed useful. Moreover, the knowledge and understanding components could be used to form the basis of a purely knowledge-based qualification should that be thought worthwhile.

USING THE STANDARDS AS A BASIS FOR CERTIFICATION OR ACCREDITATION

There are various registers available, certainly in the United Kingdom, which list the names of forensic practitioners and the areas in which they practice. In the past, the major weakness of these registers was that they were not based on true competence. Probably their major use would be as a medium for practitioners to advertise their services. Admission to such registers was often based on letters of recommendation from satisfied clients or some form of interview procedure. It is arguable whether there is a direct link between such admission procedures and true competence. If competence is defined as meeting national standards, as opposed to meeting indi-vidual organizational requirements or personal views of competence, then clearly the link is somewhat tenuous.

It could be argued that an assessment against the National Occupational Stan-dards provides a much more meaningful means, in terms of competence, of admis-sion to any register related to forensic practitioners.

In recent years, the issue of competent forensic practice within the criminal justice system has been tackled with the founding of the CRFP. The workings of the CRFP will be described in more detail later, but it uses a system of assessing practitioners on actual casework. For scientists, these assessments are against ten "essential criteria." These criteria were actually derived from the National Occupa-tional Standards, although it is doubtful whether many of its registrants or indeed its assessors appreciate that fact!

REFERENCES

1. Peter D Barnett, Ethics in Forensic Science: Professional Standards for the Practice of Criminalistics, CRC Press, Boca Raton, FL (2001).
2. Skills for Justice, A Guide to the Development of Education and Training Using National Occupational Standards.
3. Forensic Science: Implications for Higher Education, Science, Engineering, Manu-facturing Technologies Alliance (SEMTA) (2004).
4. House of Commons Science and Technology Committee, Forensic Science on Trial, Seventh Report of Session 2004, 05 HC 96-1, London, HMSO (2004).
5. P L Kirk, Journal of Criminal law, Criminology and Police Science 54, 235 (1963).

5 Council for the Registration of Forensic Practitioners (CRFP)

INTRODUCTION

Earlier, it was seen how standards can be used as a basis for certification and accreditation and that the Council for the Registration of Forensic Practitioners (CRFP) has used this principle.

The CRFP Register was launched in October 2000, in response to reports in 1993 by the Royal Commission on Criminal Justice and the House of Lords Select Committee on Science and Technology which highlighted concerns about miscarriages of justice where scientific evidence was shown subsequently to have been flawed.

The Report of the Royal Commission on Criminal Justice said:

> [I]t cannot be said that, simply because given by an expert, the evidence is necessarily correct or, indeed, credible.... We recommend that the professional bodies assist the courts in their task of assessment by maintaining a special register of their members who are suitably qualified to act as expert witnesses in particular areas of expertise.

In the House of Lords debate on the Royal Commission Report, the late Lord Dainton said:

> [T]o the Select Committee it seemed self evident that individual forensic scientists, whatever their other qualifications, should be tested and registered as fit to practise.

The House of Lords Select Committee on Science and Technology Report, *Forensic Science*, said that

> the cause of justice requires that the work of forensic scientists is of the highest possible quality. That quality in turn depends on two principal factors, namely the efficiency, tone and management of the laboratory and the technical competence and personal and professional integrity of the individuals who work there. The public is entitled to proof that there are mechanisms for assessing and maintaining both.

Also in 1993, at a meeting of the Forensic Science Sector Lead Body (now the Skills for Justice Forensic Science Committee), it was said:

> The Steering Group had considered the potential of developing a register of competent practitioners which would take account of the possession of relevant current National and Scottish Vocational Qualifications.

This indicates the intention from the outset that registration was to be based on performance.

WHY A REGISTER?

The main reasons for establishing systems and procedures to register practicing professionals are:

- To define, promote, and maintain appropriate standards of professional competence and conduct
- To ensure the safety of those affected by the practice of professionals
- To provide the public with assurance of the quality of professional practice
- To provide the courts and others with a ready means of identifying individuals who have demonstrated current competence
- To provide a mechanism for ensuring that professionals stay up-to-date and maintain competence

To achieve these aims, an assessment of an individual's performance against agreed standards of competence needs to be made. Although qualifications can provide some of the evidence required to support this assessment, they cannot provide the ultimate evidence of current competence—actual practice in real-life situations in the workplace and in the courtroom.

RECENT DEVELOPMENTS

The CRFP was established in 1999 as a regulatory body following detailed study by the forensic science community, supported by the government, of alternative mechanisms for promoting confidence in UK forensic practice.

The decision was to create a central register, a definitive indicator of the current competence of individuals, which would become a tool for the courts, and for the general public, covering successive forensic specialties until it became a map of the competent forensic community.

The CRFP register now includes some 2,400 names of forensic practitioners.

Entry to the CRFP register is through peer assessment of an applicant's competence to practice by detailed scrutiny of samples of recent casework, selected by the peer assessor. Assessment is made against agreed "essential elements of competence" relevant to the specialty for which the applicant wishes to register. These elements have been drawn up by the CRFP in consultation with leading practitioners and professional organizations, with close reference to any existing national occupational standards which may be up-to-date and relevant to the specialty in question.

The purpose of a register is to set a boundary around a profession, with those of proven current competence inside and those who have not demonstrated their competence outside. Registration is the public badge practitioners can wear to state that they

- are part of a coherent professional group.
- subscribe to high and definable professional standards.

- have had the confidence to have their competence judged by a peer through a framework applying to all forensic specialties, prepared with particular reference to the public's needs and the demand for independent assessment.
- are prepared to be judged against published standards of professional conduct, competence, and ethics, if something goes wrong and there is a complaint.
- are committed to maintaining competence and staying up-to-date so they can stay on the register when revalidated by the CRFP every four years. (Ref)

Currently there are more than 20 classifications for registration, and more are being developed. They are:

Anthropology
Archeology
Computer examination
Fingerprint development
Fingerprint examination
Fire scene examination
Image origination and examination
Odontology
Medical examination
Pediatrics
Podiatry
Road transport investigation
Scene examination
Scene examination—volume crime
Science and engineering (incorporating the eight specialties: Drugs, Firearms, Human contact traces, Incident reconstruction, Marks, Particulates, and Toxicology)
Questioned documents
Telecommunications
Veterinary science

Other categories under development are:

Nursing and allied professions
Natural sciences (geology, entomology, earth sciences, soil, and pollen metallurgy)

Each of the science and engineering specialties is divided into a number of sub-specialties, as shown in the following extract from the application documentation.

APPLICATION FORM FOR REGISTRATION: SCIENCE/ENGINEERING

Please read the note "How to Apply for Registration" and keep it by you. Then complete this form in block capitals legibly in black ink. Be aware throughout that you will have to declare your understanding that any false or misleading information may disqualify you from registration.

cr**fp**   council for the registration of
        forensic practitioners

Application form for registration: science/engineering

Please read the note *How to apply for registration* and keep it by you. Then complete this form in block capitals legibly in black ink. Be aware throughout that you will have to declare your understanding that any false or misleading information may disqualify you from registration.

Section A   Registration details

The details submitted in this section will go on the public register, and will appear as shown in the box on the first page of the explanatory note. This means that these details will be made available to the public. Therefore, please give here **only** those details that you wish to be included in the register.

CRFP is registered under the Data Protection Act 1998 and **all** information provided in this form will be held in accordance with the provisions of the Act.

Register information

Surname (including any previous surname)

Forename/s that you wish to appear in the register

Sex   Male ☐   Female ☐

Please give below the address that you wish to appear in the register

Geographical region

Please select only one from the following: London   North East
                                                   East Anglia   North West
                                                   South East   Scotland
                                                   South West   Northern Ireland
                                                   Midlands   Wales

You may, if you wish, have this line in your register entry:
The registrant has indicated availability to undertake work beyond the region shown in the entry. If you would like this, please tick this box: ☐

FOR OFFICE USE ONLY	
Office Reference Number: ☐☐☐☐☐	Date application received: ☐☐ ☐☐ ☐☐

Specialty

I am applying to be registered in the following number of specialties ☐

Note: For scientists/engineers a specialty is defined as, for example, Marks or Firearms. The further divisions are sub-specialties. CRFP assessors will need to assess your current competence in each of the sub-specialties you tick. You do not need to be competent in all the sub-specialties to achieve registration in your specialty. But we advise you to apply only in the specialties and subspecialties where you have a strong list of recent casework.

- **Scientists/engineers**

	Specialty	Sub-specialty
Drugs	☐	
Computing (see note on page 4)	☐	
Firearms	☐	
Forensic ballistics		☐
Comparison microscopy		☐
Classification		☐
Human Contact Traces	☐	
DNA		☐
Body fluids		☐
Blood distribution		☐
Hairs		☐
Other (eg. serology, animal identification: please specify)		☐
Image evaluation (see note on page 4)	☐	
Incident evaluation	☐	
Fire investigation		☐
Explosion investigation		☐
Explosives incidents		☐
Metallurgy and materials failures		☐
Traffic accident reconstruction		☐
Tyre examination		☐
Tachographs: vehicle movement analysis		☐
Tachographs: hours analysis		☐
Non-metallurgical component failure		☐
Marks	☐	
Toolmarks		☐
Footwear marks		☐
Tyre marks		☐
Packaging and manufacturing marks		☐
Other marks (eg. feet in shoes: please specify)		☐

Particulates and other traces ☐

    Fibres
    Glass
    Paint
    Explosives residues
    Gunshot residues
    Plant material
    Pollutants
    Chemical traces and stains
    Other particulate material

Questioned documents ☐
    Handwriting
    Documents
    Other (please specify)

Telecoms (see note on page 4) ☐
    Equipment evaluation
    Call data (network CDRs) evaluation

Toxicology ☐
    Toxicology
    Alcohol analysis
    Alcohol technical defence

The Digital Specialties: Computing, Imaging, and Telecoms

Computer and telecom specialists are involved in the retrieval, identification, examination, and assessment of data held in computers or telecom equipment (in general, but not always, the latter will apply to equipment connected to a public telecom network—for example, phones, fax machines, pagers, and telecom systems). Some telecom specialists work with data retrieved from physical apparatus such as phones, Subscriber Identification Module (SIM) cards, and pagers. Others scrutinize network and traffic logs in the form of call data records and undertake cell site analysis. Some practitioners perform both these functions.

Imaging specialists are involved in the origination, retrieval, identification, examination, and assessment of data held in image-recording media.

The CRFP register distinguishes between practitioners working in these specialist areas—the *digital* specialties. It also distinguishes between those whose work is essentially *investigative* and those whose work is *evaluative*. Some do both kinds of work, but more usually they do one or the other.

Investigative work includes the capture and examination of computer or telecom data—retrieving and preserving material, creating check logs, identifying and examining data, and producing information or exhibits. It also includes the origination, processing, and technical analysis of images—generating, retrieving, enhancing, restoring, optimizing, comparing, measuring, authenticating, and presenting them so that they can be used in evidence.

Evaluative work involves the assessment of data, equipment, or images in the context of other evidence in the case; the application of scientific techniques such as facial mapping; the drawing of deductions; construing significance; considering alternative hypotheses; and the expression of opinions for the benefit of the court.

These categories are described in more detail in the covering letter with this pack. These should help practitioners decide the specialty or specialties in which they wish to be registered. Special notes also guide the assessors for each specialty, in particular things to look for in deciding on a registration application.

This application form is only for specialists who do *evaluative work*. Specialists in *data capture* or *examination*, or in *image origination, processing*, or *technical analysis*, are eligible for registration in the specialties of *computer examination, imaging,* or *telecoms examination*. These have their own CRFP assessment criteria and separate application forms.

Section C: Professional Experience

In this section you must give a list of recent cases. Your assessor will ask you to provide further details of some of these. This will be the substantive part of your assessment.

It will not be possible to assess you for registration in any specialty where you have not completed at least one case during the past six months. If this is the position you are in, we suggest you wait until you have done new cases in the specialty in question, then approach us again.

If you can list at least one case in the last six months, the assessor can go ahead and may ask you for previous cases to provide extra information. But if you practice in more than one scientific specialty, we suggest you apply for registration initially in your strongest one(s). A limited list of cases in any specialty will significantly slow the progress of your application.

If you have dealt with more than fifty cases (ten in the digital specialties) during the last six months, please list just your last fifty/ten cases plus enough to include at least five where you prepared a statement for court. Tell us also how many cases, and of what type, you dealt with in total during the last six months.

Applicants for telecom call data evaluation who undertake cell site analysis must show evidence of formal qualifications and training in radio and telecommunications network engineering.

ROLE OF THE CRFP

The CRFP has three main areas of activity. These are

- to publish a register of competent practitioners.
- to ensure through periodic revalidation that forensic practitioners keep up-to-date and maintain competence.
- to deal with registered practitioners who fail to meet the necessary standards.

The great strength of the CRFP is that it is an independent body. Its formation was supported, financially, by the UK government, but the intention is that it

Applicant's name: _____   **Form 1: Caselog**

Please list here all the cases you have dealt with during the last six months (or the last fifty cases if you have dealt with more than fifty). *If you cannot list any cases for the past six months, we will not be able to assess you for registration until you have completed some new casework.*

Case Ref Number	Date You Completed Your Work	Evidence or Data Type	Did You Prepare a Formal Statement Based on the Findings?	Was Your Statement Used in Court?	Have You Presented Oral Evidence on This in Court or at a Case Conference?	Any Other Comments Relevant to the Case: For Example, Was the Finding Positive or Negative?

When you have completed your caselog, please highlight any cases which involved you in unusual work where you used techniques different from the standard ones, or which were in some way special or particularly complex.

will in time be self-supporting. The forensic professions set the standards and the CRFP ensures that they are adhered to by registrants. That is to say, it regulates the professions. Registration is voluntary and, given the judicial climate, is unlikely to become mandatory. Indeed, the CRFP has no wish that it should, although the expectation is that judges will come to expect forensic experts appearing in criminal trials to be registered and, where an individual is not registered, to explore the reasons why. That is an excellent proposal for a way forward. With this approach it will work.

As stated earlier, registration, and hence fitness to practice, relies on assessing an individual's performance on *current* casework, and several conditions are laid down to be certain that this criterion reflects current competence. This is a unique feature of the CRFP. Registration does not rely solely on the possession of academic or professional qualifications to prove competence, nor, indeed, on how long a person has been doing a job. The Science Assessment Panel has the ultimate say in whether a forensic scientist is worthy of registration.

A crucial part of the function of any register is to enable the potential users of a service to know what they are getting by way of types of specialists. Clear descriptions of the meaning of each specialty that appears on the register are therefore critical to its meaning and its proper use.

HOW IS REGISTRATION ACHIEVED?

The CRFP document "How to Apply for Registration: Science/Engineering" lists the ten essential elements against which an applicant for registration will be judged. These are:

1. Knowing the hypothesis or question to be tested
2. Establishing that items submitted are suitable for the requirements of the case
3. Confirming that the best type of examination has been selected
4. Confirming that the examination was carried out competently
5. Recording, summarizing, and collating the results of the examination
6. Interpreting the results in accordance with established scientific principles
7. Considering alternative hypotheses
8. Preparing a report based on the findings
9. Presenting oral evidence to court and at case conferences
10. Ensuring that all documentation is fit for purpose

These, supported by the more detailed guidance under each of these headings which the CRFP gives its assessors, may be considered as the "standards" against which a forensic scientist's fitness to practice is judged. They are outcome based and are derived from the National Occupational Standards for forensic science developed and agreed by the profession.

If these ten elements or criteria are compared with the units and elements of competence, the similarity is evident—but a little "digging" has to be done.

Unit 1: Prepare to Carry Out Examinations

Unit summary
> Element 1.1: Determine case requirements
> Element 1.2: Establish the integrity of items and samples
> Element 1.3: Inspect items and samples submitted for examination

Knowledge and understanding

Unit 2: Examine Items and Samples

Unit summary
> Element 2.1: Monitor and maintain the integrity of items and samples
> Element 2.2: Identify and recover potential evidence
> Element 2.3: Determine examinations to be undertaken
> Element 2.4: Carry out examinations
> Element 2.5: Produce examination notes and records

Knowledge and understanding

Unit 3: Undertake Specialist Scene Examinations

Unit summary
> Element 3.1: Establish the requirements of the investigation
> Element 3.2: Prepare to examine the scene of the incident
> Element 3.3: Examine the scene of the incident

Knowledge and understanding

Unit 4: Interpret Findings

Unit summary
> Element 4.1: Collate the results of the examinations
> Element 4.2: Interpret examination findings

Knowledge and understanding

Unit 5: Report Findings

Unit summary
> Element 5.1: Produce report
> Element 5.2: Participate in pretrial consultation
> Element 5.3: Present oral evidence to courts and inquiries

Knowledge and understanding

The CRFP has always insisted that this represents a start—a very successful start at that—and the CRFP is to be applauded for insisting that registration is based on workplace competence and not on professional or academic qualifications alone—grandfathering as a route to registration was rejected from the outset.

TABLE 5.1

Comparison of Professional Standards of Competence with CRFP Criteria

National Occupational Standards	CRFP Criteria
Unit 1	Criteria 1 and 2
Unit 2	Criterion 3
Unit 2, "Knowledge and understanding"	Criterion 4
Unit 2	Criterion 5
Unit 4	Criteria 6 and 7
Unit 5	Criteria 8 and 9
All units	Criterion 10

A SUGGESTED MODEL FOR THE DEVELOPMENT OF REGISTRATION

A next logical step could be for the CRFP to consider as one route to registration workplace performance against the National Occupational Standards for the profession.

What would be the advantage of using National Occupational Standards rather than the CRFP ten elements or criteria?

It has been discussed earlier when describing the development of National Occupational Standards that the five high-level activities or units of competence could be considered as some form of basic "standard." The disadvantage of this is that it leaves a great deal to the personal judgment of assessors, which was agreed to be undesirable. To make assessments consistent, the description of the units in terms of elements was recommended where the elements were considered to be subactivities. Taking Unit 4, "Interpret Findings," to demonstrate this, it is seen that the unit is divided into two elements:

Unit 4: Interpret Findings

Unit summary
Element 4.1: Collate the results of the examinations
Element 4.2: Interpret examination findings
Knowledge and understanding

This was then taken a stage further, and each element was described in terms of performance criteria.

Each of the elements is now described in terms of performance criteria, of which there are six performance criteria for each of the elements of competence, giving twelve in all for this single unit. These are shown below.

Element 4.1: Collate the Results of the Examinations

Performance Criteria
You must ensure that you

1. record and collate results accurately in a clear unambiguous format.
2. complete an accurate examination of the examination results.
3. use sufficient results from specified examinations.
4. summarize results to meet the examination requirements.
5. present the results clearly in a structured format.
6. confirm that the evaluation, commentary, and support information is accurate and clearly presented.

Element 4.2: Interpret Examination Findings

Performance Criteria
You must ensure that you

1. confirm that examination data are complete, comprehensive, and accurate.
2. base interpretations on the documented results and information provided about the incident.
3. consult relevant reliable sources of information at appropriate times and in an appropriate way to assist the interpretation.
4. confirm results and data for accuracy, validity, and reliability.
5. draw opinions from the results and data clearly based on agreed criteria.
6. record relevant information accurately, comprehensively, and contemporaneously.

National Occupational Standards provide some other important information, for instance the knowledge and understanding associated with the unit. For the unit under discussion, this knowledge and understanding is described as:

Knowledge and Understanding

1. The principles and factors involved in the examinations used
2. How to summarize results in relation to the examination requirements
3. How to collate and use results prepared by yourself and others
4. The importance of and ways to establish the accuracy, validity, and reliability of examination methods
5. The range, purpose, and limitations of different methods available to present results
6. How to ensure that the presentation of results will meet the needs of the end user
7. How to ensure the accuracy of the evaluation, commentary, and support information
8. How to present evaluation, commentary, and support information
9. The use and relevance of the different types of examinations
10. The scientific principles and practices on which interpretations are based
11. Why it is important to ensure the examination data are complete, comprehensive, and accurate
12. Why it is important to establish the accuracy, validity, and reliability of the examination results

13. The principles involved in processing, evaluating, and interpreting results
14. The criteria on which opinions are based, and how to record opinions
15. The sources of information available for consultation
16. How and when to access and consult sources of information
17. How the sources of information can be used to assist the interpretation
18. How to ensure that the sources of information are reliable, and the importance of reliability
19. What recording systems are available and how to use them
20. What information is relevant, and when and how it should be used
21. Why it is important to record information in a format suitable for further use
22. How to identify the need for contemporaneous records and notes, and how to make them
23. How to keep records to protect the security of information
24. Who has the right of access to information held on record

It is interesting to see that competence in interpreting findings could be demonstrated through knowledge-based activities such as dealing with a variety of theoretical scenarios. Example cases given to the potential registrant in his or her desired field of registration would provide a vehicle on which assessments could be made. This is a vital role of those who report cases, and together with this scenario assessment some form of assessment on current casework will also be highly desirable.

ASSESSMENTS USING NATIONAL OCCUPATIONAL STANDARDS

There is undoubtedly a great deal more information in the National Occupational Standards through performance criteria and knowledge and understanding than there is in the CRFP criteria and indeed assessor guidance. It is almost certain that assessors for the CRFP will have these performance criteria in mind when they carry out assessments, but it would bolster the already worthy process to publish these criteria.

One of the weaknesses in any competence assessment program is for a simple tick-box mentality to be adopted, and a rigorous system of recording assessments against performance should be in place. Such a recording program will not need the rigor of the National Vocational Qualification (NVQ) program, as described elsewhere. It will, however, need to provide a basis for third-party scrutiny of the assessment of an individual where that is needed.

AN ASSESSMENT STRATEGY FOR REGISTRATION

Were employer organizations to assess the performance of their staff on a regular basis against occupational standards, the evidence forthcoming from such a performance-monitoring scheme could be used as a significant part of the registration process. For such a scheme to be acceptable to the CRFP, the key issues that would need to be addressed would be what we mean by "regular basis"; the acceptability, or otherwise, of individuals chosen by employers to act as assessors; the methods of ensuring the consistency of performance monitoring within and across organizations; and the key involvement of the CRFP in quality assuring the assessment process wherever and by whom it is carried out.

From the point of view of transparency and perception, the independence of assessment offered by the current process is its strength, together with its principles of external scrutiny. Nevertheless, robust safeguards could be incorporated within any employer-based performance-monitoring scheme to satisfy the requirements of the CRFP, its assessment panels, and, of course, the wider public.

The CRFP could play a similar role to that of the Approved Centres under the NVQ program. The Approved Centre (CRFP) would be responsible through employing organizations to ensure that assessors and verifiers were appropriately trained and capable of carrying out the assessment and verification process. They would call regular meetings of assessors to keep systems of assessment up-to-date and to discuss any situation that presented which was in some way out of the norm. This would greatly facilitate revalidation where potential applicants could collect evidence of competent performance over the four-year period.

Registration for forensic scientists currently deals only with those scientists who report cases and present oral evidence to courts. Some major organizations operate a procedure where a reporting scientist is involved in assessing the requirements of the customer and developing a case examination strategy to meet them, and in interpreting and evaluating the scientific findings, but may not do the actual analysis or technical examination. It is likely therefore that many of the issues surrounding registration of such reporting forensic scientists can be assessed away from the job. The safety-critical features should be assessed under real conditions, and the remaining by using what Skills for Justice has called the Training Performance Standard (TPS). The safety-critical features may be assessed under real conditions using the concept of the Operational Performance Standard (OPS). The most safety-critical feature, "Presenting Evidence in Court," should be assessed in the real work environment but has proved to be difficult in terms of logistics and cost to assess effectively.

Court transcripts have been suggested as having the potential to be used as a means of assessing an individual's performance. The written word—assuming it to be correct, of course—cannot, however, reflect the ambience of the courtroom, or the disposition of judge and counsel.

In certain instances chosen at random or indeed prearranged, there may be scope for the oral evidence of the scientist to be recorded on tape, CD, or other recording media specifically for the purpose of assessing the performance of the expert witness. There would need to be a procedure developed for doing this, and it would need to be accepted by all stakeholders. In practice, this may well be an idea that goes too far.

In parts of Canada, a questionnaire-based system has been used. Questionnaires are sent to the prosecuting and defense lawyers involved in cases where an organization's scientists have given evidence, and are evaluated when returned to the organization. Response rates have proved to be in excess of 60 percent.

The most robust method of assessment of witness-box performance, undoubtedly, involves the use of assessors trained to assess against an agreed set of criteria relevant to the impartial presentation of evidence in, so far as the United Kingdom is concerned, an adversarial system of justice.

The choice of assessors for establishing a forensic scientist's suitability to present oral evidence is critical. Many of the problems associated with evidence presentation in court have often occurred where there is variance from what appears in the thoroughly checked written report. The mismatch between what appears in the written report and what is given in oral testimony can only be checked by assessors competent in the area of work in which evidence is being presented—not by legal professionals or others in court, as is sometimes suggested.

Assessments would need only to be done on a random, but regular, basis—not every time a scientist presents evidence in court.

There would need to be some effort and negotiation to set up such a procedure, but since its sole purpose is to enhance the robustness of the judiciary and to reduce the chances of costly (in more ways than one) miscarriages of justice, it is certainly worth pursuing. This would carry logistical difficulties but is worthy of pursuit.

It follows from the fact that the CRFP registers only those scientists who prepare reports for use in the justice system that there, perhaps, needs to be some registration procedure for those who assist with or carry out entirely the technical work. There are many instances where reporting scientists are fit to carry out laboratory work, and some where they are not. There are also times where some support work is so specialized and technical that it is not possible for a reporting scientist to "confirm the examination was carried out competently"; see criterion 4 of the CRFP criteria. This is a situation about which the CRFP has some concerns.

FINALLY

In the preparation of this work, the proposals in this chapter have been discussed with the chief executive officer of the CRFP, Alan Kershaw, who has expressed a desire to discuss them in more detail. This will be done.

6 Skills for Justice

The Police Standards and Skills Organisation (PSSO) was formed in 2001 and, as the standards-setting body for the policing sector, developed a comprehensive suite of National Occupational Standards (NOS) covering a wide range of policing roles. This work also addressed the requirement to include any forensic scientific activities that need to be carried out by police personnel. National Occupational Standards had already been developed by the erstwhile Science, Technology and Mathematics Council (now incorporated as a part of the Sector Skills Council for Science, Engineering, Manufacturing Technologies Alliance, or SEMTA). The PSSO considered these existing standards, seeking opinion from operational specialists as to their suitability. Although fit for purpose, they were deemed to require updating. The PSSO is now part of the Sector Skills Council for the justice sector—Skills for Justice—and the standards for crime scene examination and fingerprint specialists have now been completed [1].

Skills for Justice has also developed a similarly comprehensive National Competency Framework. This is firmly based on the National Occupational Standards but more usefully relates the requirements for competence to the actual roles of individuals.

Both the suite of NOS and the National Competency Framework are now being used by colleges, universities, and other learning providers to better shape their courses to the needs of the policing sector. This is being actively encouraged through the establishment of the Police Licensing and Accreditation Board, which aims to set up schemes of licensing or endorsement of particular courses, providing they are indeed geared to meeting the skills and knowledge specifications laid down in the National Occupational Standards.

In order for the suite of National Occupational Standards to be accepted and registered by the Regulatory Authorities Qualification and Curriculum Authority (QCA), the Scottish Qualification Authority (SQA), and so on, they are accompanied by a comprehensive assessment strategy. This specifies what type of evidence of competence can be accepted as proof of an individual's competence against particular elements of the standards, for example where knowledge-based exams can be used, where a simulation is acceptable, and where only actual practice in real conditions can be used as evidence. The assessment strategy also specifies what competence the assessors themselves need to have in order for the whole assessment process to be considered robust. Generally, this is evidenced by the assessor holding a similarly nationally recognized qualification called the "A1 unit."

This procedure and outcomes are similar to that described elsewhere in this book for NOS for scientists. The NOS for policing activities in all aspects of the work of police officers and civilian support staff are ideally placed—as with scientists described earlier—to form a focus for the development of training and education programs. The National Occupational Standards developed from the early work of

SEMTA for crime scene investigation are now accepted by the police to be the focus for all training development and for the assessment of workplace competence.

Crime scene investigation comprises "Five Units of Competence," which are:

Unit 3H4. Start the crime scene investigation process.
Unit 3H5. Attend and control the crime scene.
Unit 3H6. Examine the scene and collect evidence.
Unit 3H7. Package, store, and transport items of evidence.
Unit 3H8. Evaluate the crime scene investigation.

The full standard is reproduced with the permission of Skills for Justice.

UNIT TITLE

3H4	Start the crime scene investigation process.

SUMMARY

This unit is about starting the investigative process. You will need to be able to maintain health, safety, and welfare throughout this work.

You will need to be able to obtain the relevant information, decide the types of examination necessary, and make an initial assessment. You will also need to prepare for the examination and provide advice to others on control and preservation of the scene.

There is one element:

3H4.1	Start the investigative process.

This unit was developed by Skills for Justice.

ELEMENT

3H4.1	Start the investigative process.

PERFORMANCE CRITERIA

To meet the standard, you must:

1 Obtain the information relating to the incident from the relevant personnel and systems
2 Decide the types of examination necessary based on the information you have obtained
3 Make an initial assessment of the appropriate resources according to local operating procedures
4 Identify and take the necessary actions to maintain health, safety, and welfare
5 Correctly access and prepare any equipment that is required for the examination
6 Prioritize your work according to examination and local operating procedures
7 Obtain the necessary consent and authority to carry out the examination according to local operating procedures and legislation
8 Provide advice to relevant personnel regarding the control and preservation of the scene
9 Accurately record all the relevant information in accordance with local operating procedures

RANGE

1 **Examination**
   a Carried out by self
   b Carried out in coordination with others
2 **Resources**
   a Equipment
   b Accommodation at scene
   c Welfare requirements
   d Specialist personnel

UNIT

3H4　　Start the crime scene investigation process.

KNOWLEDGE AND UNDERSTANDING

To meet the standard, you need to know and understand:

Legal and Organizational Requirements

1 Current, relevant legislation, policies, local operating procedures, codes of practice, guidelines, and investigative process for scene examination
2 Current, relevant legislation and organizational requirements in relation to race, diversity, and human rights
3 Current, relevant legislation and organizational requirements in relation to health and safety
4 How to obtain consent and authority for scene examination

Sources of Information

5 How to obtain information relating to incidents
6 The personnel who may be able to provide information
7 How to use the information technology (IT) and databases required for the work
8 Information collection and recording techniques

Resources and Equipment

9 How to access equipment and resources
10 The types and uses of equipment and resources
11 The preparation and use of equipment for investigations
12 The specialized proficiencies: techniques and resources available, both in-house and other sources
13 How to prioritize your work load

Scene Preservation

14 The importance of and how to control and preserve scenes
15 Contamination issues and considerations

Health and Safety

16 Potential health and safety hazards at scenes
17 How to assess risks to health and safety

UNIT TITLE

3H5	Attend and control the crime scene.

SUMMARY

This unit is about attending and controlling the scene of an incident. It also covers preserving the scene for examination. You will need to be able to maintain health, safety, and welfare throughout this work.

You will need to gather information at the scene and contribute to the investigative process. You will also need to review and define the scene parameters. You will also need to consider the possibility of linked scenes.

In addition, controlling and preserving the scene will require establishing and communicating responsibilities with relevant personnel, and establishing the scene boundary. You will need to put preventative measures in place and maintain these during the examination.

There are two elements:

3H5.1	Attend the scene.
3H5.2	Control and preserve the scene.

This unit was developed by Skills for Justice.

ELEMENT

3H5.1	Attend the scene.

PERFORMANCE CRITERIA

To meet the standard, you must:

1 Identify and take the necessary actions to maintain health, safety, and welfare
2 Identify potential operational threats and risks to relevant others
3 Gather information at the scene, and contribute to the investigative process
4 Review and define the scene parameters based on all the available information
5 Consider the possibility of linked scenes and their relevance to other investigations
6 Assess the need for additional resources according to local operating procedures
7 Accurately record all the relevant information in accordance with local operating procedures
8 Confirm the necessary consent and authority have been obtained to carry out examinations according to legislation and local operating procedures

RANGE

1 Resources
   a Equipment
   b Accommodation at scene
   c Welfare requirements
   d Specialist personnel

ELEMENT

3H5.2   Control and preserve the scene.

PERFORMANCE CRITERIA

To meet the standard, you must:

1 Establish and communicate responsibilities for the scene examination with the relevant personnel
2 Establish and adjust the scene boundary and approach path as required
3 Put measures in place to prevent the damage, degradation, contamination, or loss of evidence
4 Liaise and communicate effectively with others at the scene to minimize any conflict and facilitate understanding
5 Accurately record all the relevant information in accordance with local operating procedures

RANGE

1 Conflict between
a Examinations
b Personnel
c Welfare requirements
d Roles

UNIT

3H5.2   Control and preserve the scene.

KNOWLEDGE AND UNDERSTANDING

To meet the standard, you need to know and understand:

Legal and Organizational Requirements

1 Current, relevant legislation, policies, local operating procedures, codes of practice, guidelines, and investigative process for attending and controlling the scene of an incident
2 Current, relevant legislation and organizational requirements in relation to race, diversity, and human rights
3 Current, relevant legislation and organizational requirements in relation to health and safety
4 The need to confirm consent and authority for scene examination

Liaison and Communications

5 The internal and external personnel with whom you will have to liaise
6 Lines of communication with internal and external personnel
7 Communication systems, and how these should be used

Sources of Information

8 How to obtain information relating to incidents
9 The personnel who may be able to provide information

10 How to use IT and databases
11 Information collection and recording techniques
12 How to obtain consent and authority for scene examination

Investigative Processes

13 Investigative processes and the wider context of the investigation
14 How to maintain the continuity of the investigative process
15 The types of information gathering that may be used
16 The potential for conflict of interest at the scene, and how this can be minimized
17 How to assess and determine examination requirements: scientific disciplines, specialized proficiencies, techniques, and resources
18 Incident patterns and trends, and how these can be used
19 The reasons for reviewing initial assessments
20 The potential evidence types, and when to seek advice in relation to their recovery

Scene Preservation

21 The importance of and how to control and preserve scenes, including consideration of location, weather conditions, time of day, and multiple locations
22 The nature of linked scenes, and the need to consider linked scenes
23 Contamination issues and considerations: means of prevention

Resources and Equipment

24 How to access equipment and resources
25 The types and uses of equipment and resources
26 Types of personal protective equipment
27 How to prioritize your work load

Health and Safety

28 Potential health and safety hazards at scenes
29 How to assess risks to health and safety

Identifying Operational Threats and Risks

30 The difference between threats and risks
31 How to identify potential threats and risks
32 The types of available information which are required to identify operational threats and risks

---

UNIT TITLE

3H6	Examine the scene and collect evidence.

SUMMARY

This unit is about examining the scene and collecting evidence. You will need to be able to maintain health, safety, and welfare throughout this work. In addition, you will need to record all relevant information relating to scene examination, evidence collection, and completion of the examination.

In examining the scene you will need to determine the type of examination that is necessary and use suitable examination and investigation techniques. You will need to locate and record potential evidence and maintain effective communications.

Collecting potential evidence will involve maximizing the recovery of evidence through the use of appropriate techniques. You will need to maintain the continuity, security, and integrity of items.

Completing the examination will involve ensuring all the necessary actions have been taken and evaluating the scene to prove or disprove the hypothesis. Further examination and/or additional resources may be required, and you will need to identify such a need and take the appropriate action. Finally, you will need to communicate the progress and completion of the examination to relevant personnel.

There are three elements:

3H6.1	Examine the scene.
3H6.2	Collect evidence.
3H6.3	Complete the examination.

This unit was developed by Skills for Justice.

ELEMENT

3H6.1	Examine the scene.

PERFORMANCE CRITERIA

To meet the standard, you must:

1 Determine the sequence and types of examination that are necessary
2 Identify any additional resources that are required
3 Use examination and investigative techniques that are appropriate for the scene and circumstances of the incident
4 Use examination and investigative techniques in a way that ensures potential evidence is preserved and optimized
5 Locate and record potential evidence in accordance with local operating procedures
6 Identify and take the necessary actions to maintain health, safety, and welfare
7 Identify potential operational threats and risks to relevant others
8 Record relevant information accurately and contemporaneouslyb in accordance with local operating procedures and legislation
9 Maintain effective communications concerning the progress of the examination with the relevant personnel
   a. *For example, a fingerprint or fiber.*
   b. *Meaning "at the time of the examination."*

RANGE

1 Examination
   a Carried out by self
   b Carried out in coordination with others

2 Resources
   a Equipment
   b Accommodation at scene

     c   Welfare requirements
     d   Specialist personnel
   3   Circumstances of the incident
     a   Indoor
     b   Outdoor
     c   Variations in weather conditions
     d   Possibility of contamination
     e   Degradation
     f   Damage
     g   Loss of potential evidence

ELEMENT

3H6.2   Collect evidence.

PERFORMANCE CRITERIA

To meet the standard, you must:

1   Select and use the appropriate examination techniques and equipment to maximize recovery of evidence
2   Prioritize and collect evidence in an appropriate manner and in cooperation with other relevant personnel
3   Identify the need for additional resources, and take the necessary actions to obtain them
4   Ensure that recovered items are preserved and recorded in accordance with local operating procedures
5   Establish and maintain the continuity, security, and integrity of items in accordance with organizational requirements
6   Identify and take the necessary actions to maintain health, safety, and welfare
7   Record all relevant information in relation to the collection of evidence accurately and contemporaneously

RANGE

   1   Resources
     a   Equipment
     b   Accommodation at scene
     c   Welfare requirements
     d   Specialist personnel
   2   Items
     a   Evidence
     b   Intelligence
     c   information

ELEMENT

3H6.3   Complete the examination.

PERFORMANCE CRITERIA

To meet the standard, you must:

1   Review the scene examination to ensure that all the necessary actions have been taken
2   Evaluate the scene examination to prove or disprove the examiner's hypothesis

3 Identify the need for further examination and/or additional resources, and take the necessary actions
4 Communicate the progress and completion of the examination to the relevant personnel at the appropriate time
5 Identify and take the necessary actions to maintain health, safety, and welfare
6 Record the relevant information pertaining to the examination accurately and contemporaneously

RANGE

1 **Resources**
   a Equipment
   b Accommodation at scene
   c Welfare requirements
   d Specialist personnel

UNIT

3H6.3 Examine the scene and collect evidence.

KNOWLEDGE AND UNDERSTANDING

To meet the standard, you need to know and understand:

Legal and Organizational Requirements

1 Current, relevant legislation, policies, local operating procedures, codes of practice, guidelines, and investigative process for examining scenes of incidents
2 Current, relevant legislation and organizational requirements in relation to race, diversity, and human rights
3 Current, relevant legislation and organizational requirements in relation to health and safety

Liaison and Communications

4 The internal and external personnel with whom you will have to liaise
5 Lines of communication with internal and external personnel
6 Communication systems, and how these should be used

Investigative Processes

7 Intelligence collection and recording techniques
8 Investigative processes and the wider context of the investigation
9 How to maintain the continuity of the investigative process
10 The types of investigative and interview techniques that may be used
11 How to assess and determine examination requirements: scientific disciplines, specialized proficiencies, techniques, and resources
12 The importance of reassessing in the light of what you find
13 The different types of search and examination techniques—the importance of sequential examination techniques

Scene Preservation

14 How to define the scene of an incident
15 The ways in which approach paths should be established

16   The nature of linked scenes, and the need to consider linked scenes
17   How and when scene logs are used
18   Techniques for the preservation of the scene
19   Contamination issues and considerations, and means of prevention
20   The importance of and how to control and preserve scenes, including consideration of location, weather conditions, time of day, and multiple locations

Collection of Evidence

21   The types of retrieval techniques
22   The point at which items become evidence
23   The potential evidence types, and when to seek advice in relation to their recovery
24   Types of evidence preservation techniques
25   The importance and methods of recording potential evidence
26   Screening methods, presumptive and physical tests for potential evidential material, and sampling techniques
27   Continuity, security, and integrity requirements

Resources and Equipment

28   The types and use of equipment and consumables
29   Types of personal protective equipment
30   Types of tests available
31   Types of additional expertise available
32   How to prioritize your work load

Health and Safety

33   Potential health and safety hazards at scenes
34   How to assess risks to health and safety

Identifying Operational Threats and Risks

35   The difference between threats and risks
36   How to identify potential threats and risks
37   The types of available information which are required to identify operational threats and risks

UNIT TITLE

3H6.3   Package, store, and transport items of evidence.

Summary

This unit is about packaging, storing, and transporting items of evidence. You will need to be able to maintain health, safety, and welfare throughout this work.

You will need to handle, package, and store items safely and correctly, and ensure that items are handled in a way that minimizes the risk of contamination. You will also need to select suitable methods of transport and ensure that the evidence is moved legally, securely, and safely.

There are two elements:

3H7.1   Package, store, and record evidence.
3H7.2   Transport evidence.

This unit was developed by Skills for Justice.

ELEMENT

3H7.1　Package, store, and record evidence.

PERFORMANCE CRITERIA

To meet the standard, you must:

1　Handle, package, and store physical items safely according to legislation and local operating procedures
2　Ensure that items are handled in a way that minimizes the risk of contamination
3　Identify the appropriate packaging requirements for physical items
4　Ensure that nonphysical evidencea is correctly recorded
5　Store and retain items in appropriate conditions, and ensure appropriate levels of access
6　Maintain storage facilities in accordance with health and safety requirements
7　Record relevant information accurately and correctly in accordance with organizational and legal requirements
　　a.　*For example, digital photography*

RANGE

1　Storage facilities
　　a　Transport
　　b　Static

ELEMENT

3H7.1　Transport evidence.

PERFORMANCE CRITERIA

To meet the standard, you must:

1　Select a method of transport that allows evidence to be moved legally, securely, and safely, and in a way that minimizes the risk of contamination, loss, or degradation
2　Ensure that, where necessary, evidence is segregated in a way that preserves integrity and continuity
3　Decontaminate containers and transportation in accordance with local operating procedures
4　Record relevant information accurately and correctly in accordance with organizational and legal requirements

RANGE

1　Segregation using
　　a　Special packaging materials
　　b　Segregation within vehicles
　　c　Separate transportation

UNIT

3H7　Package, store, and transport items of evidence.

KNOWLEDGE AND UNDERSTANDING

To meet the standard, you need to know and understand:

Legal and Organizational Requirements

1 Current, relevant legislation, policies, local operating procedures, codes of practice, guidelines, and investigative process for the storage and transport of evidence
2 Current relevant legislation and organizational requirements in relation to race, diversity, and human rights
3 Current, relevant legislation and organizational requirements in relation to health and safety

Collection of Evidence

4 The potential evidence types, and when to seek advice in relation to their recovery
5 Types of evidence preservation techniques
6 Continuity, security, and integrity requirements

Packaging and Storing Evidence

7 Causes of contamination and means of prevention
8 Sampling, packaging, preservation, and storage techniques
9 The importance and need for segregation of potential evidential materials

Transport of Evidence

10 Types of transport available, and factors to be considered when selecting

Resources and Equipment

11 The types and use of equipment and consumables
12 Types of personal protective equipment
13 How to prioritize your work load

Health and Safety

14 Health and safety considerations
15 Decontamination procedures

UNIT TITLE

3H8	Evaluate the crime scene investigation.

SUMMARY

This unit is about evaluating the scene investigation. You will need to maintain health, safety, and welfare throughout this work.

You will need to consider all information that may help the investigation and identify the need for further investigation and/or examination. You will also need to consider the possibility of linked scenes that may be a result of series incidents or multiple scene incidents. You will need to identify and agree items for forensic examination, and pass intelligence to appropriate sources.

There is one element:

3H8	Evaluate the scene investigation.

This unit was developed by Skills for Justice.

ELEMENT

3H8	Evaluate the scene investigation.

PERFORMANCE CRITERIA

To meet the standard, you must:

1 Participate in debriefing meetings in accordance with investigation and local operating procedures
2 Identify and access additional sources of information that may help the investigation
3 Consider all information that may help to prove or disprove matters under investigation
4 Identify the need for further examination and/or additional resources, and take the necessary actions
5 Make an evaluation of the evidence to determine whether submission for further investigation and/or examination is required
6 Consider the possibility of linked scenes and their relevance to other investigations
7 Identify and agree items to be submitted for forensic examination with relevant personnel
8 Pass intelligence to appropriate sources

RANGE

1 **Sources of information**
   a Colleagues
   b Internal databases
   c External databases
2 **Resources**
   a Equipment
   b Accommodation at scene
   c Welfare requirements
   d Specialist personnel
3 **Linked scenes**
   a Series incidents
   b Multiple scene incidents

UNIT

3H8	Evaluate the crime scene investigation.

KNOWLEDGE AND UNDERSTANDING

To meet the standard, you need to know and understand:

Legal and Organizational Requirements

1 Current, relevant legislation, policies, local operating procedures, codes of practice, guidelines, and investigative process
2 Current, relevant legislation and organizational requirements in relation to race, diversity, and human rights
3 Current, relevant legislation and organizational requirements in relation to health and safety

Liaison and Communications

4 The internal and external personnel with whom you need to liaise, and the lines of communication to use

5 Communication systems, and how these should be used
6 The purpose of debriefing meetings, and how to participate in such meetings

Evaluation

7 The need to consider emerging and new information—need to keep an open mind
8 The need to review current legislation and local operating procedures in the light of the examination
9 Additional sources of information that may help the investigation, and how to access them
10 How to carry out an evaluation of scene investigations
11 How to evaluate material recovered from the scene(s)
12 Specialized proficiencies, techniques, and resources available—both in-house and other sources
13 The nature of linked scenes, and the need to consider linked scenes
14 How to prioritize your work load

Health and Safety

15 Potential health and safety hazards at scenes
16 How to assess risks to health and safety

A TRAINING STRATEGY

In February 2006, the Police Service of England and Wales through the Association of Chief Police Officers (ACPO) developed a training strategy for those aspects of forensic science involved in policing activities. NOS had been developed for scene investigation and for fingerprinting activities; however, in addition to this, those other aspects of policing that could in some way impinge upon forensic science have been developed. The following units of competence developed by Skills for Justice refer in some way to forensic science.

1.E1.   Respond to road-related accidents.
2.C1.   Provide an initial police response to incidents.
2.C5.   Contribute to providing an initial response to incidents.
2.G1.   Manage major investigations.
2.G2.   Conduct investigations.
2.G3.   Plan and conduct allocated investigations.
2.G4.   Finalize investigations.
2.G5.   Plan and conduct financial investigations.
2.G6.   Plan and conduct road collision investigations.
2.I1.   Search individuals.
2.I2.   Search vehicles, premises, and land.
2.K1.   Escort detained persons.
2.K2.   Present detained persons to custody.
2.K3.   Authorize and manage police detention.
2.K4.   Assist with the detention of detained persons.
2.L2.   Prepare for, and participate in, a chemical, biological, radiological, or nuclear (CBRN) incident or operation.
3.H4.   Start the crime scene investigation process.
3.H5.   Attend and control the crime scene.

3.H6.   Examine the scene, and collect evidence.

3.H7.   Package, store, and transport items of evidence.

3.H8.   Evaluate the crime scene investigation.

3.H1.   Analyze, compare, and evaluate friction ridge detail.

3.H2.   Analyze, compare, and evaluate fingerprints against prints held in files and databases.

3.H3.   Verify fingerprint identifications.

In unit 2I2, "Search vehicles, premises, and land" to see where any reference is made that could require some knowledge and skills of forensic science. It comprises two elements of competence.

UNIT TITLE

2I2	Search vehicles, premises, and land.

SUMMARY

This unit is about searches of vehicles, premises, and land. The search of land could include, for example, a garden, a grass verge, or a yard.

The planning of coordinated structured searches is covered in a separate unit about planned policing operations; however, this unit is relevant to the conduct of the search itself.

The search must be conducted in a legal and ethical way, using approved search methods. You will need to establish that you have the grounds and legal authority to carry out the search. Where evidence is found, this may be seized, packaged, and stored in a manner that maintains its integrity and continuity. You will also need to complete any necessary documentation.

There are two elements:

2I2.1	Prepare to search vehicles, premises, and land.
2I2.2	Conduct searches of vehicles, premises, and land.

This unit was developed by the Police Skills and Standards Organisation.

ELEMENT

2I2.1	Prepare to search vehicles, premises, and land.

PERFORMANCE CRITERIA

To meet the standard, you must:

1   Establish that you have the grounds and legal authority to carry out the search
2   Carry out planning appropriate to the circumstances, and conduct an accurate risk assessment
3   Maintain the health and safety of yourself and others prior to the search
4   Identify the search area, confirming that the location corresponds with the details on any search authority

5   Clearly inform the appropriate individuals present of the purpose and grounds for the search, and their rights in accordance with legislation
6   Prepare for the search in an ethical manner, recognizing individual and community needs with respect to race, diversity, and human rights

RANGE

1   **Legal authority**
    a   Legal powers
    b   Warrants

In this first element, "Prepare to search vehicles, premises, and land," the performance criteria 2, 3, 4, and 5 could require knowledge of forensic science, and therefore the implications of that will need to be considered when designing training.

ELEMENT

2I2.2   Conduct searches of vehicles, premises, and land.

PERFORMANCE CRITERIA

To meet the standard, you must:

1   Conduct the search in an ethical manner, recognizing individual and community needs with respect to race, diversity, and human rights
2   Maintain the health and safety of yourself and others during and after the search
3   Deal with personal property respectfully and in accordance with current policy
4   Respond to any contingencies appropriately and in accordance with current policy and legislation
5   Liaise with all relevant parties to maintain the effectiveness of the search
6   Conduct the search using approved and appropriate search methods
7   Identify and seize any item suspected of being evidence of an offense
8   Package and store any evidence seized to maintain its integrity and continuity
9   Complete any necessary search documentation accurately and legibly during the search
10   Leave the search site in an appropriate condition, and conclude the search procedures in accordance with current legislation and policy

RANGE

1   **Contingencies**
    a   Legal (including further authorities required)
    b   Access and egress
    c   Medical and welfare
    d   Aggressive and/or abusive individuals
    e   Adverse environmental conditions
2   **Relevant parties**
    a   Internal departments
    b   External agencies or organizations

In this element, "Conduct searches of vehicles, premises, and land," performance criteria 2, 4, 5, 6, 7, 8, and 10 all suggest some requirements of forensic science knowledge and skill.

Unit

| 2I2.1 | Search vehicles, premises, and land. |

Knowledge and Understanding

To meet the standard, you need to know and understand:

Legal and Organizational Requirements

1 Current, relevant legislation, policies, procedures, codes of practice, and guidelines for searching vehicles, premises, and land
2 Current, relevant legislation and organizational requirements in relation to race, diversity, and human rights
3 Current, relevant legislation and organizational requirements in relation to health and safety
4 How to maintain the health and safety of yourself and others during the search
5 The information which must be provided to relevant person(s) during the search procedure

Preparing for Searches of Vehicles, Premises, and Land

6 The reason why you must have the grounds and legal authority to carry out the search
7 How to establish you have the grounds and legal authority to carry out the search
8 How to obtain any necessary authority for the search
9 How to gather information and intelligence for the search
10 The items and evidence you are searching for
11 The risks involved in searching vehicles, premises, and land, and how to deal with them
12 How to carry out a risk assessment

Conducting Searches of Vehicles, Premises, and Land

13 How to access search areas safely
14 How to keep damage and disruption to a minimum during searches
15 How to carry out searches of vehicles, premises, and land
16 The limitations of the search with respect to the items that are being searched for
17 The ways in which items can be hidden and disposed of immediately prior to the search
18 How to interact with and handle individuals during the search to maintain safety and the effectiveness of the search
19 The contingencies that may occur, and how to deal with them (e.g., firearms, drugs, and explosives)
20 The officer safety techniques (including the use of force) that should be used, and when it is appropriate to use them
21 How to handle, package, and store items suspected of being evidence of an offense
22 The information you must provide to others on completion of the search
23 The condition in which the search area should be left, and how to report any damage caused by the search

Documentation

24 The types of search documentation that must be completed
25 The procedures for completing and submitting search documentation

The underpinning knowledge and understanding will point to some further need for knowledge of forensic science and will therefore identify the requirements of an effective training program.

Interestingly, unit 2C1, "Provide an initial police response to incidents," provides detail of what must be achieved when responding to incidents. Clearly, carrying out this initial response to something which is an unknown could involve just about anything from a simple straightforward situation to the most serious where the initial actions could be critical in maintaining the integrity of any evidence to be used later.

The unit developed by Skills for Justice is given here.

UNIT TITLE

2C1	Provide an initial police response to incidents.

SUMMARY

This unit covers providing an initial police response to incidents. The unit is not rank specific and applies to all persons responding to incidents. The incidents covered by this unit include domestic violence, road traffic incidents, critical incidents, public order, allegations of crime, noncrime incidents, and racist incidents and other hate crime. You must be able to deal with these types of incidents.

You will need to be able to gather information on the incident. Such information may include, for example, history, dangers, and witness information. Based on the information you have obtained, you will need to be able to establish the nature of the incident, and plan your actions accordingly. This process will often happen fairly quickly en route to the incident.

You will need to take into account the health and safety of self and others during the incident. If it is a major or critical incident, and you are the first on the scene, you will need to take interim control until relieved by the appropriate person.

There are two elements:

2C1.1	Gather information, and plan a response.
2C1.2	Respond to incidents.

TARGET GROUP

This unit is not rank specific and applies to all persons responding to incidents.

This unit was developed by the Police Skills and Standards Organisation.

ELEMENT

2C1	Gather information, and plan a response.

PERFORMANCE CRITERIA

To meet the standard, you must:

1 Identify and assess relevant information on the incident
2 Establish the nature of the incident based on the available information

3 Obtain any necessary additional information for the response to the incident
4 Prioritize and plan your actions according to the nature of the incident
5 Respond to the incident within the appropriate time scales and according to current policy
6 Provide the necessary information to others regarding the incident

RANGE

1 Incident
  a Domestic violence
  b Road traffic
  c Critical incident
  d Public order
  e Allegation of crime
  f Noncrime incidents
  g Racist incidents and other hate crime

2 Others
  a Control room
  b Line management
  c Other specialists, including external agencies
  d Colleagues
  e Members of the public

ELEMENT

2C1.2   Respond to incidents.

PERFORMANCE CRITERIA

To meet the standard, you must:

1 Take into account the health and safety of yourself and others during the incident
2 Communicate any required information and intelligence to others attending the scene
3 Identify and prioritize any casualties, providing any necessary first aid within the limits of your training
4 Deal with individuals in an ethical manner, recognizing their needs with respect to race, diversity, and human rights
5 Take control of more serious incidents in accordance with current policy
6 Challenge and deal appropriately with any unacceptable behavior
7 Liaise and communicate effectively with other agencies or partnerships relevant to the incident
8 Identify and request any other resources required for the incident
9 Identify and record any potential intelligence and intelligence sources from the incident
10 Take any necessary steps to protect the scene of the incident and preserve evidence
11 Fully document all decisions, actions, options, and rationale in accordance with current policy and legislation, and submit for supervision within agreed time scales

RANGE

1 Control
  a Through to conclusion of incident
  b Until relieved by the appropriate person

   2 **Incident**
      a   Domestic violence
      b   Road traffic
      c   Critical incident
      d   Public order
      e   Allegation of crime
      f   Noncrime incidents
      g   Racist incidents and other hate crime

   3 **Agencies**
      a   Other emergency services
      b   Local authority
      c   Health and safety executive
      d   Other external investigative bodies
      e   Other nonstatutory bodies
      f   Media
      g   Armed forces

UNIT

2C1.2   Provide an initial police response to incidents.

KNOWLEDGE AND UNDERSTANDING

To meet the standard, you need to know and understand:

Legal and Organizational Requirements

1 Current, relevant legislation, policies, procedures, codes of practice, and guidelines for responding to incidents
2 Current, relevant legislation and organizational requirements in relation to race, diversity, and human rights
3 Current, relevant legislation and organizational requirements in relation to health and safety

Information and Intelligence Gathering

4 How to gather and assess information about an incident
5 How to use information and intelligence to plan your response
6 How to identify potential intelligence sources

Liaison and Communication with Others

7   How to communicate effectively with control rooms
8   The types of specialists that may need to be brought into the incident
9   The types of other agencies that may be involved in the incident
10 Systems and protocols for communicating with other agencies

The Local Community

11 The composition and diversity of the local community

Responding to Incidents

12 The types of incidents you are likely to attend, including domestic violence, road traffic, critical incidents, public order, allegation of crime, noncrime incidents, and racist incidents and other hate crime
13 The procedures for responding to different types of incidents

14   How to provide support to victims, witnesses, and other individuals at the incident
15   The type of support you can provide to victims, witnesses, and other individuals at the incident
16   How to deal with suspects who may have been involved in the incident
17   How to challenge and deal with unacceptable behavior
18   The officer safety techniques (including the use of force) that should be used, and when it is
      appropriate to use them
19   How to identify and take into account the health and safety of self and others
20   How to administer first aid within the limits of your training
21   How to protect the scene of an incident and preserve evidence

Documentation

22   The types of documentation that must be completed
23   How to complete incident-related documentation
24   The time scales within which documentation must be completed, filed, and forwarded to others

---

All of the performance criteria for the two elements of this unit require some knowledge and skills associated with forensic science, thereby providing an essential focus for designing training programs.

There is now a program of work underway in the police service to base all new training firmly on NOS. Any existing training will be mapped against NOS. This provides not only a good way to identify training requirements but also a means of assessing the workplace performance of practitioners against the standards. It will deliver a training specification that could be used by potential training providers to design training. This latter fact is now more important than it was previously. This latter fact is now more important than previously given the developments in England and Wales of the marketplace in forensic science. This has led to a decrease in the market share for the Forensic Science Service (FSS) [now essentially a profit-driven commercial company] as other mainstream and niche providers of forensic scientific products have sprung up. With the police now putting the provision of forensic science and forensic science training out to competitive tender, a process for evaluating tender responses is needed. Having appropriate (agreed) Occupational Standards and Assessment Strategies in place should enable those involved in the tender evaluation process to come to a better informed judgment as to the merits of the tender responses. Having the standards in place not only gives a clear specification for tendering but also through assessments of performance will assess the effectiveness of training.

It has been briefly mentioned that the Forensic Science Sector Strategy Group is now working under Skills for Justice and is now called the Skills for Justice Forensic Science Committee. The occupational standards for the traditional laboratory side of forensic science are to be reviewed, and a new mapping exercise carried out. This review will include a review of the individual standards developed on the early N/SVQ program. Funding has now been secured for this work and a consultant specializing in standards development work appoints it.

A new group has emerged, the United Kingdom Forensic Science Education tion Group (UKFSEG), to support those universities presenting a forensic science program.

Appendix 1: Occupational Mapping Study for the Forensic Science Sector

DG Associates

1 INTRODUCTION

1.1 This report summarizes the findings of seven months of research with the forensic science sector. Its purpose is to enable a strategic view to be formed of the education, training, and development of all staff in the sector, and to provide a consistent platform for all future work both in standards development and in the proposition of areas of competence relevant to the occupational roles within the sector. There is a growing demand for standards of competence that can be used to inform the development of training, assessment systems, and other personnel development activities in the forensic science sector.

2 BACKGROUND TO THE PROJECT

2.1 The Forensic Science Sector Committee developed a range of National Occupational Standards (NOS) and National Vocational Qualifications and Scottish Vocational Qualifications (NVQs/SVQs) in the mid-1990s. The standards and qualifications were developed to cover the functions of

Scene of incident investigation
Recovering materials of evidential value
Forensic science (levels 4 and 5) (various disciplines)
Fingerprint operations
Fingerprint identification
Managing and coordinating investigations at scenes of incident

The NVQ/SVQs were first offered in September 1996; however, due to low take-up, the qualifications were withdrawn in December 2000. During this time, some 20–30 registrations were received by the awarding body and 6–7 individuals successfully completed their qualification.

The main reason for the low take-up was considered to be the bureaucracy involved in the assessment and verification procedures. The NOS were supported and were found to be useful for structuring training and for developing learning plans for individuals in the sector.

2.2 The original functional and occupational map was produced by the Forensic Science Sector in 1991. This provided the basis for the development of the initial suite of standards and qualifications.

2.3 In recent years, there have been several significant structural changes in the sector together with an expansion of the services provided by the sector. There has been an increasing interest in the use of occupational standards which has accelerated over the last two years with the emergence of the Council for the Registration of Forensic Practitioners (CRFP).

2.4 The revised functional and occupational maps will need to take account of the changes in the sector because it is important to understand how these changes impact on the needs of the workforce, and how these will influence the future development and use of NOS and qualifications in the sector.

3 AIMS OF THE PROJECT

3.1 One aim of the project is to produce a revised functional, occupational, and qualifications map for the Forensic Science Sector and to make recommendations for future actions on occupational standards and qualifications. The outcomes of the research will provide a comprehensive map of the forensic science domain in the United Kingdom including accurate, functional identification of current areas of employment and a prediction of trends in future patterns of employment.

4 METHODOLOGY

4.1 The following methodologies were used:

- Desk research to identify key publications, strategic documents, and so on, which need to be taken into account in the research. A list of these is in Annexe 1, below.
- 354 questionnaires were distributed to different organizations in the sector, including forensic science organizations, police forces, fire investigation units within fire services, and forensic science departments within universities.
- Web and electronic communication.
- Interviews with nominated employers and organizations.
- Meetings and/or consultation workshops which brought together key groups to gain agreement on the issues in the sector and to develop the functional map.

4.2 Response to the questionnaire was very slow, and despite numerous follow-up telephone calls it proved extremely difficult to get a good level of response and even more difficult to get a comprehensive response. A number of organizations refused to supply any information, saying either that they were too busy or that they were not interested in the work.

4.3 The report that follows summarizes the results of all of the research carried out in the sector. The results of the questionnaire exercise are recorded in Annexe 2.

5 STRATEGIC CHANGES IN THE SECTOR

5.1 Since the production of the original functional and occupational maps in 1991, the sector has grown at a rate not previously experienced. The growth has come about as a result of advances in technology (including the development of the National DNA Database), changes in the attitude of the courts toward forensic evidence, and the development of new disciplines to reflect analysis and interpretation services required, for example computers, mobile phones, and facial reconstruction.

5.2 A major change affecting the UK workforce is devolution. The establishment of devolved administrations for each UK country provides an added dimension in the drive for quality services. The different needs and systems of the four countries, particularly the criminal and civil justice systems, need to be balanced in the development of National Occupational Standards.

5.3 The CRFP was founded in 1998, and its register was launched in October 2000. The CRFP is an independent registration body whose objective is to promote public confidence in forensic practice within the United Kingdom. It aims to achieve this by

- publishing a register of competent forensic practitioners.
- ensuring through periodic revalidation that forensic practitioners keep up-to-date.
- dealing with registered practitioners who fail to meet the necessary standards.

The CRFP has developed and is using a system involving the assessment of current competence to accept individuals onto the register. The system is not the same as assessment for competence-based qualifications; however, there are similarities, and the concept of assessing competence has now been clearly accepted in the sector.

At present the number of practitioners successfully registered with the CRFP is over 400, some 10 percent of the overall number of application packs that have been issued, which stands at approximately 4,000.

5.4 Forensic science has become a popular choice of subjects for first-degree students, resulting in a significant increase in undergraduate courses at both colleges and universities. In 1991, only two first-degree courses were available in forensic science; by comparison, 162 undergraduate courses were available to students at the commencement of the 2002–2003 academic year, and a further 52 courses will be available for the 2003–2004 academic year, bringing the total to 214 degree courses (see Annexe 3).

5.5 The Human Rights Act came into force in October 2000. UK citizens are able to seek protection of their rights (under the European Convention on Human Rights) within the UK court system. The act places a new onus on public bodies (and their private contractors) to ensure that their policies and practices are in accordance with human rights legislation.

6 LEARNING AND DEVELOPMENT INITIATIVES

6.1 There have been a number of key education and training policy initiatives over the last few years that will affect the sector.

6.2 LEARNING TO SUCCEED (1999)

This white paper sets out a vision for lifelong learning [1]. It aims to ensure that all young people have the skills, attitudes, and qualities that provide a secure foundation for lifelong learning, work, and citizenship. In addition it advocates a framework for the development of lifelong learning for everyone to improve employability in a changing skills market.

6.3 LEARNING AND SKILLS ACT 2000

This act established the Learning and Skills Councils. These bodies have a responsibility for planning, funding, and quality assuring all further education and training for those aged sixteen and over. The Learning and Skills Council (LSC) published a Workforce Development Strategy in December 2002 [2]; the strategy sets out a threefold approach for developing the skills of the workforce so as to increase productivity, support advances in enterprise and innovation, and improve levels of social inclusion. The LSC intends to take action to

- raise informed demand for employment-related skills among individuals and employers.
- support improvements in the responsiveness and flexibility of the supply side.
- contribute to the development of an underpinning framework of better skills and labor market intelligence, responsive vocational qualifications, and improved links to the wider educational agenda.

6.4 SKILLS FOR SCOTLAND

Skills for Scotland will draw together the work of various national training agencies and the private sector to create a comprehensive and fully integrated skills strategy for Scotland.

6.5 EDUCATION AND LEARNING WALES (ELWA)

The National Council—ELWa has been responsible since April 2001 for the planning, funding, and promotion of all post-sixteen education and training except higher education. This includes further education, work-based learning, school sixth forms, and adult and continuing education.

6.6 THE NORTHERN IRELAND PROGRAMME FOR GOVERNMENT

One of the most significant developments in Northern Ireland has been the publication of the Executive's Programme for Government [3]. This sets out the plans and priorities for tackling problems and improving public services over a three-year period from April 2001. In order to achieve the goal of making a positive difference to the lives of people, some of the executive's priorities include:

Investing in education and skills
Growing as a community
Securing a competitive economy

7 FORENSIC SCIENCE

7.1 The forensic science sector is difficult to define, and presently there is no accepted definition of "forensic science." The Forensic Science Sector Committee considered that it was important to use the project to start a debate concerning the adoption of an agreed definition of forensic science. For the purposes of this project, the following definition was provided for individuals in the sector to consider and comment on: "assessing the value of evidence of single, possibly nonreplicable items of information about specific hypotheses referring to an individual event" [4].

This definition was considered by a few people to be acceptable, but the majority of responses stated that the definition was too narrow and did not reflect the whole forensic process. The definition offered appears to deal only with the examination and interpretation of potential evidence; it does not include identifying the potential evidence in the first place, nor does it include reporting and giving evidence in court.

Several alternative definitions were offered by those consulted; these are recorded in Annexe 4.

7.2 In the context of agreeing a definition of forensic science, it is worth noting the dictionary definitions of the words "science" and "forensic":

Science: 1. knowledge 2. systematic and formulated knowledge 3. physical or natural sciences collectively 4. branch of knowledge, organised body of the knowledge that has been accumulated on a subject 5. expert's skill as opposed to strength or natural ability.

Forensic: of or used in courts of law or in forensic science etc. (Concise Oxford Dictionary).

7.3 The concerns in the sector seem to be centered on what are described as emerging forensic disciplines such as computer investigations, technical equipment investigations, and facial reconstructions. Looking at the above definitions for the word "science," in particular definition 4, it can be seen that new disciplines may emerge and may continue to emerge that may be described as science. Any new discipline could be recognized when the body of knowledge is such that it may be considered to be organized in a systematic manner. The debate therefore could more rightly be said to be needed about what constitutes an organized and systematic body of knowledge and who will be the determinant of the body of knowledge.

7.4 It is considered that the definition that is finally agreed upon must reflect all of the services offered by the forensic community, including scene examination and giving evidence in court.

7.5 Scientific investigation is said to consist mainly of

- scene investigation to identify potential evidence.
- recovery of potential evidence at scenes of incidents and in the laboratory.
- detailed examination and analysis of recovered materials using a wide range of techniques.
- interpretation of findings including the use of statistics.
- writing reports and statements of evidence.
- giving evidence in court.

In addition, work in the sector requires an understanding of relevant parts of the legal process, including the rules of evidence. There is also a need for continual research to be carried out in and on behalf of the sector to develop new and improved techniques.

7.6 The forensic process fundamentally consists of three distinct stages, as can be seen in Figure A1.1.

Scene Investigation

The effective and efficient examination of a scene of incident is regarded as one of the critical steps in an investigation, and the importance of the scene as a source of information that can be used for scientific analysis and interpretation cannot be overstated. Scenes of incident are attended by different groups of people; in the event of a crime scene, the police will be in attendance and they will request the attendance of a forensic scientist based on practical circumstances.

The forensic scientist performs a different role from that of the police scenes of crime officer (SOCO). The role of the SOCO is primarily to locate and maximize the collection of evidence and intelligence, whereas the scientist may need to reconstruct events from the evidence, suggest and examine possible further explanations for the evidence, and act in a consultancy role to the senior investigating officer.

Other people who may attend a scene of incident include loss adjusters, insurance investigators, and private practitioners.

The Examination Stage

The examination stage is often carried out within a laboratory; however, depending on the type of potential evidence involved, it may need to be performed at the scene of incident. The examination stage is concerned with assessing the significance of recovered evidence through the deployment of a wide range of examination methods. The selection of examination methods will depend upon the types of evidence involved and the state of the evidential material, for example burnt, smoke damaged, or water logged.

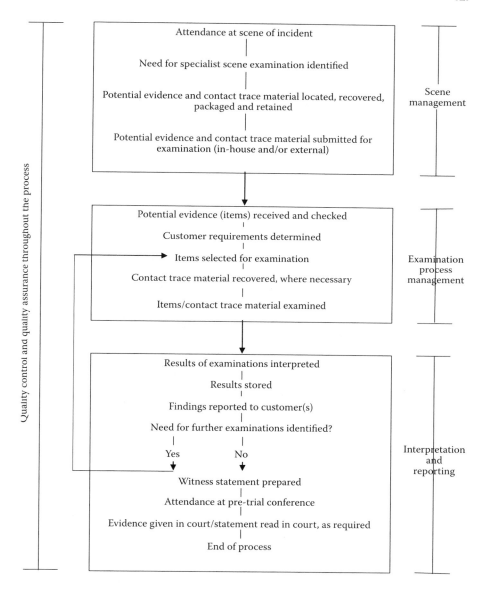

Quality control and quality assurance throughout the process

Attendance at scene of incident

Need for specialist scene examination identified

Potential evidence and contact trace material located, recovered, packaged and retained

Potential evidence and contact trace material submitted for examination (in-house and/or external)

Scene management

Potential evidence (items) received and checked

Customer requirements determined

Items selected for examination

Contact trace material recovered, where necessary

Items/contact trace material examined

Examination process management

Results of examinations interpreted

Results stored

Findings reported to customer(s)

Need for further examinations identified?

Yes   No

Witness statement prepared

Attendance at pre-trial conference

Evidence given in court/statement read in court, as required

End of process

Interpretation and reporting

FIGURE A1.1   The forensic process.

INTERPRETATION AND REPORTING

The interpretation and reporting stage is concerned to ensure that valid conclusions are drawn from the examinations performed and that reports provided are easy to understand, as precise as possible, and scrupulously correct. Interpretations will be subject to questioning and cross-examination, and reports may need to be presented in a court of law.

8 THE STRUCTURE OF THE SECTOR

8.1 There is currently no consistent framework across the United Kingdom for the collection of workforce data. Forensic science cannot be identified as an occupational area within any national statistics that are currently gathered and reported. Forensic scientists are not identified as an occupational role within the Standard Occupational Classification. For this reason, a questionnaire seeking to gather workforce data was developed and circulated to 354 organizations that have a direct involvement in the sector. The findings of that research are included in full in Annexe 2 and are summarized below.

8.2 Following numerous follow-up telephone calls and e-mails to the original list of organizations that were sent the questionnaire, a total of sixty-two responses was obtained for a 17.5 percent response rate. Some organizations refused to assist with the survey, saying they either were too busy or were uninterested. Many of the responses received were incomplete, and comprehensive responses proved impossible to gain despite follow-up contact with the organizations concerned. Particular gaps in the data provided are in the age breakdown and ethnic breakdown of the workforce.

8.3 The information about the age breakdown of the workforce that was received shows that there is a large number of workers in the sector aged between twenty-six and thirty (1,810 employees); the next largest age group is between forty-one and fifty (1,550 employees). The age group between thirty-one and forty has only 772 employees, which seems to indicate that there was significant growth in the sector approximately 5–6 years ago, or that large numbers of young people move out of the profession in their late twenties to early thirties. Either way, there is an apparent imbalance in the age distribution of the workforce. This may not be causing any problems at the moment; however, it may be difficult in the future to find staff who have sufficient experience of working in the sector for promotion to managerial roles.

8.4 The largest group of employers in the sector is the police forces, who between them employ some 3,745 personnel in England and Wales who are involved in the forensic process. Actual numbers employed are not available for Scotland and Northern Ireland; however, it is considered that the total number of personnel employed across the four countries will be approximately 5,000. Most of these staff are civilians, but many police forces still have police officers working as scenes of crime officers.

8.5. The next largest group of employers is the public sector forensic science laboratories. Prominent amongst these is the Forensic Science Service, which employs 2,761 personnel overall with some 1,399 qualified people employed in professional or associate professional roles (a definition of occupational roles is available in Annexe 5). The majority of work undertaken by the Forensic Science Service comes from the police forces, although a growing amount of work is undertaken on behalf of organizations on the defense side of legal proceedings. Other employers in this group include:

• The Forensic Science Northern Ireland laboratory with some 100 professional and associate professional staff; 139 staff overall

- Four forensic science laboratories in Scotland employing approximately 175 professional and associate professional staff; 281 staff overall
- The Forensic Explosives Laboratory employing 32 professional and associate professional staff; 44 staff overall

8.6. The third main group of employers is the fire services, which employ fire investigation staff. The number of fire investigation staff employed within ten of the fire services is 189. There are sixty-three fire services throughout the United Kingdom; therefore, the total number of people employed within fire investigation units is likely to be in the region of 1,100.

8.7. The fourth group of employers is the private sector. This group includes a range of employers from self-employed individuals to quite large forensic laboratories, such as the Laboratory of the Government Chemist and Forensic Alliance. Based on responses to the survey questionnaire, it is considered that there may be as many as 1,000 people employed in professional and associate professional occupations, with 2,000 staff employed overall.

8.8. In all there are about 8,000 personnel working in the sector in the occupational categories of professional and associate professional (not counting police surgeons, who number approximately 1,000), and a further 3,500 staff employed in management and support functions.

8.9. It is interesting to compare the numbers employed in 2002 with the numbers identified in the 1991 Occupational Mapping report [5]. The number of employees identified in 1991 was 1,831; however, this figure was only derived from respondents to the survey and it does not include all organizations in the sector. A better comparison to make is between the percentage of the workforce employed in different occupational categories (see Table A1.1). It should be noted that there have been some changes in the occupational definitions used in the Standard Occupational Classifications; however, the changes are not of a fundamental nature and should not affect the validity of the comparison.

Table A1.2 gives a further breakdown by gender:

8.10. Due to the changes in the Standard Occupational Classification, it is worth reporting here the changing structure of male and female employment in 1991 and 1996–1997 (Table A1.3).

8.11. The statistics reported in Table A1.2 and Table A1.3 illustrate to a large extent what would be expected from a comparison of the structure of a professional sector with the national workforce. It is worth noting, however,

TABLE A1.1
The Overall Structure of the Workforce

	1991 (%)	2002 (%)
Managers	9	16.7
Professionals	51.6	22.8
Associate professionals	19.2	36.1
Administrative and secretarial	13.2	15.6
Others	7.1	8.9

TABLE A1.2
The Structure of the Workforce by Gender

	Male		Female	
	1991 (%)	2002 (%)	1991 (%)	2002 (%)
Managers	12.7	22.9	4.2	10.6
Professionals	61.8	24.6	38.3	21
Associate professionals	15.4	33.5	24.2	38.5
Administrative and secretarial	3.1	9	26.3	22
Others	7	9.9	7	8

- the growth in managerial occupations in the sector, which is significantly greater than the national growth.
- the significant reduction in professional occupations, which is counter to national employment.
- the growth in associate professional occupations, which is considerably greater than the national growth.

Some of the apparent decline in professional occupations and growth in associate professional occupations may be explained by changes made to the Standard Occupational Classification between 1990 and 2000. Another explanation for the apparent decline could be the trend toward specialization and concentration on interpretation work (paragraph 10.3) and the growth in some repetitive work (paragraph 10.2).

TABLE A1.3
The Changing Structure of Male and Female Employment in England and Wales, 1991 and 1996–1997: A Comparison of SOC90 and SOC2000

	Male				Female			
	SOC90 1991 (%)	SOC2000 1991 (%)	SOC90 1996/7 (%)	SOC2000 1996/7 (%)	SOC90 1991 (%)	SOC2000 1991 (%)	SOC90 1996/7 (%)	SOC2000 1996/7 (%)
Managers	19	16.5	19.5	18	12	8	11.75	9
Professionals	9	9.75	11	12	8	7.8	9.5	9.6
Associate professionals	8	12	9	13	10	11.5	11	13
Administrative and secretarial	6.5	5	6.5	4.9	28	27.5	25	24

Source: Standard Occupational Classification 2000, vol. 1, London, 2000.

9 ROLES AND RESPONSIBILITIES

9.1 A draft functional map was developed by a working group whose membership included representatives of all four groups of employers in the sector. Two consultative workshops were held to review and comment on the draft functional map; the map was subsequently amended. The final functional map is available at Annexe 6.

9.2 The field research identified 406 different job titles within the sector, although some of the job titles are only differentiated by the type of department they are employed within (e.g., assistant forensic scientist—drugs and assistant forensic scientist—DNA). Other job roles are differentiated by the level of responsibility attached to them, for example officer, reporting officer, senior officer, principal officer, higher officer, deputy chief officer, and chief officer. When these types of duplication of job titles are accounted for, some 118 job titles have been identified within the sector. Of the 118, there are approximately 58 job titles that are directly involved in forensic science work and 60 that are involved in managing and supporting the forensic science work. The full list of job titles identified in the sector, together with their respective Standard Occupational Classification number, is included at Annexe 10.

9.3 The job titles have been plotted against the functional map to illustrate the functions carried out by different occupations. The results of the mapping are shown at Annexe 7. This analysis helps to demonstrate those functions that will need National Occupational Standards to be developed at different levels to capture the differences in responsibility, autonomy, skills, and knowledge and understanding. An example of this is function A3.4, "Conduct and record examinations." This function is likely to be carried out by at least the following people in the sector:

Assistant forensic scientist
Forensic scientist (reporting officer)
Senior forensic specialist
Forensic examiner—team leader
Consultant forensic scientist
Principal scientist

9.4 Whilst some of the functions performed by people holding different job titles might be almost identical, there are other jobs which will perform the same function but in a way which requires different levels of responsibility, decision making, skills, and knowledge and understanding. The National Occupational Standards must be able to accommodate these differences.

10 IMPORTANT AND CHALLENGING ISSUES FACING THE FORENSIC SCIENCE SECTOR—LEARNING AND DEVELOPMENT

10.1 A series of telephone interviews, together with findings from the questionnaire and the two consultation workshops, were used to try to gain an understanding of the issues facing the sector in the next few years. The main findings are summarized below, the questionnaire responses are provided in full in Annexe 8, and the findings from the workshops are reported in Annexe 9.

10.2   RECRUITMENT

There does not seem to be any lack of applicants for science-related job vacancies in the sector; indeed, the biggest complaint was that there are too many applicants. The problems seem to be more concerned with the abilities, attitudes, and expectations of new recruits. A general concern was the apparent lack of practical skills by many new recruits; practical skills are not taught at school, college, or university.

There is a perceived mismatch between the jobs available in the sector and the course content of some degree courses. The number of degree courses has increased dramatically over the last decade, as reported in paragraph 5.4 (above), and forensic science seems to have become a "sexy" subject. The increased number of graduates is, however, not matched by an equal increase in the number of jobs in the sector. This situation is exacerbated by the fact that employers reported that they would prefer to recruit graduates who have a traditional science-related degree rather than a "forensic" degree. It would appear that a large number of young people are studying for and achieving a degree that does not prepare them adequately for work in the sector, and the degree that they achieve is not valued by potential employers.

It was further reported that some recruits are overqualified for the jobs that they are asked to do and that they quickly become dissatisfied. Some interviewees stated that they personally had applied for jobs that they were overqualified for simply as a means of gaining employment in the sector. It was reported that it is much easier to move to a better job in the sector once you are working in the sector.

Young graduates are apparently now looking for career progression within 2–3 years of starting work in the sector, and they do not expect to stay at the same level of work much beyond this period of time.

Forensic science is portrayed in many television programs as being exciting and stimulating, whereas the reality is that some jobs are very routine and require constant attention to detail—aspects of work that are not usually associated with the words "exciting" and "stimulating."

10.3   SKILLS AND KNOWLEDGE REQUIREMENTS

It was reported that there is the potential for overspecialization in some areas. Whilst this may prove useful in the short term, in the longer term, specialists can become too narrow and there is a danger that they may lose the abilities that enable them to work in different areas.

A concern was also raised that due to the pressure of work, some forensic officers are having to concentrate their skills and abilities into interpretation and reporting work and that they no longer do any examination and analytical work themselves. It is considered that this will lead to deskilling in some situations and that job satisfaction is at risk. Pressures of work are leading to the introduction of more routine into work practices and forensic science becoming more of a mechanical process.

It was considered that the development and use of DNA profiling have totally transformed the way in which forensic science and the whole forensic process are managed and performed. It has affected staffing levels, the balance of skills required, the selection of evidence at a scene of incident, and the value placed on such evidence. A concern was voiced about the extent of concentration and reliance on DNA, and that there is a danger of going too far, which may end up destroying what is currently a very valuable analytical technique.

10.4   Job Satisfaction and Retention

It has already been reported under recruitment (above) that some young graduates are applying for jobs that they are overqualified for in order to gain employment in their chosen sector. If these young people are not able to move to a more challenging job role quickly enough, then they often leave the sector altogether, or at best they stay and some become demoralized and unhappy.

There is a certain amount of "poaching" going on with older, more experienced workers being encouraged to move to the private sector, where the rewards are greater and the work is structured in a more interesting way.

10.5   Keeping Up-to-Date

It was reported that some groups of workers in the sector have been left behind by developments in the application and use of forensic science. Specific examples that were quoted are DNA, fingerprinting, and imaging technology. Information technology and technical support have developed at a far greater pace than some groups of workers have kept up with. If this situation continues, it is likely that some restructuring of work roles may need to take place to compensate for the lack of skills, knowledge, and understanding in some parts of the sector.

Some concerns were voiced about the quality of training courses available to the sector, and some individual internal training departments are having to retrain people who have already attended training.

10.6   Graduates

The introduction of many new degree-level courses that include an element of forensic science is causing concern in the sector. Expectations of work in the sector are unlikely to be realized by many young graduates, and employers are unaware of what value they can place on the qualifications.

10.7   Career Opportunities

It was reported that there are few career opportunities for people working in the public forensic science laboratories or, rather, that a career path does not exist. The police reported quite the opposite, saying that the introduction of a career path for scenes of crime officers has been beneficial in recruitment, training, and retention.

11 IMPORTANT AND CHALLENGING ISSUES FACING THE FORENSIC SCIENCE SECTOR: POLICY, STRUCTURE, AND SYSTEMS

11.1 The sector has grown significantly within the last ten years, and there are now many more organizations involved in carrying out forensic science. Another notable change is that the public laboratories also involve themselves in defense work as well as in prosecution work. All of the individual organizations are likely to be engaged at some time or other in developing and using databases and in developing and adapting techniques. There could potentially be a large amount of duplication of development work. Ways to share the development and use of databases and to share the research and development work associated with new techniques would benefit all organizations in the sector.

11.2 All interviewees commented on the workload, which is apparently growing without a corresponding increase in resources. Everyone complained about the pressures associated with forensic work and that they are having to manage the demand for high-quality work and faster and faster turnaround times with greater turnover of staff and less resources. It was suggested that there needs to be some way of regulating demand.

11.3 The proposed common forensic science service in Scotland is giving rise to concern because the outcome of consultations is not yet known. The proposals came into effect in April 2007. Some restructuring has taken place with the formation of centers of excellence. Staff are naturally concerned about how they will be affected by any restructuring.

11.4 There is a concern that the current concentration on DNA evidence is detracting from other types of evidence and that DNA is being used for some cases which would previously have been investigated by other disciplines. A certain amount of pessimism was expressed about the development of DNA analysis and the DNA database and that at some point the analysis will go too far and the credibility of this evidence will be damaged in the eyes of the public. It was suggested that a certain amount of caution should be exercised with presenting DNA evidence so as not to overplay what is an extremely valuable means of identification.

11.5 ACCOUNTABILITY

All interviewees commented on the emergence of CRFP. Many interviewees reported that CRFP has the potential to be very good for the sector and that it has placed a driver for quality into organizations. However, there is also a feeling that as a result of registration, some new disciplines may gain recognition as being established forensic science disciplines when in actual fact a discipline may only just be emerging. This could be misleading to the courts and other potential users of the discipline.

Whilst the majority of interviewees and questionnaire respondents were aware of CRFP, there was much less understanding of the process that they would go through to gain registration.

Many organizations are working toward, and others have achieved, recognition against United Kingdom Accreditation Service (UKAS) standards. It was stated that more and more time is taken up every year in compliance with quality standards and legislation. Health and safety legislation is apparently having a greater impact on the sector than has previously been the case. It is not known if this is due to the introduction of new techniques and equipment, or if it is as a result of the evidential material that is now collected, submitted, and examined.

12 NATIONAL OCCUPATIONAL STANDARDS

12.1 It is clear that the future of the sector is very much about responding to the growing demand for and delivering high-quality services. The various government policies and workforce strategies recognize that this can only be achieved through investing in staff, and improving the learning and development opportunities, so as to establish a competent workforce. There is a growing demand for National Occupational Standards in the sector, and standards are starting to be recognized as a means of benchmarking competence, knowledge, understanding, and skills.

12.2 It was previously mentioned in paragraph 2.1 (above) that there has been low take-up of the NVQs and SVQs which were developed in 1996–1998, the main reason for this being perceived bureaucracy of assessment and verification. This situation is not unique to forensic science, and many other occupational sectors have experienced the same difficulties. Originally National Occupational Standards were primarily developed for use in NVQs/SVQs, and possible use in wider applications was not promoted. This situation has changed, largely as a result of an independent review of the UK National Occupational Standards program, commissioned by the regulatory bodies and reporting in 2001. The review was charged with investigating the effectiveness of the standards program, recommending cost-effective arrangements to minimize bureaucracy, encourage take-up, and help promote the key features of the NVQ/SVQ system.

12.3 Whilst some of the review's recommendations were concerned with internal Qualifications and Curriculum Authority (QCA) and Scottish Qualification Authority (SQA) systems, there are some recommendations that are extremely relevant to this report. The review recommended that in future, National Occupational Standards should make a greater contribution to the skills agenda than has previously been the case. National Occupational Standards can provide:

- Competence frameworks which can enhance the continuing professional development of individuals
- The basis for setting targets for learning and achievement which can be used to benchmark the performance of sectors, industries, and individual companies
- Employment-led standards which can be used to develop curricula, qualifications, apprenticeships, and learning programs in ways that closely reflect the skills needed to promote employability and productivity

12.4 The review also recognized that there is no tension between using National Occupational Standards as a basis for qualifications and having a wide range of other applications. It was further suggested that National Occupational

Standards and qualifications should be used as strategically important tools linking a variety of sector skills initiatives.

12.5 The independent review of the UK National Occupational Standards program has opened the way for standards-setting bodies to develop, promote, and use National Occupational Standards in a wide range of initiatives and developments depending upon the needs of different sectors. The National Occupational Standards that have been developed in the forensic science sector have only previously been used for the purpose of structuring qualifications. Whilst these standards are no longer recognized in qualifications within the National Qualifications Framework, there would be nothing to stop the sector from reviewing how the standards might contribute to other needs in the sector. The original standards could also form the basis of a review to determine the need for a wider range of qualifications, which may or may not include NVQs/SVQs, in the sector.

12.6 National Occupational Standards can be used to help to develop a "common language," which can articulate:

- How different workers, agencies, and organizations share boundaries or functions—essential for team working where functions overlap
- Specialist areas, where staff have a unique role
- Competence—essential in the management of risk and delivery of services

The development of a common language should help to deliver other policy initiatives within the sector leading to the wider strategic use of National Occupational Standards.

12.7 Presently, the forensic science sector owns the National Occupational Standards that were developed for the qualifications listed in paragraph 2.1 (above). In reviewing any of the National Occupational Standards developed to date, it will be important to establish joint working arrangements so that the outputs of the work are acceptable to all people in the sector.

12.8 One of the first tasks in any future development work must be to explore where there are shared outcomes and functions, but also where outcomes differ. The occupational job titles have been mapped to the key functions from the functional map (Annexe 7). This should provide a useful basis for agreeing a set of jointly owned National Occupational Standards and which standards should fall within specific sector responsibility.

12.9 It has been identified that the Police Standards Setting Body (SSB) has started to review the National Occupational Standards for scenes of incident and fingerprinting; however, the Forensic Science Standards Setting Body has not been directly involved in this work. It is recommended that the Forensic Science Standards Setting Body should contact the Police SSB to clarify the position with the standards review and the intended outcomes of the work.

12.10 The fire service is represented by the Local Government Standards Setting Body. Joint working arrangements have been established between this body and the Forensic Science Standards Setting Body, so as to ensure that the outcomes of the project, to develop National Occupational Standards in fire and explosion investigation, are acceptable to all people working in the area of fire investigation.

13 RECOMMENDATIONS

The section draws on the information and data gathered during the research phases of the project. The recommended actions should assist the sector to prepare for and cope with the issues identified in sections 10 and 11 of this report (above). The recommendations have been grouped under seven themes.

THEME 1: NATIONAL OCCUPATIONAL STANDARDS (NOS)

NOS can be used for a variety of purposes and in a variety of ways. They can be used

- to inform the development of new training programs.
- to inform the review and revision of existing training programs.
- to map new roles and functions against.
- to assist in role development and structuring.
- to inform organization development and structuring.
- in recruitment and selection processes and procedures.
- in appraisal systems.
- in personal development plans.

The sector has previously only used NOS in the formation of NVQs/SVQs, although more recently work has been undertaken to broaden the usage beyond qualifications. It is essential to have a "demand-pull" system in place to ensure the capability of the workforce to meet the sector challenges of the future.

Recommendation 1. A strategic promotion policy should be encouraged across the sector to help sell the benefits of NOS.

Recommendation 2. Specific guidance should be targeted at the policy makers in the sector to help them understand the potential and importance of NOS.

Recommendation 3. Promote the use of NOS in developing training and in reviewing and revising existing training.

Recommendation 4. Promote the use of NOS in recruitment and selection procedures.

Recommendation 5. Promote the use of NOS in appraisal systems and personal development plans.

Recommendation 6. Utilize information technologies to enable different organizations and individuals in the sector to access information about NOS and their application.

Recommendation 7. Explore the potential to develop qualifications other than NVQs/SVQs for the sector, for example Vocationally Related Qualifications (VRQs) and foundation degrees. Involving employers in the development of foundation degrees should ensure that the skills developed are matched with employer demand, which in turn will lead to increased employability.

THEME 2: THE GENERIC FORENSIC SCIENCE SECTOR NOS

The generic forensic science sector NOS have been approved since January 2002; however, not many people in the sector are aware of their existence. The generic NOS have been used to form the basis of work to develop NOS for fire and explosion investigations. Through this work the need has been identified to supplement the generic NOS with a schedule, setting out the fire- and explosion-specific knowledge and understanding and the scope of activities or applications needed to show competence in the function.

Recommendation 8. Promote the availability of the generic forensic science NOS.
Recommendation 9. Develop case study materials to show how the generic NOS can be used across a wide range of different forensic disciplines.
Recommendation 10. Analyze the job titles, provided through this report (Annexe 10), against the generic forensic science NOS to identify those jobs that are not covered by the standards. Particular emphasis could be placed on new jobs, for example those concerned with work for the National DNA Database.

THEME 3: OTHER NOS DEVELOPED BY THE SECTOR FOR THE SECTOR

NOS have previously been developed within the sector for scenes of incident, recovering material of potential evidential value, scene of incident management, fingerprint services, fingerprint identification, law enforcement technical support units, and several specific disciplines—at levels 4 and 5. The majority of these NOS were incorporated into a range of different NVQs and SVQs; they have not been updated and are now no longer included in the National Qualifications Framework. The exception to this is the law enforcement technical support units NOS, which were approved in 2001 and are still to be submitted to QCA and SQA for accreditation as a National/Scottish Vocational Qualification. The Police Standards and Skills Organisation has been undertaking a review of the scenes of incident, fingerprint services, and fingerprint identification NOS.

Recommendation 11. The Forensic Science Standards Setting Body to contact the Police Standards Setting Body to clarify the position with the standards review and the intended outcomes of the work.
Recommendation 12. The Forensic Science Standards Setting Body to decide if it wishes to retain ownership of the NOS previously developed, to determine if there is a need to update them, and to identify the best means of completing such work.

THEME 4: USE OF NOS DEVELOPED BY OTHER STANDARDS-SETTING BODIES

A whole range of different jobs have been identified in the sector that will be able to make use of standards developed by other standards-setting bodies. There are NOS available for the following functions: administration, research, management, customer service, marketing, personnel, training, health, and safety. The majority of these NOS should be directly relevant to the job titles identified in these functions.

Recommendation 13. Promote the availability of cross-sector NOS to relevant personnel in the sector.
Recommendation 14. Analyze the research jobs in the sector against the NOS for research functions, and identify if there is a need to tailor the standards or if they can be used as they are.

THEME 5: CAREERS IN FORENSIC SCIENCE

The report has identified a perceived mismatch between the qualifications that young people achieve and the qualifications that employers expect of them. There is no apparent career structure in some parts of the sector, and it would appear that young people are entering the sector with false expectations of the type of work they will be required to do.

Recommendation 15. Develop and publish potential career paths in the forensic science sector, the recommended entry routes, and progression opportunities.
Recommendation 16. Review the graduate apprenticeship framework that was previously developed in the sector, and explore the advantages and disadvantages of launching the framework in the sector.
Recommendation 17. Research the academic qualifications available to young people wishing to start a career in the sector with the intention of publishing the information for the benefit of both employers and young people alike. The research should include mapping the qualifications against the relevant NOS.
Recommendation 18. Organize a focus group meeting to explore and eliminate the apparent mismatch between academic qualifications, employer expectations, and the expectations of young people.
Recommendation 19. Research the extent and nature of practical skills expected of young people, and identify the most appropriate means of developing such skills.

THEME 6: THE DEVELOPMENT OF THE PROFESSION

The report has identified some concerns regarding new and emerging disciplines in the sector; it has also identified growth areas in the sector, together with the concerns that growth brings for more traditional forensic science approaches.

Recommendation 20. Explore the potential for greater synergy between CRFP, National Occupational Standards, and assessment methods.
Recommendation 21. Research and recommend a procedure or system to recognize when an analytical method or investigative technique has developed such a body of knowledge to qualify it as forensic science.
Recommendation 22. Conduct a skills performance analysis in the sector to identify if the current trend to more specialization is likely to continue, to identify the impact of specialization on the skills of the existing workforce, and to recommend actions to ensure that the workforce is adequately equipped to deal with future demands on the sector.

THEME 7: OVERALL MANAGEMENT

It is essential that sufficient time is taken to ensure adequate preparations are made to carry out the above recommendations. The time needed to establish management arrangements, establish membership of various working groups and consultation groups, set dates for meetings, and so on should not be underestimated.

There must be clarity of the outcomes expected of any work undertaken, and the role and responsibility of all participants in delivering these must be clear at the outset. Good project management skills will be critical to the achievement of the desired outcomes.

ANNEXE 1: PUBLICATIONS AND DOCUMENTS CONSULTED DURING THE PROJECT

Title	Author	Date Published
Under the Microscope	HMI—Constabulary	July 2000
Under the Microscope: Refocused	HMI—Constabulary	June 2002
Using Forensic Science Effectively	Association of Chief Police Officers and Forensic Science Service	June 1996
Forensic Science and Crime Investigation	Police Research Group	June 1996
Report of the Forensic Science Working Group		November 1997
DNA: Present and Correct	Forensic Science Service	
The Scenes of Crime Handbook	Forensic Science Service	
Professional Standards of Competence: Forensic Science	Forensic Science Steering Group	January 2002

ANNEXE 2: RESULTS OF THE QUESTIONNAIRE EXERCISE

1 THE SURVEY INSTRUMENT

1.1 The survey instrument was targeted at 354 organizations overall. Contact details for the organizations were obtained from the Forensic Science Society World List and a directory of Police Forces and Fire Services. The details for the universities and colleges were drawn from the University Careers Advisory Service (UCAS) Web site. A total of 62 organizations responded to the survey, giving a response rate of 17.5 percent. (Universities were included in the survey because it is known that some of them carry out forensic science casework.)

1.2 Table A1.4 shows the split of the different types of organizations that responded.

1.3 Table A1.5 shows the response rate for each type of organization.

2 ANALYZING THE WORKFORCE

2.1 Number of Full-Time Forensic Staff Employed

Respondents were asked to quantify the number of permanent employees in their organization. Sixty (96.8 percent) respondents provided figures, which are shown in Table A1.6.

TABLE A1.4
Split of Organization Types

	Number Received	%
Education	6	9.7
Fire	10	16.1
Forensic science organizations	30	8.4
Police	16	25.8
Total	62	100.0

The total number of employees covered by the survey is 4,785. The number of full-time employees is 4,675, and part-time employees 110.

It should be noted that the fire services figures only relate to personnel working within fire investigation units. It should also be noted that the "sales and customer service" category has been omitted from the following charts, as not many people are employed in this category by the organizations which responded to the survey (5 employees out of 4,785).

Scientific support staff numbers for the police forces in England and Wales have recently been provided by Centrex. These are shown in Table A1.7.

These figures can be compared with the staff numbers collected during the Occupational Mapping study, which is shown in Table A1.8.

See Annexe 5 for the definition of the job titles, as provided in the Standard Occupational Classification.

Figure A1.2 shows that 61.5 percent of forensic organizations have fewer than eleven employees, with a further 19.2 percent having between eleven and fifty employees. This totals 80.7 percent of the forensic organizations having fifty or fewer employees. The rest of the forensic organizations have either between 101 and 500 (7.7 percent) employees, and one organization has more than 1,000 employees.

The police respondents indicated that 66.7 percent have fewer than fifty employees directly involved in forensic science work, with the remaining 33.3 percent having between 51 and 500 employees. No police respondents indicated that they had over 500 employees.

The responses from the fire service participants are purely indicating the staff of the fire investigation departments. The results show that 40 percent of the fire

TABLE A1.5
Response Rate for Each Organization Type

	Number Sent Out	Number Received	%
Education	63	6	9.5
Fire	63	10	15.9
Forensic science organizations	140	30	21.4
Police	88	16	18.2
Total	354	62	17.5

TABLE A1.6
Full-Time Employees by Organization Type

Number of Forensic Employees	Number Overall	%
Forensic science organizations	3,426	73.3
Police	986	21.1
Fire	189	4.0
Education	56	1.6
Totals	4,675	100.0

TABLE A1.7
Police Force Scientific Support Staff Numbers

	Description	Total by Job Category	Occupational Category Total	% of Workforce
Managers	Scientific Support Manager	50	50	1.3
Professional	Fingerprint experts	629	629	16.8
Associate professionals	Photographic staff	292	3,066	81.9
	Crime scene examiner (CSE)	1,746		
	Fingerprint lab staff	165		
	Fingerprint trainees and ten-print technicians	356		
	Assistant CSE	507		
Totals		3,745	3,745	100.0

Source: Provided by Centrex.

TABLE A1.8
Police Force Scientific Support Staff Numbers Obtained from This Survey

	Occupational Category Total	% of Workforce
Managers	54	5.3
Professionals	194	19.2
Associate professionals	680	67.2
Administration	66	6.5
Sales	0	0.0
Other	18	1.8
Totals	1,012	100.0

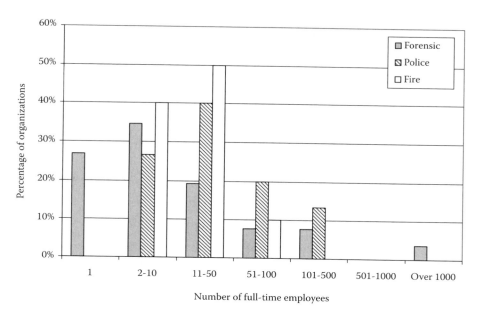

FIGURE A1.2 Distribution of organizations by type and size.

services have ten or fewer fire investigation officers, 50 percent have fifty or less, and 10 percent have more than fifty.

2.2 Number of Part-Time Forensic Staff Employed

The number of part-time staff employed by the respondents is shown in Table A1.9.
From Table A1.9, it can be seen that part-time employees are primarily used by the forensic science organizations.

2.3 Changes in Workforce Size

The survey asked if the size of the workforce has changed over the last twelve months. 56 (90.3 percent) respondents answered this question. Over half of the respondents (55.4 percent) indicated that the workforce has increased in this period, and a small

TABLE A1.9
Part-Time Employees by Organization Type

Number of Forensic Employees	Number Overall	%
Forensic science organizations	71	64.5
Police	26	23.6
Fire	0	0.0
Education	13	11.8
Totals	110	100.0

TABLE A1.10

Changes in Workforce Size

	% of Total
Increased	55.4
Decreased	5.4
No change	39.3
Totals	100

percentage (5.4 percent) stated that a decrease in staff has been experienced. (See Table A1.10.)

2.4 Recruitment during the Last Twelve Months

Respondents were asked if their organization had recruited any new staff over the last twelve months. 55 (88.7 percent) responses were received to this question, of which 61.8 percent stated that they had recruited in this period; the others had not.

2.5 Numbers Recruited during the Last Twelve Months

Organizations were requested to supply numbers of new recruits by occupational category and to indicate the source and age of the new employees. The total number of new recruits is shown in Table A1.11.

Almost 80 percent of the new recruits are employed in the professional and associate professional categories. 3.3 percent of managers have been recruited over the last year. Of the 218 professional and associate professional recruits, 128 (58 percent) are employed by the police forces. This may be due to the recruitment drive for volume scene of crime officers.

Figure A1.3 shows the breakdown of new recruits by age and qualification and/or experience.

All responding organizations stated that their managers are over twenty-five years of age; over half report that they do not expect managers to have any experience in forensic science.

Over 22 percent of responding organizations fill professional vacancies with graduates, regardless of age or previous work experience. 51 percent of participants

TABLE A1.11

Numbers Recruited during the Last Twelve Months

	Number	% of Total
Managers	9	3.3
Professional	110	40.1
Associate professionals	108	39.4
Administration and secretarial	27	9.9
Other occupations	20	7.3
Totals	274	100

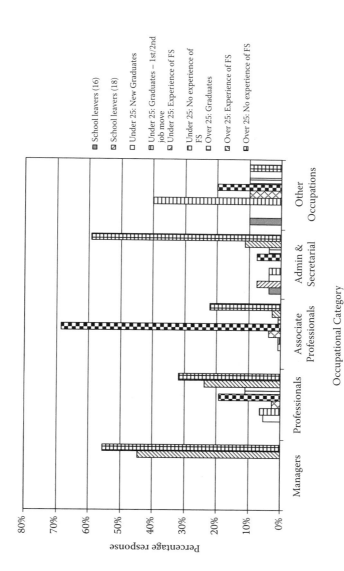

FIGURE A1.3 Source of new recruits.

state that, when recruiting professionals, no previous experience in forensic science is required. 66.3 percent of recruits for professional posts are over twenty-five years of age.

68.5 percent of associate professionals in the sector are recruited under the age of twenty-five, with no experience of forensic science; a further 22 percent are over the age of twenty-five, also with no experience. This totals 90 percent of associate professionals in the sector being recruited without previous experience of forensic science.

Almost 60 percent of participating organizations recruit people over twenty-five years of age and with no experience of forensic science into administrative and secretarial posts. A further 14.8 percent recruit individuals over twenty-five, either with experience or a degree.

It can be seen from Figure A1.3 that only the administrative and secretarial category in the sector recruits school leavers, at age sixteen or eighteen.

2.6   Temporary and Seasonal Workers Employed

Respondents were asked if their organization employs seasonal or temporary workers. Fifty-nine (95.2 percent) respondents answered this question, out of which fourteen (23.7 percent) responded in the affirmative.

Of the fourteen organizations which stated that they do employ temporary workers, eight (57.1 percent) were able to give details of numbers employed, and a total of forty-seven employees were reported. Clearly, temporary and seasonal workers are not often used in the forensic science sector.

2.7   Male-Female Split by Job Category

Organizations were asked to provide the age breakdown of the workforce by gender and occupational category. Sixty (96.8 percent) organizations surveyed responded to this question.

Figure A1.4 shows the gender breakdown by job category. The "sales and customer service" category has been removed from the charts due to the low number of employees (five) in this category.

The forensic science organizations have a fairly even male-female split in all occupational categories with the exception of administrative and secretarial, which has 71.4 percent female and 28.6 percent male. In the managerial and senior official category, there are slightly more men (57.5 percent), but the professional and associate professional categories have more female employees (51.4 and 60.7 percent, respectively).

The police forces employ more males than females in all occupational categories except administrative and secretarial (68.2 percent female, 31.8 percent male). In the managerial and senior official category, the breakdown of males and females is 85 and 15 percent, respectively, whereas the associate professional roles are more evenly shared with a split of 54.9 percent male and 45.1 percent female.

Responses from the fire service indicate that no females are employed in the fire investigation teams. All occupational categories show a 100 percent male base. The reason given for this is that fire investigation teams tend to be composed of senior ranking officers, and no females have, as yet, reached the required level in the management structure. Several fire services explained that they are keen to redress the balance.

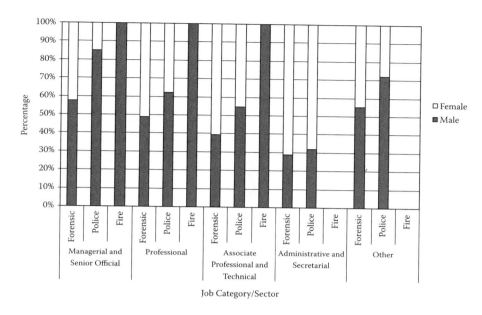

FIGURE A1.4   Gender split of occupational categories.

The total number of male employees represented by Figure A1.5a is 2,366. This figure shows the distribution of male employees across the occupational categories. The total number of female employees represented by Figure A1.5b is 2,419. This figure shows the distribution of female employees across the occupational categories.

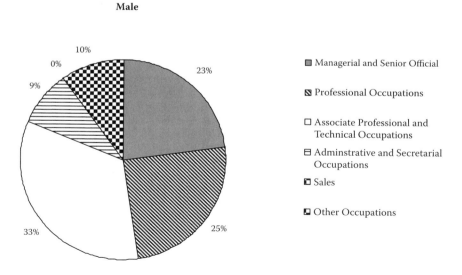

FIGURE A1.5A   Breakdown of male occupational categories.

Female

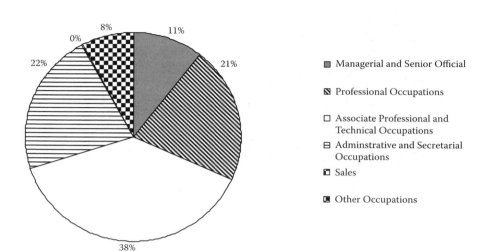

FIGURE A1.5B   Breakdown of female occupational categories.

As seen in Figure A1.6, there are very few employees in the sector, in any occupational category, under the age of twenty or over the age of sixty. The majority of the workforce is aged twenty-six to thirty or forty-one to fifty; these age groups account for 1,810 and 1,550 employees respectively, which is over 70 percent of the employees surveyed.

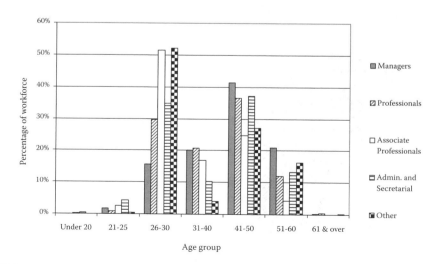

FIGURE A1.6   Age by occupational category.

The twenty-six to thirty age group shows high percentages of employees in the associate professional and other categories; however, these employees appear not to stay with the organizations, as the next age group, thirty-one to forty, has significantly reduced numbers (772 employees). Managers and professionals appear to stay with the companies, however, showing a steady increase in numbers until reaching the fifty + age bracket.

There are very few managers in the sector aged under thirty; the trend for managers seems to follow that of other occupational categories, but a decade later.

3 Staff Development

3.1 How Employees Are Kept Up-to-Date

Respondents were asked how they keep their employees up-to-date with new developments in forensic science. A total of fifty-six organizations (90.3 percent) replied to this question.

For each organization type, a summary of the main methods used to keep knowledge current is given below. Other comments from this question in the survey can be found in Appendix 6.

Forensic science organizations responded that employees are kept up-to-date by journals, training courses, conferences, meetings, seminars, and literature. The Internet is also used.

All the **police forces** responded to this question and appear to use a wide range of methods. Employees are kept up-to-date by attending courses—at the Centrex National Training Centre, Durham University, and other locations. Seminars, attendance at scientific meetings, circulating documentation, conferences, the Internet, and journals were also listed as methods used to keep up-to-date with developments in forensic science.

Fire services: All staff receive training in fire investigation. In one fire service, 70 percent of staff had completed the University of Central Lancashire Certificate in Forensic Science Studies. The fire services also reported that seminars and training courses are used to keep forensic knowledge up-to to-date.

Universities and colleges tend to use conferences, journals, and courses. Other methods of keeping knowledge current were given as liaison with local Forensic Science Society (FSS) staff, corporate membership of the FSS, police scientific investigations, and HQ pathologist and collaborative research projects.

3.2 Training Plans

Fifty-three (85.5 percent) respondents completed the question covering training plans (see Table A1.12). A high proportion of respondents have a formalized training plan for employees (83.0 percent). 93.8 percent of the responding police forces have a training plan, whilst 69.6 percent of the forensic science establishments have a formal plan. The majority of the forensic organizations that do not have a training plan are single practitioners with less than ten staff.

TABLE A1.12
Training Plans

	% of Total
Yes	83.0
No	17.0
Total	100

3.3 Training Budget

When asked if a training budget is in operation, fifty-three (85.5 percent) responses were received. A large proportion of respondents have a formalized training budget. 20.5 percent of the organizations that have a training plan do not have a training budget. (See Table A1.13.)

80 percent of colleges and universities have a training budget.
100 percent of fire services have a training budget.
93.3 percent of police forces have a training budget.
39.1 percent of forensic science organizations have a training budget. (The forensic science organizations which do have a training budget range from a 2-person company to a 137-person laboratory.)

3.4 Training by Job Category

Respondents were asked to identify the training methods used for the various occupational categories. Forty-seven (75.8 percent) respondents answered this question.

Staff in **managerial** occupations are more likely (29.1 percent) to be trained on the job, in-house, or by an external training provider (both 22.2 percent). Less than 15 percent of respondents use college and university to train managers, and a small percentage (8.5 percent) engage in open learning.
In the **professional** category, a similar pattern evolves. On-the-job learning is the most popular method (25.4 percent), with in-house courses also often used (20.6 percent). Almost 20 percent of professionals undertake training at college or university, and a similar proportion through external training providers. This category makes the most use of open learning; 10.3 percent of respondents claimed to use this method.

TABLE A1.13
Training Budgets

	% of Total
Yes	69.8
No	30.2
Total	100

Associate professionals are the highest users of external courses (26.8 percent) of all the occupational categories. On-the-job learning and in-house learning are also popular (22.0 percent and 23.2 percent). 18.3 percent of this category use colleges and universities to further their education.

33.3 percent of the **administrative and secretarial** staff learn on the job, and 30.7 percent are trained in-house. External courses are used to a lesser degree for this group.

Employees in the **other** occupation category are more likely to receive training on the job (33.3 percent) and in-house (28.2 percent).

Overall, the sector makes high use of on-the-job training (27.9 percent), in-house learning (24.2 percent), and external training providers (21.1 percent). College and university courses are attended by 16.2 percent, while open learning (8.0 percent) and other methods (2.7 percent) are less popular.

3.5   Other Training Methods Used

Training methods other than those listed above include:

Managerial: Alternative forms of management training to the methods listed above were Continuing Professional Development (CPD) with the Royal College of Pathology, attendance at international symposia, and so on, and benchmarking through Scottish and UK Forensic Science liaison groups.

Professional: Two alternatives were given for professional training: national or international seminars and conferences.

Associate professionals: CPD with the Royal College of Pathology.

Administrative: Conferences.

3.6   Does Training Lead to Qualifications?

Respondents were asked if any of the training provided by their organization leads to a qualification. Fifty-two (83.9 percent) responses were received to this question, and of these, 61.5 percent stated that employees do gain a qualification. (See Table A1.14.)

A number of qualifications were listed in the survey, and respondents were asked to indicate which, if any, employees are encouraged to achieve. A total of thirty-one responses were received; the breakdown of qualifications identified is shown in Table A1.15.

TABLE A1.14
Does Training Lead to Qualifications?

	% of Total
Yes	61.5
No	38.5
Total	100

TABLE A1.15
Which Qualification Does Training Lead To?

	% of Total[a]
MBA	21.9
Customer service diploma	3.1
Management diploma	31.3
Forensic Science Society diploma	28.1
Science-related degree	37.5
Business administration certificate	18.8
Durham University diploma in crime scene investigation	43.8

[a]Calculated out of thirty-one positive responses.

A further 33 percent offered qualifications not listed above. These are listed below by organization type.

Forensic organizations
- Computer Literacy and Information Technology
- Information Business Technology 2/3
- Basic telematics and intermediate telematics
- European information technology (IT) qualification
- Bachelor or master of science degree in biomedical science
- Master of science degree
- Scottish Vocational Qualifications

Police
- A number of staff hold degrees; however, this is not a prerequisite for their employment
- Fingerprint expert registration
- Photographic qualifications (i.e., Higher National Certificate [HNC], Higher National Diploma [HND], City & Guilds [C&G], British Institute of Professional Photography [BIPP])
- Police continuous development program

Fire
- Forensic Science Society certificate

Education
- PhD
- Teaching qualifications

3.7 Qualifications Expected

The survey asked what qualifications employees are expected to attain in each of the occupational categories. Thirty-nine (62.9 percent) responses were received to this question. 48.4 percent of organizations in the sector expect their managers to achieve at least a degree, and in a further 22.6 percent of cases a postgraduate degree, as part of their work. The other 29.0 percent expect their managers to attain a professional qualification. (See Figure A1.7.)

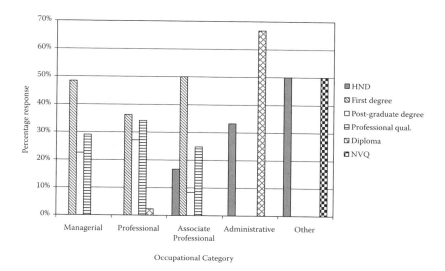

FIGURE A1.7   Qualifications expected by occupational category.

A small percentage of organizations in the sector expect their professionals to achieve at least a diploma (2.3 percent), but most expect a degree (36.4 percent), a postgraduate degree (27.3 percent), or a professional qualification (34.1 percent).

Half of the responding organizations expect their associate professionals to achieve a degree, with a further 8.3 percent requiring them to achieve a postgraduate degree. 25 percent of organizations expect their associate professionals to achieve a professional qualification. 16.7 percent require them to achieve an HND.

Organizations which stated a requirement for administrative and secretarial staff to gain a qualification indicated a preference for an HND or a diploma (33.3 and 66.7 percent respectively).

In "other" roles, respondents do not expect their employees to achieve a degree or professional qualification, although HNDs and NVQs are expected.

"Other" requirements listed include:

Forensic science organizations
- Administrative: relevant keyboard and Internet skills, "O" grade/ standard grade, Ordinary National Certificate (ONC)
- Associate: laboratory experience, Membership of the Royal College of Pathologists (MRC) pathology, statistical knowledge, degree, HND, HNC, diploma (crime scene examination)
- Managerial: look for experience over qualifications, degree plus indus- trial experience, MRC pathology, degree and professional registration, CRFP, honors degree minimum
- Professional: CRFP, degree in facial mapping and fingerprint expert status qualification, degree plus industrial experience, degree and pro- fessional registration, honors degree minimum, postgraduate

Police

- Qualifications not presently included as an expectation of employment, but presently under consideration
- Administrative: three highers, Higher National Diploma in Business Administration (HND), ONC, CLAIT, CRFP where appropriate, IBT 2
- Associate: HNC, photographic qualification, science-based A level
- Managerial: CRFP
- Other: HND graphical subjects or imaging
- Professional: CRFP, Durham University diploma in crime scene examination, FSS diploma, National Training Centre diplomas in scene of crime and fingerprints, teaching certificate or degree

Fire

- The Fire Service (nationally) is introducing an Integrated Personal Development System (IPDS) which will identify roles, development, and CPD—lifelong learning. Currently, personal development is an individual choice, with different people at different levels undertaking their own CPD.
- We have internal progression qualifications and courses that are necessary. We also have personnel asking to undertake other professional qualifications specific to their current or proposed role.
- The professional qualifications required at management level are a Fire Service College course in management, the Institute of Fire Engineers, and Institute of Supervisory Management.
- The professional qualifications named at professional level were the membership of its Institute of Fire Engineers and the Fire Service College Fire Investigation Skills.

Education

- Experience is more important than qualifications for administrative staff.

3.8 Training Provision

Respondents were asked to give details of the provision made for employee training. Thirty-three (53.2 percent) responses were received. The spread of provision offered in the sector can be seen in Table A1.16.

The most popular provision for training is the funding of courses, with 55.9 percent responses across the various occupational categories. Associate professionals particularly appear to benefit from this incentive (71.4 percent). Paid study leave and in-house training are also regularly provided.

TABLE A1.16
Training Provision

	Managerial (%)	Professional (%)	Associate Professional (%)	Administrative or Secretarial (%)	Other (%)
In-house	24.0	21.9	0	0	33.3
Training paid for	52.0	53.1	71.4	50.0	33.3
Paid study leave	8.0	12.5	14.3	50.0	33.3
Allocate mentor	16.0	12.5	14.3	0	0

TABLE A1.17
Performance Monitoring

	Managerial (%)	Professional (%)	Associate Professional (%)	Administrative or Secretarial (%)	Other (%)
Annual appraisal	55.9	48.1	31.6	47.4	42.9
Performance assessment	17.6	25.9	31.6	26.3	42.9
Internal Progress Review and objective setting	2.9	3.7	5.3	5.3	28.6
Personal development plan	23.5	22.2	31.6	21.1	14.3

Additional comments received:

Fire
- Professional: pay for training (Joint training with police SO.COs)

3.9 Performance Monitoring

The question concerning performance monitoring received forty-two (67.7 percent) responses. The most frequently used method of performance monitoring is the annual appraisal (47.6 percent). (See Table A1.17.)

The following alternatives were offered.

Forensic science organizations
- Monitoring casework
- Success in casework
- All: annual appraisals, ad hoc meetings, personal development review and personal assessment, career grade structure
- Associate: all externally validated through UKAS and Investors in People
- Managerial: appraisal, weekly and monthly review, appraisal every three months, action and development plans and targets (IIP)
- Professional: appraisal; line managers; reviews weekly, monthly, or every six months; action and development plans and targets (IIP)

Police
- Administrative: continuous supervision, dip sampling of work, and quality awareness checking
- Associate: quality assurance (QA) tests, on-the-job QA visits, and specific monitoring of workload and results from computerized data
- Managerial: action and development plans and targets (IIP), ad hoc meetings, specific monitoring of workload and results from computerized data
- Other: monitoring quality of output, supervisory control
- Professional: dip sampling of work, ad hoc meetings
- Professional: quality assurance tests

TABLE A1.18
Career Opportunities

	Managerial (%)	Professional (%)	Associate Professional (%)	Administrative or Secretarial (%)	Other (%)
As vacancies arise	25.0	13.6	5.3	33.3	0
Promotion to next level	75.0	86.4	94.7	66.7	100.0

Fire
- All: personal development plan
- Performance management system
- Best value scrutiny

Education
- All: informal monitoring
- All: mentoring
- All: workload model

3.10 Career Opportunities

The survey asked what career progression opportunities exist in each of the job categories. A total of thirty-nine (62.9 percent) organizations responded. 85.0 percent of all respondents stated that promotion to the next level is the most common form of career progression. (See Table A1.18.)

Several respondents provided the following alternatives.

Forensic science organizations
- Administrative: move to similar posts in police support structure.

Police
- Administrative: career progression limited at present in this category, move to operational trainee grade, move to similar posts in police support structure.
- All: all posts are competitive and can be open to anyone with the necessary criteria.
- Associate: none.
- Managerial: none.
- Other: career progression very limited, although it depends on qualifications held.

Fire
- All: all uniformed staff are able to progress through ranks and take various qualifications. Nonuniform staff have the same opportunities but are unable to swap to uniform posts.
- All: progression is available to all.
- All: there are regular opportunities for uniform personnel. However, there are not as many opportunities for our support staff within the Fire Service, but they may apply for other public sector positions.

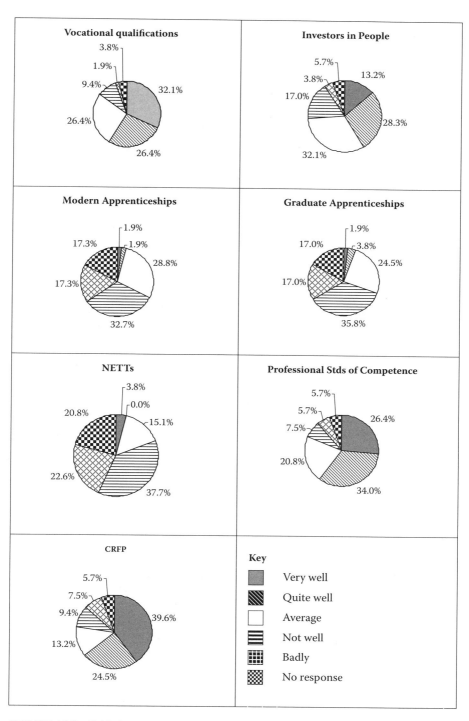

FIGURE A1.8 Initiatives.

Education
- Administrative: little opportunity for career progression for secretaries within sector.
- Associate: IT manager; increased autonomy and independence rewarded for effort and initiative.
- Professional: as vacancies arise, progression to fee-earning status, and salaried and then equity membership.

3.11 Education and Training Initiatives

Organizations were asked how well informed employees are on specific education and training initiatives. A total of fifty-three (85.5 percent) organizations responded to this question.

Of all the initiatives listed, respondents replied that they are best informed about the Professional Standards of Competence and CRFP. 60.4 percent of respondents claim to be very well or quite well informed about the Professional Standards of Competence, and 64.2 percent are very well or quite well informed about the CRFP.

Figure A1.8 shows the responses received.

ANNEXE 3: LIST OF UNIVERSITIES OFFERING DEGREE COURSES

Degree Courses (48 universities or colleges offering 162 courses, 2002–2003)

Anglia Polytechnic University	The University of Kent at Canterbury
Bournemouth University	The University of Manchester Institute of Science and Technology
Coventry University	The University of Strathclyde
Cranfield University (Royal Military College of Science)	The University of Surrey
De Montfort University	University College, London
Edinburgh University	University of Abertay Dundee
Glasgow Caledonian University	University of Bradford
Halton College (RAF College)	University of Cambridge, Duckworth Laboratory
Heriot-Watt University, Edinburgh	University of Central Lancashire
King's College, London	University of Derby
Liverpool John Moores University	University of East London
London Guildhall University	University of Glamorgan
Loughborough University	University of Greenwich
Sheffield Hallam University	University of Lincoln
South Bank University	University of Liverpool
Staffordshire University	University of North London
The Manchester Metropolitan University	University of Northumbria at Newcastle
The North East Wales Institute of HE	University of Portsmouth
The Nottingham Trent University	University of Sheffield
The Robert Gordon University	University of Teeside
The University of Birmingham	University of Wales, Swansea
The University of Huddersfield	University of West England (Bristol)
The University of Hull	University of Wolverhampton

Colleges Running BTEC Courses

Cornwall College
De Montfort University

Colleges and Other Institutions Running Other Forensic Courses (short or part-time courses)

Cranfield University
Dundee College

Harrogate College
Henley College Coventry

Colleges Running BTEC Courses

Lancaster & Morecambe College
Sheffield Hallam University
Sutton Coldfield College
University of Derby
University of Glamorgan
University of Teesside

Gloucestershire College of Arts and Technology
Jewel & Esk Valley College

Colleges and Other Institutions Running Other Forensic Courses (short or part-time courses)

Lyndhurst Centre
New College Nottingham
North Tyneside College
South East Essex College
Tavistock & Portman NHS Trust

ANNEXE 4: ALTERNATE DEFINITIONS OF FORENSIC SCIENCE

The following alternate definitions were offered:

- Scientific investigation that provides information or evidence which may be used in the legal process (forensic science organization).
- The use of scientific methods to identify and evaluate evidence to assist the investigative and judicial process (forensic science organization).
- The use of science to support the legal process (forensic science organization).
- Informing intelligence and assisting justice through the use of science in an impartial manner (forensic science organization).
- Applying scientific procedures and processes in order to identify individuals or draw conclusions as to how an incident occurred (police).
- To find, record, and identify trace evidence from scenes of crime (police).
- Examination and assessment of scenes and submitted articles of evidence (police).
- Analysis and/or examination of information or items from the crime scene, victim, or suspect (police).
- Systematic investigations into individual events, assessing scene evidence, collating and interpreting information relating to the event, all in order to determine the cause of fire (fire).
- Eliminating the possibility of other causes of fire and arriving at a supposed cause based on a preponderance of probability. Where doubts exist, and it is warranted, other experts are called on to help (fire).

ANNEXE 5: DEFINITION OF OCCUPATIONAL ROLES

Occupational Category	Brief Description
Managers and senior officials	Occupations whose main tasks consist of the direction and coordination of the functioning of organizations and businesses, including internal departments and sections, often with the help of subordinate managers and supervisors. Working proprietors in small businesses are also included in this category.
Professional occupations	Occupations whose main tasks require a high level of knowledge and experience in the natural sciences, engineering, life sciences, social sciences, humanities, and related fields. The main tasks consist of the practical application of an extensive body of theoretical knowledge, increasing the stock of knowledge by means of research, and communicating such knowledge by teaching methods and other means.

Occupational Category	Brief Description
Associate professional and technical occupations	Occupations whose main tasks require experience and knowledge of principles and practices necessary to assume operational responsibility and to give technical support to professionals in the natural sciences, engineering, life sciences, social sciences, humanities, and related fields and to managers. The main tasks involve the operation and maintenance of complex equipment; legal, financial, and design services; the provision of IT services; providing skilled support to health professionals; and serving in protective service occupations. Occupations could include forensic technicians, laboratory technicians, and scenes of crime officers.
Administrative and secretarial occupations	Occupations within this major group undertake general administrative, clerical, and secretarial work, and perform a variety of specialist client-orientated clerical duties. The main tasks involve retrieving, updating, classifying, and distributing documents, correspondence, and other records held electronically and in storage files; typing and word processing and otherwise preparing documents.
Skilled trades occupations	Occupations whose tasks involve the performance of complex physical duties that normally require a degree of initiative, manual dexterity, and other practical skills. The main tasks of these occupations require experience with, and understanding of, the work situation, the materials worked with, and the requirements of the structures, machinery, and other items produced.
Personal service occupations	Occupations whose tasks involve the provision of a service to customers, whether in a public protective or personal care capacity. The main tasks associated with these occupations involve the care of the sick and the elderly; the supervision of children; the care of animals; and the provision of travel, personal care, and hygiene services.
Sales and customer service occupations	Occupations whose tasks require the knowledge and experience necessary to sell goods and services, accept payment in respect of sales, replenish stocks of goods in stores, and provide information to potential clients and additional services to customers after the point of sale. The main tasks involve a knowledge of sales techniques, knowledge of the product or service being sold, and familiarity with cash and credit handling procedures and record keeping associated with those tasks.
Process, plant, and machine operators	Occupations whose main tasks require knowledge and experience necessary to operate and monitor an industrial plant and equipment, to assemble products from component parts according to strict rules and procedures, and to subject assembled parts to routine tests.
Elementary occupations	Occupations which require the knowledge and experience necessary to perform mostly routine tasks, often involving the use of simple handheld tools and, in some cases, requiring a degree of physical effort

.ANNEXE 7: FUNCTIONAL AND OCCUPATIONAL MAPPING

A1: Plan and Manage Scene Investigations

This Functional Area Is Applicable To

National Occupational Standards were developed for this functional area in 1997. A qualification structure was developed for the proposed qualification: "Managing and coordinating investigations at scenes of incident" (level 4).

Crime Scene Enquiry Centre Officer

A1: Plan and Manage Scene Investigations

This Functional Area Is Applicable To

Crime Scene Investigator/Scene of Crime
Examiner, Assistant, Officer, Principal, Senior,
Assistant Senior, Chief
Detective Constable, Sergeant (Marks)
Detective Inspector (Identification Bureau
Manager) (Firearms)
Fire Investigation Officers
Fire Officer
Firearms Examiner
Forensic Biologist
Forensic Chemist
Forensic Document Examiner, Document
Examiner
Forensic Examiner
Forensic Examiner/SOCO (Firearms) (Marks)
Forensic Investigator (Customs and Excise)
(Crime Scene) (Fingerprints), Assistant (FIDO)
(Drugs) (Fingerprints) (Photography) (Crime
Scene), Principal (Crime Scene) (Fingerprints)
(Logistics) (Photography), Senior (Crime Scene)
(Fingerprints) (Biology) (Chemistry) (DNA
Database) (Quality)
Forensic Specialist, Senior Forensic Specialist
Forensic Vehicle Examiner
Forensic Scientist, Forensic Scientist (Reporting
Officer [RO]) (Court Reporting), Trainee, Assistant
(C&E) (DNA) (Drugs) (Evidence Recovery Unit)
Scenes of Crime/Fingerprint Officer
Scenes of Crime/Photographer
Scientist, Principal, Senior—Biology, Chemistry,
DNA, Document Examination, DNA
Troubleshooting (Unit)
Watch Commander

A2: Evaluate and Examine the Scene of Incident

This Functional Area Is Applicable To

National Occupational Standards were developed for
this functional area in 1996, and an NVQ/SVQ
level 3, "Investigating Scenes of Incident," was
accredited.

A higher level unit was also developed for specialist
scene examination and was accredited within the
level 4 and level 5 NVQ/SVQ Forensic Science in
1997—in three specific disciplines. A unit for
specialist scene examination was included in draft
standards that were developed in 1998 for:

- Drugs
- Accident investigation
- Firearms

A2: Evaluate and Examine the Scene of Incident	This Functional Area Is Applicable To
• Trace material	
Fire and explosion incidents	Associates, Senior Associates
	CE Investigators
	Computer Crime Network Investigator
	Crime Scene Custodian IT Officer
	Crime Scene Investigator/Scene of Crime Examiner, Assistant, Officer, Principal, Senior, Assistant Senior, Chief
	Detective Constable, Sergeant (Marks)
	Detective Inspector (Identification Bureau Manager) (Firearms)
	Dog Handler, Hydrocarbon Dog Handler
	Fire Investigation Officers
	Fire Officer
	Fire Surveyor
	Firearms Examiner
	Forensic Biologist
	Forensic Chemist
	Forensic Document Examiner, Document Examiner
	Forensic Examiner
	Forensic Examiner/SOCO (Firearms) (Marks)
	Forensic Investigator (C&E) (Crime Scene) (Fingerprints), Assistant (FIDO) (Drugs) (Fingerprints) (Photography) (Crime Scene), Principal (Crime Scene) (Fingerprints) (Logistics) (Photography), Senior (Crime Scene) (Fingerprints) (Biology) (Chemistry) (DNA Database) (Quality)
	Forensic Scientist, Forensic Scientist (RO) (Court reporting), Trainee, Assistant—(C&E) (DNA) (Drugs) (ERU)
	Forensic Specialist, Senior Forensic Specialist
	Forensic Vehicle Examiner
	Photographer, Senior Photographer, Chief Photographer
	Photographic Assistant
	Photographic Officers, Higher
	Scenes of Crime/Fingerprint Officer
	Scenes of Crime/Photographer
	Scientific Officer, Assistant Scientific Officer, Senior Assistant Scientific Officer, Principal, Senior, Higher
	Scientific Support Assistant, Officer, Senior Officer
	Scientist, Principal, Senior—Biology, Chemistry, DNA, Document Examination, DNA Troubleshooting (Unit)
	Senior Clinical Scientist, Principal
	VCSI (Volume Crime Scene Investigators)
	Watch Commander

A3: Conduct Investigations of Potential Evidence	This Functional Area Is Applicable To
National Occupational Standards were developed for this functional area in 1996 (A3.1, 3.3, and 3.4) and an NVQ/SVQ level 3, "Recovering Materials of Evidential Value (Laboratory Based)," was accredited.	
The functional area was also included in the higher level standards that were developed and accredited within the level 4 and level 5 NVQ/SVQ Forensic Science in 1997—in three specific disciplines. The higher level standards were tailored to accommodate the needs of several different disciplines: • Drugs • Accident investigation • Firearms • Trace material • Fire and explosion incidents Tailored standards were also developed in the area of fingerprinting at level 2 and at level 4. These qualifications were accredited in 1997.	
The higher level standards have since been revised and are included within the Professional Standards of Competence—Forensic Science level 4, which was approved by QCA/SQA in January 2002.	Analyst, Senior Analyst, Data Analyst, DNA Analyst, Financial Analyst, Forensic Analyst, Principal Analyst, Assistant Financial Analyst Associates, Senior Associates C&E Investigators DNA Database Scientists Facial Identification Officer Fingerprint Officer, Senior, Chief, Assistant Fingerprint Expert Fire Investigation Officers Fire Surveyor Firearms Examiner Forensic Analytical Specialist Forensic Biologist Forensic Chemist Forensic Document Examiner, Document Examiner Forensic Examiner Forensic Examiner/SOCO (Firearms) (Marks) Forensic Investigator (C&E) (Crime Scene) (Fingerprints), Assistant (FIDO) (Drugs) (Fingerprints) (Photography) (Crime Scene), Principal (Crime Scene) (Fingerprints) (Logistics) (Photography), Senior (Crime Scene) (Fingerprints) (Biology) (Chemistry) (DNA Database) (Quality) Forensic Odontologist Forensic Researcher Forensic Scientist, Forensic Scientist (RO) (Court Reporting), Trainee, Assistant—(C&E) (DNA) (Drugs) (ERU)

A3: Conduct Investigations of Potential Evidence

This Functional Area Is Applicable To

Forensic Specialist, Senior Forensic Specialist
Forensic Support Officer
Forensic Vehicle Examiner
Laboratory Assistant, Attendant,
  Attendant—Research
Nurse/Phlebotomist
Photographer, Senior Photographer, Chief
  Photographer
Scenes of Crime/Fingerprint Officer
Scenes of Crime/Photographer
Scientific Officer, Assistant Scientific Officer,
  Senior Assistant Scientific Officer, Principal,
  Senior, Higher
Scientific Support Assistant, Officer, Senior
  Officer
Scientist, Principal, Senior—Biology,
  Chemistry, DNA, Document Examination,
  DNA Troubleshooting (Unit)
Section Leader for Biology, DNA, Drugs,
  General Chemistry, Toxicology
Senior Clinical Scientist, Principal
Technician—Laboratory, Senior Laboratory,
  Accounting, Chemical Laboratory, Chemical
  Treatment Laboratory, Darkroom, Anatomical
  Pathology, C&E, DNA Support Lead, DNA
  Support, Fingerprint Chemical Development,
  Fingerprint, Fingerprint Laboratory, Forensic
  Laboratory, Mortuary, Photographic,
  Postgraduate Research, Postdoctoral Research,
  Scenes of Crime, Senior, Video

A4: Interpret and Report Findings of the Investigations

This Functional Area Is Applicable To

National Occupational Standards were developed and accredited within level 4 and level 5 NVQ/SVQ Forensic Science in 1997. The qualifications were available for three different disciplines (i.e., Blood and Body Fluids, Marks and Impressions, and Questioned Documents).

The standards were tailored to accommodate the needs of several different disciplines:

- Drugs
- Accident investigation
- Firearms

Analyst, Senior Analyst, Data Analyst, DNA Analyst,
  Financial Analyst, Forensic Analyst, Principal Analyst,
  Assistant Financial Analyst
Associates, Senior Associates
C&E Investigators
Computer Crime Network Investigator
Crime Scene Match Reporting Officer
DNA Database Scientists
Facial Identification Officer

A4: Interpret and Report Findings of the Investigations

- Trace material
- Fire and explosion incidents
- Law enforcement technical support
- Fingerprints

The standards have since been revised and are included within the Professional Standards of Competence—Forensic Science level 4, which was approved by QCA/SQA in January 2002

This Functional Area Is Applicable To

Fingerprint Officer, Senior, Chief, Assistant
Fingerprint Expert
Fire Investigation Officers
Fire Surveyor
Firearms Examiner
Forensic Analytical Specialist
Forensic Biologist
Forensic Chemist
Forensic Document Examiner, Document Examiner
Forensic Examiner
Forensic Examiner/SOCO (Firearms) (Marks)
Forensic Investigator (C&E) (Crime Scene) (Fingerprints), Assistant (FIDO) (Drugs) (Fingerprints) (Photography) (Crime Scene), Principal (Crime Scene) (Fingerprints) (Logistics) (Photography), Senior (Crime Scene) (Fingerprints) (Biology) (Chemistry) (DNA Database) (Quality)
Forensic Odontologist
Forensic Researcher
Forensic Scientist, Forensic Scientist (RO) (Court Reporting), Trainee, Assistant—(C&E) (DNA) (Drugs) (ERU)
Forensic Specialist, Senior Forensic Specialist
Forensic Support Officer
Forensic Vehicle Examiner
Information Scientist, Assistant Information Scientist, Senior Information Scientist
Intelligence Officer, Scientific Intelligence Officer, Assistant Intelligence Officer, DNA Intelligence Officer, Forensic Intelligence Officer
Laboratory Assistant, Attendant, Attendant—Research
Liaison Officer—DNA, Assistant DNA, Detective Sergeant
Scenes of Crime/Fingerprint Officer
Scenes of Crime/Photographer
Scientific Officer, Assistant Scientific Officer, Senior Assistant Scientific Officer, Principal, Senior, Higher Scientific Support Assistant, Officer, Senior Officer
Scientist, Principal, Senior—Biology, Chemistry, DNA, Document Examination, DNA Troubleshooting (Unit)
Section Leader for Biology, DNA, Drugs, General Chemistry, Toxicology
Senior Clinical Scientist, Principal
Technician—Laboratory, Senior Laboratory, Accounting, Chemical Laboratory, Chemical Treatment Laboratory, Darkroom, Anatomical Pathology, C&E, DNA Support Lead, DNA Support, Fingerprint Chemical Development, Fingerprint, Fingerprint Laboratory, Forensic Laboratory, Mortuary, Photographic, Postgraduate Research, Postdoctoral Research, Scenes of Crime, Senior, Video

B1: Research and Develop New and Modified Practices, Methods, and Techniques	This Functional Area Is Applicable To
Standards developed by other "expert groups" are available for this functional area.	Forensic Researcher Research and Liaison Assistant Research Assistant, Research Assistant in Forensic Hematology Research Fellow Researcher—Senior, Senior Management, Senior Nonmanagement Senior Development Scientist

B2: Implement Protocols, Methods, and Procedures to Improve the Scientific and Technical Services	This Functional Area Is Applicable To
Standards developed by other "expert groups" are available for this functional area.	Deputy to Chief Scientist Forensic Researcher Research and Liaison Assistant Research Assistant, Research Assistant in Forensic Hematology Research Fellow Researcher—Senior, Senior Management, Senior Nonmanagement Senior Development Scientist

C1: Meet the Needs of the Customer	This Functional Area Is Applicable To
Standards developed by other "expert groups" are available for this functional area.	Customer Programs Coordinator Customer Services Coordinator Deputy to Chief Scientist Director of Forensic Science Unit International Market Coordinator Local Quality Coordinator Market Research Executive Marketing Communications Executive Marketing Coordinator Section Leader for Biology, DNA, Drugs, General Chemistry, Toxicology Senior Development Scientist Marketing Services Coordinator National Quality Leader NDNAD Custodian Quality Advisor, Coordinator Partners Principal Member—Equity, Nonequity

C2: Build And Develop Relationships And Networks	This Functional Area Is Applicable To
Standards developed by other "expert groups" are available for this functional area.	All occupations

C3: Manage Resources	This Functional Area Is Applicable To
Standards developed by other "expert groups" are available for this functional area.	Communications Officer, Senior Communications Officer

Contracts Assistant

Corporate Document Controller

Deputy to Chief Scientist

Director of Forensic Science Unit

Divisional Officer—Various Sections

DNA National Services Support

Financial Director (Office Manager)

Graphics Officer

Head of Branch, Biology, Chemistry, Community Protection, Department, DNA Database, Quality, Fingerprint Bureau, Forensic Science, Forensic Services, Information and Support, Information Services, IT Group, Section, Deputy Head of Forensic Support Unit, Head of Forensic Unit

IT Helpdesk Operator

IT Specialist

Manager—Business Development, Business, Corporate Communications, Crime Scene Investigation Unit, Customer Service Department, Customer Services, DNA Administration, DNA IT Administrative Support, DNA Deputy Unit (Paternity), DNA Support, DNA Support Services, DNA Unit, Enabling Program, ERU, Finance, Fingerprint Bureau, Fingerprint, Fingerprint (FP) Unit, General, IT—Telecoms, IT, Laboratory, Library Services, Local Estates, Market Research and Analysis, Market Sector, Marketing—Communications, Customer Programs, National Logistics, National Service Constituency Program, Office, Operations, People Development, Personnel, Photographic, Photographic and Imaging, Project Support, Quality Systems, Recovery and Intelligence, Sales, Research, Scene of Crime, Crime Scene, Scientific Support and Troubleshooting Unit, Scientific Support and Troubleshooting Project, Scientific Support, Service Delivery (SD) Project, SD Senior Project, Service Development Program, Site Support, Stores, Procurement, Submissions and Identification, Technical, Technical Training, Training Course, Training Services

Managing Director (computer manager)

Operations Controller

Partners

Personal Assistant, DNA

Principal Member—Equity, Nonequity

Procurement Officer, Senior

Program Support Officer

Project Officer

Receptionist, Receptionist-Telephonist

Safety Advisor

Secretary Forensic Science Unit, Scientific Secretary, Secretarial Support, Team Secretary, Personal Secretary, Typist

Section Leader for Biology, DNA, Drugs, General Chemistry, Toxicology

Senior Development Scientist

Site Services Assistant

C3: Manage Resources	This Functional Area Is Applicable To
	Station Officer, Arson Task Force
	Stores Assistant
	Submissions officer
	Supervisor—Accounting Catering, Crime Scene IT Enquiry Centre, CS Match Reporting, CSI, Scene of Crime, Darkroom, DNA Process, FP, Site Support, Stores
	Team Leader - Fingerprint Bureau, Chemistry, DNA, DNA Database, General Biology, Crime Scene, Forensic Examiner, Personnel Administration, Night Shift Leader
	Unit Head—CSI, Computer examination, FP, Forensic Support, Forensic, Imaging, SSL
	Administration Assistant, Officer, Support, Team Administrator, Crime Scene Administrator, CS Site Administrator, Major Crime Scene Administrative Officer, DNA Administrative Officer, DNA Administrator, DNA—IT Administrative Support Assistant, HR Team Administrator, Library Administrative Assistant, Library Administrative Officer, Personnel Administrator, Quality Assurance (QA) Group Administrator, Site Administrator, Training Services Administrator

C4: Manage and Develop Individuals and Self	This Functional Area Is Applicable To
Standards developed by the Employment National Training Organisation (NTO) and the Learning and Development NTO are available for this functional area.	All occupations

ANNEXE 8: ISSUES FACING THE SECTOR— QUESTIONNAIRE RESPONSES

1 MAIN CONCERNS RELATED TO STAFFING

The survey asked organizations to identify their main concerns relating to recruiting staff, both for 2002 and the following two years. 36 (58.1 percent) respondents provided details for this question. (See Figure A1.9.)

The biggest fear is in keeping skills up-to-date; slightly over 20 percent see this as a problem. This concern did not seem to rectify over the following years and was still a major concern in 2004.

Most of the concerns are constant over the next three years, failing to resolve but not getting any worse. The main issues over the coming years are all related to retaining staff of different sorts.

Other areas of concern which were identified are listed below:

Forensic science organizations
- Development of staff
- Impact of changes in employment law, for example working hours and job share
- Demography of workforce

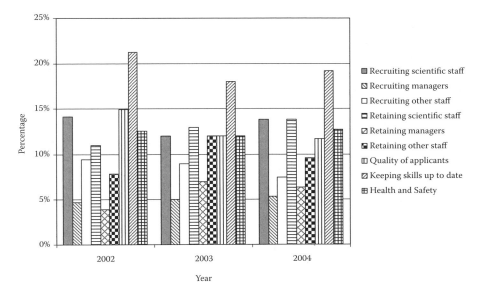

FIGURE A1.9 Main concerns related to staffing.

Police
- Need to train staff or initiate apprentice scheme to fill future vacancies
- 2–3 years before up to acceptable standard
- Relates mainly to fingerprint staff recruitment
- Sickness and absence management

Education
- Our area is relatively new, and while many have aspirations, few have relevant experience.
- We have little difficulty recruiting staff, but a poor career structure and relatively low pay are poor for morale.

2 IMPORTANT AND CHALLENGING ISSUES OVER THE NEXT FIVE YEARS

Forensic science organizations
- Accreditation
- Changes in legal requirements, registers, and so on, which can lead to the disadvantage of defendants in criminal trials
- New civil procedure rules in civil courts
- CRFP
- ACF proposals, National Health Service Education for Scotland proposals
- Funding: proper fees and expenditure in legal aided work
- Greater reliance upon technology to get more results; higher expectations
- Keeping abreast of the requirements of the ever changing needs of the insurance industry, maintaining our preeminent position in the market
- Wolfe reforms
- Legal aid fees

- Alternative Dispute Resolution
- Liability
- Single joint expert appointment
- Possibly a knock-on effect from the U.S. courts' decision to allow litigation against independent experts
- Promoting the concept of "comparative forensic medicine"
- Surviving
- Incorporation of questioned document examination as a branch of forensic science
- Dedication of staff to volume crime

Police forces

- Change to nonnumeric standard in fingerprint ID
- Creation of a Scottish forensic science laboratory service involving four existing labs
- Scottish DNA database and some functions currently carried out by non-laboratory staff in some forces
- Development and enhancement of DNA evidence
- Digital imaging, a common police service
- Increase in criminality and the continuous requirement for greater detailed examination of crime scenes, especially an increase in violent incidents
- Managing growth
- Maximizing forensic potential within financial constraints
- Move toward common police service solution and civilianization of police posts
- Legislative changes
- Staff retention and development
- The recovery of physical evidence at crime scenes using sensitive technology without any contamination issues arising
- The rising demand for forensic evidence, and the cost to supply it
- Joint fire training
- Competency testing
- CRFP
- Greater awareness and acceptance by the police service of health and safety
- National Automated Fingerprint Identification System
- Working time regulation
- The advent of new technology and procedures

Fire services

- Proposed legislation on the reform of fire safety
- Arson reduction and detection: Arson Control Forum
- How we move forward in becoming more professional at fire investigation and are recognized by the courts and others for that
- CRFP
- Legislative power and duty to investigate fire in new Fire Safety Bill
- Integration with police, SOCO, and military for team scene examiners
- Introducing more practical scene examination training

Educational organizations
- Accreditation of degrees in forensic science
- Developing expertise, particularly in crime scene simulations and analysis
- Developing external links
- Developing quality forensic science research and supervising students in final-year research projects
- Initiating research
- Maintaining student recruitment levels
- Moving to a new multiuser lab
- Staff levels and increasing workloads, replacement of equipment
- Retaining our very reputable MSC and undergraduate courses: many new ones, especially undergraduates with the benefit of a high level of finance or resources
- The plethora of new organizations springing up
- CRFP
- Occupational standards
- National reorganization and changes in working practices of police and forensic science
- Foundation training

ANNEXE 9: ISSUES FACING THE SECTOR—CONSULTATION WORKSHOP COMMENTS

Managing scientific and technological advances and their impact, for example facial recognition (pseudo experts); CRFP okay for traditional. Could go too far. Will new experts creep in by the back door?

Big stress to produce databases and to use—may be of little use in the fullness of time.

Qualifications and the proliferation of academic institutions + accreditation (who does it) + police different way.

National pay rates for SOCOs—why not?

Quality of work versus resources available/greater turnover of staff/faster and faster turnaround times.

Accreditation—why is it presumed that you forget what you have learned when leaving the Forensic Science Service?

Demand and capacity of services.

Succession planning—experienced people retiring/lot of new people—don't seem to have control on the intake and growth. Imbalance of age and experience.

Does plethora of courses mean people will find employment outside of main labs?

Private SOCO services and lab services (outsourcing)

What happens when government money runs out? Politics of funding—big issue.

Forces facing cutbacks in next two years.

Review custodianship of DNA database.

Potential for forces to provide own services. Restructuring of forces—group together for regional lab.

Practical abilities of recruits. Usually straight from university—don't have the practical skills. Universities don't develop the practical skills, and it is not done in schools.

Need to rectify knowledge put out by National Police Training—concerns about the basic training.

Lots of people apply for SOCO posts with a forensic degree.

Lab technicians—taking people with degrees who are ambitious—don't have the practical skills. People overqualified. Getting a lot of very unhappy people.

Big divide between DNA staff and reporting officer jobs.

Generation X—was a career but not now. 2–3 years and then move on. Instant gratification culture.

Mismatch of jobs and expectations. Would like to see accreditation of in-house training toward a degree. May help to keep people in the sector.

No longer need the skills/knowledge in the sector as used to do.

Reporting officers don't do the bench work anymore—concentrate on interpretation. They are losing the ability to do the practical work. Lab work may go away—may only be done if you have to go to the scene.

Definition of roles—may get to rely on types of evidence more likely to have high impact.

Qualifications and accreditation may help to iron out problems of quality/long-term turnaround times. Should organizations only use accredited labs? Not realistic. Have to look at what clients get for their money.

Careers—limited opportunities. Still struggling—for career progression, have to move to management. Some people get on rapidly—but very few.

Career path in SOCO—yes—is expanding. 30–35 percent growth in last three years. Career path has developed as a result of civilianization.

Recognition: may need to change and move for career opportunities.

Comparison with medicine, however, specialize early on.

Growing recruitment into the private sector.

The Forensic Science Service has grown out of all recognition. Enormous growth in private organizations/size and number of such organizations. Can't expect to develop careers in the way that they used to. Flexibility and rapid change mitigate against this.

Would like to see recruitment possibilities throughout the whole forensic process—opportunities across the whole of the forensic process, for example police, private sector. National journal of opportunities.

Common Police Service—Forensic Science. Huge implications. Rationalization. Report to Scottish Executive by February/March. Implementation now—2005.

Legislation—nonexistent in Scotland presently—under police powers now.

Sixteen-point system—nonnumerical system not yet applied in Scotland.

Accreditation—the processes—UKAS, all will be. Working more tightly to work practices. Takes more time and costs more. Has changed practices.

CRFP—assessment of people. May encourage specialization. Expects to have to sit tests/exams.

Concern that fire qualifications will become a private sector money spinner–priesthood that only certain people will be able to achieve the qualifications. Will cut out the fire services.

Relationship between fire service and private sector not good.

Demand for services—increasing workload, decreasing resources.

Must be some way of regulating demand—charging?

Unified forensic lab, scenes, and identification in Strathclyde, however, the only one to have this—will be affected when rationalization happens. May have police officers—but will lead to civilianization.

Technical changes—led by the Forensic Science Service (e.g., new equipment). DNA database—have to satisfy UKAS but also the Forensic Science Service criteria to input to the database.

Retention—been losing to private sector. Headhunting going on regularly—specialist and reporting officers—been losing experienced and highly qualified people.

Fire reports—common styles of doing. National issue.

DNA—impact on every aspect of forensic science. Have to be more strict with our anticontamination practices. Should DNA evidence be looked at first: DNA could go too far—re: can tell who was in a room at any one time. How can link to crime? Communication and training needed across the agencies—re: implications of DNA.

DNA is now sorting out some fibers cases. Looking to retain our skills in the rationalization.

Health and safety—getting more and more difficult to comply with. Soaking up more of our efforts every year.

Specialization—is increasingly happening. Relates to senior people retiring, poaching, accreditation, repetitive tasks. Job satisfaction. More production line orientated.

Scottish protocol—written and agreed between fire and police in absence of legislation. Is foundation for the future.

Funding for common forensic science service—external and internal. Internally have to fight for our own funding which will account for local variations. Rationalization could be good.

Dispute—fire, how it is resolved could have major implications for the future. Relationship with the police could break down entirely in fire service itself.

Legal issues—some could make forensic science easier—not perfect fit. Minor changes could make science practically easier to do. Some is happening—we as a sector could drive this more.

Fire service—target to achieve in arson reduction over specified time period.

Mismatch between forensic degrees and jobs/recruitment. Look for experience much more than qualifications. Don't think we sell what we do properly—must attract the real scientists.

Growth in courses has not affected Strathclyde University yet. Doing postgraduate stuff therefore not affected. Have lost some graduates who have gone straight into lecturing in university. Would prefer solid science-related degree rather than "forensic" degree. Forensic science should be at master's level.

ANNEXE 10: LIST OF ALL JOB TITLES

FORENSIC SCIENCE ORGANIZATIONS

Directly Involved in Forensic Science	SOC Code
Analyst	2112
Anatomical Pathology Technicians	3218
Assistant DNA Liaison Officer	2321
Assistant Forensic Scientist	2112
Assistant Forensic Scientist—DNA	2112
Assistant Forensic Scientist—C&E	2112
Assistant Forensic Scientist—Drugs	2112
Assistant Forensic Scientist—ERU	2112
Assistant Intelligence Officer	2321
Assistant Researcher	2112
Assistant Scientific Officer	2321
Associates	2112
Biomedical Scientists	2117
Constable	3312
Consultant	2129
Consultant Crime Scene Investigator	3319
Consultant Fingerprint Experts	2129
Consultant Forensic Imaging and Facial Mapping	2129
Consultant Forensic Scientist	2129
Consulting Forensic Engineer	2129
CS Team Leader	113
Data Analyst	3539
Deputy Head of Forensic Unit	1112
Deputy to Chief Scientist	2112
Director of Forensic Science Unit	1112
DNA Analyst	2112
DNA Database Scientists	2112
DNA Support Lead Technician	3111
DNA Support Technician	3111
DNA Team Leader	113
DNA Troubleshooting Scientist (Unit)	2112
DNA Unit Manager	113
Document Examiner	2112
Firearms Examiner	3312
Forensic Analytical Specialist	2112
Forensic Biologist	2112
Forensic Chemist	2112
Forensic Consultant	2112
Forensic Document Examiner	2112
Forensic Examiner—Team Leader	2112
Forensic Investigator (C&E)	2112
Forensic Laboratory Technician	3111
Forensic Odontologist	2129
Forensic Scientist: Court Reporting	2112
Forensic Scientist: Advanced Court Reporting	2112
Forensic Scientist/Reporting Officer	2112
Forensic Specialist	2129
Forensic Support Officer	4113
Head of Biology	1112
Head of Branch	1112

Directly Involved in Forensic Science	SOC Code
Head of Chemistry	1112
Head of Department Section: Biology	1112
Head of Department Section: Chemistry	1112
Head of Department Section: DNA Database	1112
Head of Department Section: Quality	1112
Head of Forensic Science	1112
Head of Forensic Unit	1112
Head of Information and Support	1112
Head of Section	1112
Higher Photographic Officers	3434
Higher Scientific Officer	2321
Information Scientist/Assistant Information Scientist	4112
Inspector	1172
Intelligence Officer	2321
Lab Attendant—Research	8138
Laboratory Attendant	8138
Laboratory Assistant	8138
Operations Manager	1121
Operations Controller	3131
Partners	1114
Photographic Officers	3434
Photographic Technician	3434
Principal Analyst	2112
Principal Member—Equity	2112
Principal Member—Nonequity	2112
Principal Scenes of Crime Officer	3319
Principal Scientific Officer	2321
Principal Scientist	2112
Procurement Officer	3541
Researcher	2329
Researcher Management	1137
Scenes of Crime Officer	3319
Scientific Officer	2321
Scientist	2112
Section Leader for Biology	2112
Section Leader for DNA	2112
Section Leader for Drugs	2112
Section Leader for General Chemistry	2112
Section Leader for Toxicology	2112
Senior Analyst	2112
Senior Associates	2329
Senior Consultant	2129
Senior Development Scientist	2112
Senior Forensic Scientist: Biology	2112
Senior Forensic Scientist: Chemistry	2112
Senior Forensic Scientist: DNA Database	2112
Senior Forensic Scientist: Quality	2112
Senior Forensic Specialist	2129
Senior Information Scientist	2112
Senior Scientific Officer	2321
Senior Scientist	2112
Senior Scientist: Biology	2112
Senior Scientist: Chemistry	2112
Senior Scientist: DNA	2112

Directly Involved in Forensic Science	SOC Code
Senior Scientist: Document Examination	2112
Senior Researcher—Management	1137
Senior Researcher—Nonmanagement	2321
Sergeant	1172
Team Leaders: General Biology	2112
Team Leaders: DNA	2112
Team Leaders: Chemistry	2112
Team Leaders: DNA Database	2112
Technician	3111
Trainee Forensic Scientist	2112

Not Directly Involved in Forensic Science	SOC Code
Accounting Supervisor	4122
Accounting Technician	3537
Accounts Payable Clerk	4122
Accounts Receivable Clerk	4122
Administrative Assistant	4112
Administrative Officer	4150
Administrative Support	4150
Assistant Financial Analyst	3534
Business Development Manager	1142
Business Manager	1142
Cashier	7112
Catering Assistant	9223
Catering Supervisor	9223
Chief Inspector	1172
Civil Paternity Certifying Officer	4150
Cleaner	9233
Clerical Assistant	4113
Clerical/Liaison Officer	4113
Clerical/Word Processing Officer	4113
Communications Officer	2129
Contracts Assistant	4131
Corporate Communications Manager	1132
Corporate Document Controller	4131
Crime Scene Administrator	4150
Crime Scene Custodian IT Officer	3132
Crime Scene Enquiry Centre Officer	4150
Crime Scene IT Enquiry Centre Supervisor	4150
Crime Scene Match Reporting Officer	4150
CS Match Reporting Supervisor	4150
CS Site Administrator	4112
CSD Manager	113
CSD Administrator	4112
Customer Programs Coordinator	7212
Customer Services Coordinator	7212
Customer Services Manager	1142
Detective Sergeant Liaison Officer	1172
Director	1112
DNA Administration Manager	1152
DNA Administration Officer	4150
DNA Administrator	4150
DNA Deputy Unit Manager (Paternity)	113

Not Directly Involved in Forensic Science	SOC Code
DNA IT—Administrative Support Assistant	4112
DNA IT—Administrative Support Manager	1152
DNA National Services Support	4150
DNA Night Shift Leader	4150
DNA Personal Assistant	4215
DNA Process Supervisor	8114
DNA Support Manager	113
DNA Support Services Manager	1121
Enabling Program Manager	1121
ERU Manager	113
Finance Manager	1131
Financial Analyst	3534
Financial Director (Office Manager)	1131
Financial Services Officer/Administrative Assistant	4112
General Manager	1239
Graphics Officer	4113
Head of Information Services	1112
Head of IT Group	1112
Human Resources (HR) Officer—Policy	4113
HR Officer—Projects	4113
HR Team Administrator	415
Implementation and Improvement Specialist	2321
International Market Coordinate	3543
Invoice Officer	4113
IT—Telecom Manager—Huntingdon	1136
IT Helpdesk Operator	3132
IT Manager	1136
IT Specialist	3131
IT Training Officer	3563
Lecturer in Forensic Science	2312
Library Administrative Assistant/Officer	4135
Library Services Manager	1239
Local Estates Manager—Chepstow	1231
Local Estates Manager—Huntingdon	1231
Local Estates Manager—Wetherby	1231
Local Quality Coordinator—Chepstow	3115
Local Quality Coordinator—Wetherby	3115
Major Crime Service Administrative Officer	4112
Managing Director (computer manager)	1136
Market Research and Analysis Manager	1132
Market Research Executive	1132
Market Sector Manager	1132
Marketing Communications Executive	3543
Marketing Coordinator	3543
Marketing Manager—Communications	1132
Marketing Manager—Customer Programs	1132
Marketing Services Coordinator	3543
National Logistics Manager	1162
National Quality Leader	3115
National Service Constituency Program Manager	1112
National DNA Database Custodian Quality Advisor	2321
National DNA Database Custodian Quality Co-Coordinator	3115
Office Manager/Liaison Officer	1152

Not Directly Involved in Forensic Science	SOC Code
People Development Manager	1135
People Development Officer	4135
Personal Assistant	4215
Personal Secretary to Staff Officer and Projects Officer	4215
Personnel Administration Team Leader	4150
Personnel Administrator	4150
Personnel Advisor	4150
Personnel Manager	1135
Program Support Officer	4113
Project Officer	4113
Project Support Manager	1121
QA Group Administrator	4150
Quality Systems Manager	1141
Receptionist-Telephonist	4216
Safety Advisor	3567
Sales Manager	1132
Scientific Secretary	4215
Scientific Support and Troubleshooting Project Manager	1112
Scientific Support and Troubleshooting Unit Manager	1112
SD Project Manager	1137
SD Senior Project Manager	1137
Secretary Forensic Science Unit	4215
Senior Communications Officer	4113
Senior Lecturer in Forensic Science	2311
Senior Procurement Officer	3541
Senior Technical Trainer	2321
Senior Training Consultant	1135
Service Development Program Manager	1112
Site Administrator	4150
Site Services Assistant	4112
Site Support Manager	1122
Site Support Supervisor	1122
Specialist Advisor	2321
Staff Officer	4113
Stores Assistant	9149
Stores Manager—Procurement	1162
Stores Supervisor	9149
Team Administrator	4150
Team Secretary	4215
Technical Trainer	3563
Technical Training Assistant	4150
Technical Training Manager	1135
Training Consultant	3563
Training Coordinator	3563
Training Course Manager	1135
Training Services Administrator	4150
Training Services Manager	1135
Typist	4217

POLICE

Directly Involved in Forensic Science	SOC Code
Assistant / Senior Assistant Scientific Officer	3111
Assistant Crime Scene Examiners	3319
Assistant Forensic Investigator (FIDO) (Drugs)	2322
Assistant Forensic Investigator (Fingerprints)	3312
Assistant Forensic Investigator (Photography)	3434
Assistant Forensic Investigators (Crime Scene)	3319
Assistant Scenes of Crime Officer	3319
Assistant Senior Scenes of Crime Officer	3319
CE Investigators	2131
CE Technicians	3111
Chemical Laboratory Technician	3111
Chemical Treatment Laboratory Technician	3111
Chief Fingerprint Officer	3312
Chief Photographer	3434
Chief Scenes of Crime Officer	3319
Computer Crime Network Investigator	2132
Computer Examination Unit Head	2132
Crime Scene Investigator (CSI)	3319
CSI Supervisors	3319
CSI Unit Head	1112
CSI Unit Managers	1112
Darkroom Supervisor	3434
Darkroom Technician	3434
Deputy Head of Forensic Support Unit	1112
Detective Constable (Marks)	1172
Detective Inspector (Firearms)	1172
Detective Inspector (Identification Bureau Manager)	1172
Detective Sergeant (Marks)	1172
DNA Clerical Assistant	4112
DNA Clerks	4150
DNA Forensic Trainer	3563
DNA Intelligence Officer	2321
DNA Liaison Officer	4113
Document Examiner	2112
Facial Identification Officer	2321
Fingerprint Officer	3312
Fingerprint Assistant	4131
Fingerprint Assistant / Fingerprint Technician	4131
Fingerprint Bureau Manager	1113
Fingerprint Chemical Development Technicians	3111
Fingerprint Expert	1172
Fingerprint Laboratory Technician	3111
Fingerprint Manager	1112
Fire Surveyor	3312
Firearms Examiner	3312
Forensic Analyst	2112
Forensic Clerical Assistant	4112
Forensic Examiner/SOCO (Firearms)	2112
Forensic Examiner/SOCO (Marks)	2112
Forensic Intelligence Officer	2321
Forensic Investigation Clerk	4150

Directly Involved in Forensic Science	SOC Code
Forensic Investigators (Crime Scene)	3319
Forensic Investigators (Fingerprints)	3312
Forensic Researcher	2322
Forensic Submissions Assistant	4112
Forensic Submissions Clerk	4150
Forensic Submissions Officer	4113
Forensic Support Officer	4113
Forensic Vehicle Examiner	2112
FP Clerks	4131
FP Supervisors	3312
FP Unit Head	1112
FP Unit Manager	1112
Head of Fingerprint Bureau	1112
Head of Forensic Services	1112
Head of Forensic Support Unit	1112
Imaging Unit Head	1112
Laboratory Manager	1137
Laboratory Technician	3111
Mapping Officers	2321
Mortuary Technician	3111
Photo Manager/Technicians	3434
Photographer	3434
Photographic and Imaging Manager	1152
Photographic Assistant	3434
Photographic Manager	1152
Photographic Officers	3434
Photographic Technician	3434
Principal Forensic Investigator (Crime Scene)	3319
Principal Forensic Investigator (Fingerprints)	3312
Principal Forensic Investigator (Logistics)	2322
Principal Forensic Investigator (Photography)	3434
Principal Scenes of Crime Officer (including H/SOC and Forensic Services Manager	3319
Recovery and Intelligence Manager	1112
Scene of Crime Manager	3319
Scenes of Crime/Fingerprint Officer	3319
Scenes of Crime/Photographer	3319
Scenes of Crime Clerk (HQ only)	3319
Scenes of Crime Examiners	3319
Scenes of Crime Officer	3319
Scenes of Crime Supervisors	3319
Scenes of Crime Supervisors/Crime Scene Managers	3319
Scenes of Crime Technicians	3319
Scientific Intelligence Officer	2321
Scientific Support Assistant	4112
Scientific Support Manager	1136
Senior Fingerprint Officer	2112
Senior Forensic Investigator (Crime Scene)	3319
Senior Forensic Investigators (Fingerprints)	3319
Senior Laboratory Technician	3111
Senior Photographer	3434
Senior Scenes of Crimes Officer	3319
Senior Scientific Support Officer	2321
Scientific Support Laboratory Unit Head	1112

Directly Involved in Forensic Science	SOC Code
Submissions and Identification Manager	1121
Team Leader—Fingerprint Bureau	2112
Volume Crime Scene Investigator (VCSI)	3319
Video Technician	3111

Not Directly Involved in Forensic Science	SOC Code
Clerical	4150
Clerk	4150
DNA Administrative Officer/Clerk	4150
Receptionist	4216
Submissions Officer	2321
Training and Development Coordinator	3563

FIRE

Directly Involved in Forensic Science	SOC Code
Divisional Officer—Litigation Section	1173
Dog Handler	6139
Fire Investigation Officers	1173
Hydrocarbon Dog Handler	6139
Research and Liaison Assistant	2322
Station Officer—Arson Task Force	3313

Not Directly Involved in Forensic Science	SOC Code
Appliance Commander	1173
Area Commander	1173
Brigade Commander	3218
Clerical Officer—Administrative (Nonuniform)	4113
Divisional Officer	1173
Head of Community Protection	1173
Fire Officer	1173
Station Commander	1173
Station Officer	3313
Subofficer	3313
Watch Commander	1173

EDUCATION

Directly Involved in Forensic Science	SOC Code
Biomedical Scientist (Grade 1, 2, and 3)	2117
Nurse/Phlebotomist	3211
Postdoctoral Research Technician	2321
Postgraduate Research Technician	2321
Principal Clinical Scientist	2112
Professor of Forensic Archaeology and Anthropology	2311
Professor of Forensic Toxicology	2311
Research Assistant	2323
Research Assistant in Forensic Hematology	2323
Research Fellow	2311

Directly Involved in Forensic Science	SOC Code
Senior Clinical Scientist	2112
Senior Technician	3119
Technician	3119
Trainee Biomedical Scientist	2112

Not Directly Involved in Forensic Science	SOC Code
Administration Officer	2317
Clerical Staff	4150
Demonstrator	7129
Head of Department	2311
Lecturer	2311
Personal Assistant to Professor	4215
Principal Lecturer	2311
Secretarial Support	4215
Senior Lecturer	2311
Senior Lecturer in Hematology	2311
Technical Manager	1136

REFERENCES

1. Learning to succeed, presented by the Secretary of State for Education and Employment by command of Her Majesty. June 1999, Cmd 4392.
2. Learning and Skills Council (LSC) Draft Workforce Development Strategy, (presented May 2002).
3. Northern Ireland Executives report for government. April 2001.
4. Robertson & Vignaux, Interpreting Evidence, Chichester, UK: Wiley (1995).

Appendix 2: Recovery of Material of Evidential Value— Laboratory Based

THE FORENSIC SCIENCE LEAD BODY CONSORTIUM

The Forensic Science Lead Body Consortium is made up of representatives of the forensic science sector including those from both public service laboratories and private practices. The scientific support area of police work, scenes of crime personnel, and fingerprint bureau workers are included, and representatives of the Association of Chief Police Officers (ACPO) are present on the lead body. Academia is also represented. The lead body guides the activities of working groups of practitioners who develop the standards with the support of a consultant.

The National and Scottish Vocational Qualification (N/SVQ) system offers a structure of qualifications based on units at a range of levels and are based on nationally defined standards of competence. The standards describe what an individual must do to be recognized as occupationally competent. Although they require the demonstration of conceptual and factual knowledge, they are concerned primarily with the ability of individuals to apply this knowledge in a work setting.

Forensic science is a diverse subject and for the purposes of the standards development program, the following definition has been agreed: "Forensic science is the application of non medical science to determine the value of evidence, including crime scene evidence, and to support the investigation process and the courts" [Occupational and Functional Mapping Study, 1991].

Two qualifications are now available at level 3. These are:

- Investigating scenes of incidents
- Recovering material of evidential value—laboratory based

The former qualification is aimed at those serving in the scene of crime units of police forces, and the latter at those searching items in the laboratory for traces of evidence. The qualification "Recovering material of evidential value—laboratory based" has six mandatory units and one additional unit. The mandatory units are:

- Prepare to carry out laboratory-based recovery.
- Carry out laboratory-based recovery of materials.
- Contribute to the operational effectiveness of the working environment.
- Provide information and documentation.
- Establish and maintain effective working relationships.
- Contribute to the maintenance of health and safety in the workplace.

The additional unit is:

- Carry out primary analysis of recovered material.

QUALIFICATION STRUCTURE FOR RECOVERING MATERIAL OF EVIDENTIAL VALUE—LABORATORY BASED

MANDATORY UNITS

RM1. Prepare to carry out laboratory-based recovery.

Element 1.1. Obtain and confirm instructions.
Element 1.2. Prepare equipment and work area.
Element 1.3. Obtain and confirm items for examination.

RM2. Carry out laboratory-based recovery of materials.

Element 2.1. Inspect items submitted for recovery.
Element 2.2. Recover materials.
Element 2.3. Prepare recovered material for analysis and comparison.
Element 2.4. Complete the recovery process.

RM3. Contribute to the operational effectiveness of the working environment.

Element 3.1. Monitor and maintain operational effectiveness of the work area.
Element 3.2. Monitor and maintain functional effectiveness of equipment, instruments, and reagents.
Element 3.3. Maintain a working knowledge of trends and developments within the area of responsibility.

RM4. Provide information and documentation.

Element 4.1. Provide examination records and summaries.
Element 4.2. Provide administrative records.

ISI7. Establish and maintain effective working relationships.

Element 7.1. Maintain and enhance working relationships with colleagues.
Element 7.2. Establish and maintain working relationships with one's immediate manager.

RM5. Contribute to the maintenance of health and safety in the workplace.

Element 5.1. Contribute to the safety of the workplace.
Element 5.2. Contribute to the health and safety of personnel.

ADDITIONAL UNIT

RM6. Carry out primary analysis of recovered material.

Element 6.1. Prepare to analyze recovered material.
Element 6.2. Perform primary analysis of recovered material.

MANDATORY UNITS

UNIT RM1: PREPARE TO CARRY OUT LABORATORY-BASED RECOVERY

Element 1.1 Obtain and Confirm Instructions

The Standard

Performance Criteria

a. Understanding of case requirements and instructions received are confirmed with relevant personnel.
b. Details of items submitted are confirmed to be appropriate for the work to be undertaken.
c. The sequence of the various aspects of the laboratory work is planned, agreed, and prioritized with relevant personnel in order to maximize recovery of materials and minimize contamination, damage, degradation, and loss.
d. Relevant information is accurately, legibly, and comprehensively recorded onto appropriate documentation.

Range Statements

1. Instructions received: written and oral
2. Relevant personnel: line manager, other specialists, and case supervisor
3. Items submitted: chemical, biological, and physical

Evidence Requirements

The candidate should be able to demonstrate competence over a period of time across all the performance criteria and range statements. Competence is to be demonstrated in real work situations. Where opportunities for work-based assessments are not readily available, realistic simulations of the work activity may be used, although these should be set up and assessed in the normal working environment. The candidate should be able to explain the reasons for all his or her actions and cover "what if" scenarios. Candidates should also be able to answer oral or written questions covering items specified in the "Knowledge and Understanding" specification.

Knowledge and Understanding Specification

Principles, Methods, and Techniques Relating To …

- Confirming items submitted are appropriate for the work requested and for the work to be carried out (b) (range 1 and 3)
- Contamination dangers and how these can be avoided (c) (range 2)
- Recording of information (a and d)
- The need for and importance of continuity (a and d) (range 1 and 2)
- The importance of establishing the case requirements and information (a) (range 1)
- Code of Ethics: the need for impartial judgments (c)
- Effect of recovery techniques on different types of potential evidence (c) (range 2)

Information and Data About ...

- Potential evidence types (a, b, and c) (range 1 and 3)
- Contamination dangers (c) (range 1)
- Recovery techniques (c) (range 1 and 2)

Assessment Guidance

Competence will be demonstrated across a range of different cases by a combination of observation in the work environment, oral questioning, and a review of the portfolio evidence.

Unit RM1: Prepare to Carry Out Laboratory-Based Recovery

Element 1.2: Prepare Equipment and Work Area

The Standard

Performance Criteria

a. Work area selected is appropriate for the effective and efficient recovery of potential evidential material.
b. Work area is free of contamination and is prepared in accordance with health and safety requirements and the investigation to be carried out.
c. Adequate supply of consumables, tools, and protective clothing is available for the recovery techniques which are to be employed.
d. Equipment and reagents required are available and are confirmed functional and safe in accordance with manufacturer's instructions and health and safety requirements.
e. Equipment faults are identified, and relevant actions are taken to rectify the fault within the individual's area of responsibility.
f. Equipment faults identified outside of the individual's area of responsibility are reported promptly to the relevant person.
g. Personal preparation and anticontamination requirements are carried out safely in accordance with statutory requirements.

Range Statements

1. Work area preparation: clean, clear, decontaminated, confirmed functional, confirm required services operational
2. Consumables: writing and drawing materials, sample containers, sample collection materials, reagents, controls, standards, repackaging equipment, cleaning materials
3. Equipment rectification: report, record, isolate, replace, remedy, request specialist assistance
4. Anticontamination requirements: cleaning, clothing, work area, equipment
5. Tools: forceps, scalpels, magnifying glass, needles, brushes, scissors
6. Personal preparation: use of personal protective equipment, hygiene
7. Report equipment faults: written, oral
8. Equipment: electrical, optical, manual

Evidence Requirements

The candidate should be able to demonstrate competence over a period of time across all the performance criteria and range statements. Competence is to be demonstrated in real work situations. Where opportunities for work-based assessments are not readily available, realistic simulations of the work activity may be used, although these should be set up and assessed in the normal working environment. The candidate should be able to explain the reasons for all his or her actions and cover "what if" scenarios. Candidates should also be able to answer oral or written questions covering items specified in the "Knowledge and Understanding" specification.

Knowledge and Understanding Specification

Principles, Methods, and Techniques Relating To ...

- Operation of equipment (d, e, f) (range 3 and 5)
- Cleaning and preparation requirements for the work area and equipment (a and b) (range I)
- Contamination dangers, and how these can be avoided (a, b, and g) (range 4)
- Code of ethics: the need for impartial judgments (a and b)
- Use of consumables (c) (range 2)
- Reporting faults (e and f) (range 7)
- Use of personal protective equipment (g) (range 6)

Information and Data About ...

- Types of equipment (d) (range 5 and 8)
- Types of consumables and amounts (c) (range 2)
- Manufacturers and laboratory instructions in relation to use of equipment (d, e, f) (range 3, 5, and 8)
- Cleaning and preparation procedures (a and b) (range 1 and 4)
- Statutory requirements: Health and Safety at Work Act and COSHH Regulations (g) (range 6)
- Contamination dangers (a, b, and g) (range 1, 2, 3, 4, 5, 6, and 8)

Assessment Guidance

Competence will be demonstrated across a range of different cases by a combination of observation in the work environment, oral questioning, and a review of the portfolio evidence.

Unit RM1: Prepare to Carry Out Laboratory-Based Recovery

Element 1.3: Obtain and Confirm Items for Examination

The Standard

Performance Criteria

- a. Items to be examined are safely and securely received from storage facilities.
- b. Details of storage, handling, and transfer of items are documented to maintain continuity in accordance with legal requirements.

   c. Packaging problems are identified, and consultations are undertaken with relevant personnel to determine the nature of the problem and its resolution.
   d. Movement of contaminating materials within the laboratory is avoided where possible, and adequate measures are taken to avoid contamination.
   e. Details of packaging are accurately documented to ensure integrity and continuity of items.
   f. Process is carried out safely and with due attention to minimizing hazards to self and others in accordance with statutory requirements.

Range Statements

1. Packaging: container, seals, labeling
2. Packaging problems: inappropriate labeling, inadequate seals, integrity of packaging and seals, danger of contamination, inappropriate packaging
3. Contaminating materials: particulate, fibrous, liquids, gases, cross contamination, personal contamination
4. Continuity: dates, times, names, location
5. Health and safety considerations: item type, condition of item, personal safety, safety of others
6. Relevant personnel: line manager, case supervisor, other specialists
7. Items for examination: chemical, biological, physical

Evidence Requirements

The candidate should be able to demonstrate competence over a period of time across all the performance criteria and range statements. Competence is to be demonstrated in real work situations. Where opportunities for work-based assessments are not readily available, realistic simulations of the work activity may be used, although these should be set up and assessed in the normal working environment. The candidate should be able to explain the reasons for all his or her actions and cover "what if" scenarios. Candidates should also be able to answer oral or written questions covering items specified in the "Knowledge and Understanding" specification.

Knowledge and Understanding Specification
Principles, Methods, and Techniques Relating To …

- Effect of packaging materials on different types of potential evidential materials (a, b, and c) (range 1, 2, 6, and 7)
- Contamination dangers, and how these can be avoided (a, c, and d) (range 3, 5, and 6)
- Avoiding and minimizing potential hazards (a and f) (range 5)
- Health and safety considerations (a and f) (range 5)
- Storage requirements (a and b) (range 2)
- Security and continuity of items (b and e) (range 4 and 7)
- Code of ethics: the need for impartial judgments (c and d)

Information and Data About …

- Types of packaging materials (a, b, and c) (range 1)
- Types of potential evidential materials (a, b, and c) (range 7)

- Contamination dangers (a, c, and e) (range 3 and 6)
- Statutory requirements: Health and Safety at Work Act and COSHH Regulations (a and f) (range 5 and 6)
- Storage facilities (a and b)
- Legal requirements in relation to continuity (b and e) (range 4)

Assessment Guidance

Competence will be demonstrated across a range of different cases by a combination of observation in the work environment, oral questioning, and a review of the portfolio evidence.

Unit RM2: Carry Out Laboratory-Based Recovery of Materials

Element 2.1: Inspect Items Submitted for Recovery

The Standard

Performance Criteria

a. Identity of submitted items is confirmed against documentation, and any problems are reported to the relevant personnel.
b. Removal of items from packaging and subsequent handling are safe, avoid contamination and cross contamination, and minimize loss of potential evidential material.
c. Recovery plan is confirmed against agreed prioritization and sequence of laboratory work, and is adjusted as necessary in light of observations made.
d. Appropriate location techniques are employed to detect potential evidential material, and located material of potential significance is reported to relevant personnel before continuing with the process.
e. Existence and location of evidential material, where detected, are recorded accurately in accordance with organizational requirements.
f. Continuity and integrity of items are maintained throughout the inspection process.
g. Inspection process is carried out safely and with due attention to minimizing hazards to self and others in accordance with statutory requirements.

Range Statements

1. Locating potential evidential material: by visual recognition aided and unaided
2. Health and safety considerations: item type, condition of item, personal safety, safety of others
3. Recording information format: written, drawn, photographic
4. Relevant personnel: line manager, case supervisor
5. Common evidence types: chemical, biological, physical

Evidence Requirements

The candidate should be able to demonstrate competence over a period of time across all the performance criteria and range statements. Competence is to be demonstrated

in real work situations. Where opportunities for work-based assessments are not readily available, realistic simulations of the work activity may be used, although these should be set up and assessed in the normal working environment. The candidate should be able to explain the reasons for all his or her actions and cover "what if" scenarios. Candidates should also be able to answer oral or written questions covering items specified in the "Knowledge and Understanding" specification.

Knowledge and Understanding Specification

Principles, Methods, and Techniques Relating To ...

- Potential conflict in examination methods of different evidence types (b, d, and g) (range 1 and 5)
- Scientific principles generally and specifically related to the types of investigations to be carried out (b, d, and g) (range 1, 2, and 5)
- Health and safety considerations (b and g) (range 1, 2, and 5)
- Contamination dangers, and how these can be avoided (b, f, and g) (range 5)
- The need for and importance of continuity (a, e, f) (range 3)
- Code of ethics: the need for impartial judgments (a–g)

Information and Data About ...

- Potential evidence types (b, d, and g) (range 5)
- Search and detection techniques (d) (range 1, 2, and 5)
- Statutory requirements: Health and Safety at Work Act and COSHH Regulations (b and g) (range 4)
- Limitations of own abilities and the need for consultation (a, c, and d) (range 4)
- Contamination dangers (b, f, and g) (range 5)
- Continuity requirements and procedures (e and f) (range 3)

Assessment Guidance

Competence will be demonstrated across a range of different cases by a combination of observation in the work environment, oral questioning, and a review of the portfolio evidence.

UNIT RM2: CARRY OUT LABORATORY-BASED RECOVERY OF MATERIALS

Element 2.2: Recover Materials

The Standard

Performance Criteria

a. Examination is carried out in the agreed sequence to ensure detection and optimum recovery.
b. Methods selected and employed optimize recovery, minimize loss, and avoid contamination.
c. Samples of materials are handled safely and securely in a manner commensurate with their size and nature.
d. Relevant information is accurately, comprehensively, and contemporaneously recorded onto appropriate documentation.

e. Continuity and integrity are maintained throughout the recovery process.
f. Samples of materials, records, and (where appropriate) items are carried forward for further examination and analysis in accordance with investigation requirements.
g. Recovery process is carried out safely and with due attention to minimizing hazards to self and others in accordance with statutory requirements.
h. Nonrepeatable tests are carried out in the presence of relevant personnel.

Range Statements

1. Recovery techniques: tape lifts, shaking, sweeping, vacuuming, manual removal, swabbing
2. Samples of materials: microscopic, macroscopic, bulk
3. Recording of observations and items format: written, drawn, photographic
4. Examination methods: presumptive testing, visual aided, physical, visual unaided
5. Health and safety considerations: item type, condition of item, personal safety, safety of others
6. Common evidence types: chemical, biological, physical
7. Recovery process: use of equipment, use of reagents, sampling, use of tools
8. Relevant personnel: line manager, case supervisor
9. Equipment: electrical, optical, manual

Evidence Requirements

The candidate should be able to demonstrate competence over a period of time across all the performance criteria and range statements. Competence is to be demonstrated in real work situations. Where opportunities for work-based assessments are not readily available, realistic simulations of the work activity may be used, although these should be set up and assessed in the normal working environment. The candidate should be able to explain the reasons for all his or her actions and cover "what if" scenarios. Candidates should also be able to answer oral or written questions covering items specified in the "Knowledge and Understanding" specification.

Knowledge and Understanding Specification
Principles, Methods, and Techniques Relating To ...

- Recovery techniques associated with different evidence types (a, b, c, and h) (range 1, 6, and 8)
- The need for control and reference samples (b and c) (range 2)
- Code of ethics: the need for impartial judgments (a–h)
- Potential conflict in examination methods of different evidence types (a and b) (range 4 and 6)
- Judgments necessary to optimize recovery, minimize loss, and avoid contamination (a, b, and c) (range 1, 2, 4, 5, 6, and 7)
- Use of equipment, reagents, and tools (b and c) (range 1, 4, 7, and 9)
- Recording information (e and f) (range 3)
- Health and safety considerations (g) (range 5 and 8)

- Scientific principles generally and specifically related to the types of investigations to be carried out (a, b, and c) (range 1, 2, 3, 4, 5, 6, and 7)
- Contamination and cross-contamination dangers, and how these can be avoided (a, b, c, and e) (range 1, 2, 4, 5, 6, and 7)
- The need for and importance of continuity (d, e, f) (range 3)

Information and Data About …

- Evidence types (a, b, c, and h) (range 6)
- Recovery techniques, including control and reference samples (a, b, c, and h) (range 1 and 2)
- Types of equipment, reagents, and tools (b and c) (range 9)
- Recording requirements (e and f) (range 3)
- Statutory requirements: Health and Safety at Work Act and COSHH Regulations (g) (range 7 and 8)
- Limitations of own abilities, and implications of exceeding these (a, b, and d) (range 1–7)
- Contamination and cross-contamination dangers (a, b, c, and e) (range 1, 2, 4, 5, 6, and 7)
- Continuity requirements (d, e, f) (range 3)

Assessment Guidance

Competence will be demonstrated by performance in the workplace across all of the recovery techniques listed in range 1 and all of the common evidence types listed in range 6.

Unit RM2: Carry Out Laboratory-Based Recovery of Materials

Element 2.3: Prepare Recovered Material for Analysis and Comparison

The Standard

Performance Criteria

1. Analytical requirements and instructions are obtained, and difficulties in carrying out the instructions are clarified with the relevant personnel.
2. Selection and preparation of recovered material for analysis and comparison are carried out in the agreed sequence, and optimum recovery is achieved.
3. Methods selected and employed avoid contamination, minimize loss, and present materials and samples in a manner appropriate to their size and nature and the type of analysis to be carried out.
4. Materials and samples selected and prepared are of the appropriate size and condition, representative, and suitable for analysis and comparison.
5. Relevant information is accurately, comprehensively, and contemporaneously recorded onto appropriate documentation.
6. Continuity and integrity are maintained throughout the process.
7. Preparation process is carried out safely and with due attention to minimizing hazards to self and others in accordance with statutory requirements.
8. Nonrepeatable tests are carried out in the presence of relevant personnel.

Range Statements

1. Instructions: written, oral
2. Relevant personnel: line manager, other specialists, case supervisor
3. Samples of materials: microscopic, macroscopic, bulk
4. Information recording format: written, drawn
5. Examination methods: visual aided, visual unaided, physical
6. Health and safety considerations: item type, condition of item, personal safety, safety of others
7. Preparation process: use of equipment, use of reagents, use of tools, sampling, isolation

Evidence Requirements

The candidate should be able to demonstrate competence over a period of time across all the performance criteria and range statements. Competence is to be demonstrated in real work situations. Where opportunities for work-based assessments are not readily available, realistic simulations of the work activity may be used, although these should be set up and assessed in the normal working environment. The candidate should be able to explain the reasons for all his or her actions and cover "what if" scenarios. Candidates should also be able to answer oral or written questions covering items specified in the "Knowledge and Understanding" specification.

Knowledge and Understanding Specification

Principles, Methods, and Techniques Relating To ...

- Analytical capabilities of techniques selected (a, d, and h) (range 5)
- Interaction or interference of techniques employed with any subsequent analysis (a, d, and h) (range 5)
- Contamination dangers, and how they can be avoided (c, f) (range 3, 5, and 6)
- Code of ethics: the need for impartial judgments (a–h)
- Recording information (e, f) (range 4)
- The need for and importance of continuity (e and f) (range 4)
- Health and safety considerations (g) (range 8)
- Achieving optimum recovery (b) (range 3 and 5)
- Preparing recovered material for analysis and comparison (b, d, and g) (range 7)
- Interpreting instructions (a) (range 1 and 2)

Information and Data About ...

- Examination methods (a, d, and h) (range 5)
- Preparation processes (b) (range 7)
- Contamination dangers (c and f) (range 3, 5, 6, and 7)
- Recording requirements and documentation (e and f) (range 4)
- Statutory requirements: Health and Safety at Work Act and COSHH Regulations (g) (range 6 and 8)

Assessment Guidance

Competence will be demonstrated within a specialist area of preparing materials for analysis or comparison by a combination of observation in the work environment, oral questioning, and a review of the portfolio evidence.

UNIT RM2: CARRY OUT LABORATORY-BASED RECOVERY OF MATERIALS

Element 2.4: Complete the Recovery Process

The Standard

Performance Criteria

a. Items and samples are handled, packaged, and stored in a way which prevents contamination, cross contamination, and loss of evidence.
b. Items and samples are uniquely labeled and accurately recorded.
c. The continuity of items and samples is maintained.
d. Items and samples are stored in safe and secure conditions and are accessible to relevant persons.
e. Relevant information is accurately, comprehensively, and contemporaneously recorded onto appropriate documentation.
f. Packaging and storage of items and samples are carried out with due regard to safety consideration in accordance with statutory requirements.

Range Statements

1. Items and samples: to include different types of items which will have different packaging, handling, labeling, safety, and storage requirements
2. Health and safety considerations: item type, condition of item, personal safety, safety of others
3. Relevant personnel: line manager, case supervisor, other specialists
4. Recording information: written, drawn, photographic
5. Common evidence types: chemical, biological, physical

Evidence Requirements

The candidate should be able to demonstrate competence over a period of time across all the performance criteria and range statements. Competence is to be demonstrated in real work situations. Where opportunities for work-based assessments are not readily available, realistic simulations of the work activity may be used, although these should be set up and assessed in the normal working environment. The candidate should be able to explain the reasons for all his or her actions and cover "what if" scenarios. Candidates should also be able to answer oral or written questions covering items specified in the "Knowledge and Understanding" specification.

Knowledge and Understanding Specification

Principles, Methods, and Techniques Relating To ...

- Establishing and maintaining continuity and security (a–f) (range 4)
- Avoiding and minimizing potential hazards (f) (range 1, 2, and 5)
- Selection of packaging materials (a) (range 1)

- Packaging items (a) (range 1, 2, and 5)
- Storing items (a) (range 1 and 5)
- Preservation of items and samples (a, d, f) (range 1 and 5)
- Contamination dangers, and how they can be avoided (a and d) (range 1, 2, and 5)
- Recording information (e) (range 4)
- Health and safety considerations (f) (range 2)

Information and Data About ...

- Continuity and security requirements (a–f) (range 4)
- Statutory requirements: Health and Safety at Work and COSHH Regulations (0) (range 2)
- Types of packaging materials (a) (range 1)
- Evidence types (a) (range 5)
- Storage requirements and facilities (a, d, and f) (range 1 and 5)
- Contamination dangers (a and d) (range 1, 2, and 5)
- Personnel who have access to items and sample (d) (range 3)

Assessment Guidance

Competence will be demonstrated across a range of different cases by a combination of observation in the work environment, oral questioning, and a review of the portfolio evidence.

Unit RM3: Contribute to the Operational Effectiveness of the Working Environment

Element 3.1: Monitor and Maintain Operational Effectiveness of the Work Area

The Standard

Performance Criteria

a. Work area is checked and confirmed for operational effectiveness according to organizational and work requirements.
b. Problems with the work area are identified and rectified within the individual's responsibility in accordance with organizational requirements.
c. Problems with the work area that are outside the individual's area of responsibility are reported promptly to the relevant person.
d. Services, equipment, instruments, and consumables are confirmed available and accessible according to designated work area, work, and organizational requirements.
e. Problems in the availability and accessibility of services, equipment, instruments, and consumables are reported promptly to the relevant person.

Range Statements

1. Work area: work surfaces, floor, designated activity areas
2. Operational effectiveness: routine activity, specialized activity, noncontamination

3. Work requirements: types of activity to be carried out, anticontamination requirements
4. Organizational requirements: procedures, instructions
5. Services: electricity, water, gas, vacuum lines
6. Equipment: electrical, optical, manual
7. Instruments: forceps, scalpels, magnifying glass, needles, brushes, scissors
8. Consumables: bench-covering paper, reagents
9. Work area problems: risk of contamination, faulty lighting, services breakdown

Evidence Requirements

The candidate should be able to demonstrate competence over a period of time across all the performance criteria and range statements. Competence is to be demonstrated in real work situations. The candidate should be able to explain the reasons for all his or her actions and cover "what if" scenarios. Candidates should also be able to answer oral or written questions covering items specified in the "Knowledge and Understanding" specification.

Knowledge and Understanding Specification
Principles, Methods, and Techniques Relating To ...

- Contamination and cross-contamination dangers, and how they can be avoided (a, b, and c) (range 1, 3, 6, 7, 8, and 9)
- Health and safety considerations (a, b, and c) (range 1–9)
- Checking and confirming operational effectiveness of the work area (a) (range 1 and 3)
- Confirming availability of services, equipment, instruments, and consumables (d and e) (range 6, 7, and 8)
- Identifying and rectifying problems in the work area (c) (range 4 and 9)

Information and Data About ...

- Contamination and cross-contamination dangers (a, b, and c) (range 1, 3, 6, 7, 8, and 9)
- Cleanliness procedures (a, b, and c) (range 1, 2, and 3)
- Organizational policies and procedures (a, b, and c) (range 4)
- Designated work areas and requirements (a, b, and c) (range 1 and 3)
- Types of services (d and e) (range 5)
- Types of equipment (d and e) (range 6)
- Types of instruments (d and e) (range 7)
- Types of consumables (d and e) (range 8)

Assessment Guidance

Competence will be demonstrated during observations in the work environment, oral questioning, and a review of the portfolio evidence, which should include peer and supervisor reports.

Unit RM3: Contribute to the Operational Effectiveness of the Working Environment

Element 3.2: Monitor and Maintain Functional Effectiveness of Equipment, Instruments, and Reagents

The Standard

Performance Criteria

a. Equipment, instruments, and reagents are checked and confirmed in working order according to manufacturer's instructions and health and safety requirements.

b. The need to clean and calibrate equipment and instruments is identified and carried out in accordance with manufacturer's instructions and organizational requirements.

c. Worn and damaged equipment and instruments are identified, relevant remedial action is taken, and the relevant person informed.

d. Reagents which are out of date and unfit for use are identified, disposed of, and replaced in accordance with health and safety and organizational requirements.

e. Equipment, instruments, and reagents are legibly and indelibly labeled according to organizational and health and safety requirements, and are safely and securely stored in a designated location.

f. Relevant documentation is complete, accessible as required, and filed in a designated location.

g. Incomplete and missing documentation is identified, located, and filed in the designated location; discrepancies are reported to the relevant person for action.

h. Action is taken in the event of abnormal occurrences and malfunctions to minimize hazards and to record and report the occurrence.

Range Statements

1. Equipment and instrument checks: sterilization, calibration, cleanliness, random check, regular check
2. Documentation: records, operational instructions, warning instructions
3. Organizational requirements: procedures, instructions
4. Health and safety considerations: personal safety, safety of others, hazardous equipment, instruments, and reagents
5. Equipment: electrical, optical, manual
6. Instruments: forceps, scalpels, magnifying glass, needles, brushes, scissors
7. Abnormal occurrences and malfunctions: unexpected reagent reaction, faulty equipment, faulty ultraviolet light, services breakdown
8. Remedial action taken with worn and damaged equipment and instruments: replace, repair, dispose of

Evidence Requirements

The candidate should be able to demonstrate competence over a period of time across all the performance criteria and range statements. Competence is to be demonstrated

in real work situations. The candidate should be able to explain the reasons for all his or her actions and cover "what if" scenarios. Candidates should also be able to answer oral or written questions covering items specified in the "Knowledge and Understanding" specification.

Knowledge and Understanding Specification

Principles, Methods, and Techniques Relating To …

- Checking and confirming equipment, instruments, and reagents are in working order (a) (range 1, 5, and 6)
- Cleaning and calibrating equipment and instruments (b) (range 1, 3, 5, and 6)
- Replacing, repairing, and disposing of worn and damaged equipment and instruments (c) (range 5, 6, 7, and 8)
- Disposing of and replacing reagents (d) (range 7)
- Labeling equipment, instruments, and reagents (e) (range 4)
- Recording information (f) (range 2)
- Filing documentation (g) (range 2)
- Minimizing hazards (h) (range 1, 4, and 7)
- Health and safety considerations (a, d, e, and h) (range 4)

Information and Data About …

- Types of equipment, instruments, and reagents (a, b, c, d, and e) (range 5 and 6)
- Organizational policies and procedures (b and d) (range 3)
- Health and safety requirements (a, d, e, and f) (range 4)
- Equipment and instrument checks (a, b, c, and e) (range 1, 5, and 6)
- Reagent checks (d) (range 1)
- Documentation requirements (g) (range 2)
- Emergency procedures (h) (range 7)

Assessment Guidance

Competence will be demonstrated during observations in the work environment, oral questioning, and a review of the portfolio evidence, which should include peer and supervisor reports.

UNIT RM3: CONTRIBUTE TO THE OPERATIONAL EFFECTIVENESS OF THE WORKING ENVIRONMENT

Element 3.3 Maintain a Working Knowledge of Trends and Developments within Area of Responsibility

The Standard

Performance Criteria

a. A variety of sources of information are identified and regularly reviewed for usefulness and developments regarding recovery methods, procedures, and practices.
b. Opportunities are taken to establish and maintain contacts with those who may provide useful and relevant information.

c. Relevant information is obtained and retained in accordance with organizational requirements and the needs of one's own area of responsibility.
d. Up-to-date information is accessible and is made available to relevant personnel in accordance with organizational requirements.

Range Statements

1. Information sources: colleagues, written, computerized, published, national, local, internal to organization, external
2. Information: both quantitative and qualitative
3. Organizational requirements: procedures, instructions
4. Relevant personnel: colleagues, line manager, other specialists
5. Developments in: practices, knowledge, technology

Evidence Requirements

The candidate should be able to demonstrate competence over a period of time across all the performance criteria and range statements. Competence is to be demonstrated in real work situations. The candidate should be able to explain the reasons for all his or her actions and cover "what if" scenarios. Candidates should also be able to answer oral or written questions covering items specified in the "Knowledge and Understanding" specification.

Knowledge and Understanding Specification

Principles, Methods, and Techniques Relating To …

- Potential areas of development (a) (range 1 and 2)
- Recovery techniques (a) (range 3)
- Establishing and maintaining useful contacts (b) (range 1)

Information and Data About …

- Sources of information, including useful contacts (a, b, and d) (range 1 and 2)
- Organizational policies and procedures (c) (range 3)
- Needs of own area of responsibility (c) (range 3 and 4)

Assessment Guidance

Competence will be demonstrated during observations in the work environment, oral questioning, and a review of the portfolio evidence, which should include peer and supervisor reports.

UNIT RM4: PROVIDE INFORMATION AND DOCUMENTATION

Element 4.1: Provide Examination Records and Summaries

The Standard

Performance Criteria

a. Information is offered and disseminated at an appropriate time and place.
b. Information given is current, relevant, and accurate.

   c. Information is supplied in the form requested, and is presented in a manner and at a level and pace to support understanding.

   d. Records and summaries are structured logically and present the data in appropriate formats according to organizational requirements.

   e. Records and summaries include all necessary information and avoid repetition.

   f. Recommendations are expressed within area of expertise and based firmly on results.

   g. Records and summaries are expressed in understandable and unambiguous language.

Range Statements

1. Organizational requirements: procedures, instructions
2. Records and summaries: oral, written, illustrations, photographs, sketches, graphs

Evidence Requirements

The candidate should be able to demonstrate competence over a period of time across all the performance criteria and range statements. Competence is to be demonstrated in real work situations. The candidate should be able to explain the reasons for all his or her actions and cover "what if" scenarios. Candidates should also be able to answer oral or written questions covering items specified in the "Knowledge and Understanding" specification.

Knowledge and Understanding Specification

Principles, Methods, and Techniques Relating To …

- Use of language: relevance and acceptance to end users (g) (range 3)
- Code of ethics: the need for impartial judgments (a–g) (range 1)
- Records and summaries (b, c, d, e, f, and g) (range 1, 2, and 3)
- Dissemination of information (a) (range 2)
- Presentation of information and data (b, c, and d) (range 2)
- Structuring records and summaries (d) (range 1 and 2)

Information and Data About …

- Organizational policies and procedures (d) (range 1)
- Recording formats and use (c, e, and g) (range 2)

Assessment Guidance

Competence will be demonstrated across a range of different cases by a combination of observation in the work environment, oral questioning, and a review of the portfolio evidence. The documentation provided in the portfolio should be linked to the cases assessed for units 9 and 10.

Unit RM4: Provide Information and Documentation

Element 4.2: Provide Administrative Records

The Standard

Performance Criteria

    a. Records are provided according to work allocated and organizational requirements.

    b. Records are completed within the required time scale using accepted formats.

    c. Problems in providing records are identified and actioned according to organizational requirements.

    d. Records are accurate and legible, and include all relevant information according to legal and organizational requirements.

    e. Records are accessible as required and filed in a designated location.

Range Statements

    1. Accepted formats: written, computerized
    2. Organizational requirements: procedures, instructions
    3. Administration records: transfer, continuity, storage, receipt, instructions, submissions
    4. Legal requirements: statute law, local jurisdiction

Evidence Requirements

The candidate should be able to demonstrate competence over a period of time across all the performance criteria and range statements. Competence is to be demonstrated in real work situations. The candidate should be able to explain the reasons for all his or her actions and cover "what if" scenarios. Candidates should also be able to answer oral or written questions covering items specified in the "Knowledge and Understanding" specification.

Knowledge and Understanding Specification

Principles, Methods, and Techniques Relating To …

    • Code of ethics: the need for impartial judgments (a–e) (range 2)
    • Providing records in acceptable formats (b and d) (range 1 and 2)
    • Filing requirements (e) (range 3)

Information and Data About …

    • Organizational policies and procedures (a, c, and d) (range 2)
    • Recording formats and use (b and d) (range 1)
    • Legal requirements in relation to record keeping (d) (range 3 and 4)

Assessment Guidance

Competence will be demonstrated across a range of different cases by a combination of observation in the work environment, oral questioning, and a review of the portfolio evidence. The documentation provided in the portfolio should be linked to the cases assessed for units 9 and 10.

Unit ISI7: Establish and Maintain Effective Working Relationships

Element 7.1: Maintain and Enhance Working Relationships with Colleagues

The Standard

Performance Criteria

   a. Efforts are made to establish and maintain productive working relationships.
   b. Opinions and information are exchanged and shared with colleagues.
   c. Advice and help are offered and received in a manner which does not give offense.
   d. Differences of opinion and conflict are resolved in ways that maintain productive working relationships.
   e. Differences of opinion and conflict which cannot be resolved are recorded in accordance with organizational requirements.
   f. Promises and undertakings made to others concerning work and associated commitments are honored, given time, cost, resource, and priority commitments.
   g. Suggestions and recommendations for improving working conditions and practices to enhance the environment and relationships are passed to the appropriate person as soon as it is practicable.

Range Statements

   1. Organizational requirements: procedures, instructions
   2. Colleagues are those with whom the individual works: closely on a day-to-day basis, occasionally, within the immediate work environment, outside the immediate work environment
   3. Communications: oral, written, formal, informal

Evidence Requirements

The candidate should be able to demonstrate competence over a period of time across all the performance criteria and range statements. Competence is to be demonstrated in real work situations. The candidate should be able to explain the reasons for all his or her actions and cover "what if" scenarios. Candidates should also be able to answer oral or written questions covering items specified in the "Knowledge and Understanding" specification.

Knowledge and Understanding Specification

Principles, Methods, and Techniques Relating To …

   • Principles of effective communication (a–g) (range 3)
   • Own strengths and weaknesses (a–g) (range 1, 2, and 3)

Information and Data About …

- Organizational policies and procedures (a) (range 1)
- One's own and others' job specifications (a, f, and g) (range 1 and 2)
- Communication channels within the organization (a–g) (range 1, 2, and 3)

Assessment Guidance

Competence will be demonstrated during observations, by questioning, and by the compilation of a portfolio. Forms of evidence will include personal logs, reports, and witness testimony from colleagues.

Unit ISI7: Establish and Maintain Effective Working Relationships

Element 7.2: Establish and Maintain Working Relationships with One's Immediate Manager

The Standard

Performance Criteria

- a. Immediate manager is kept informed in an appropriate level of detail about activities, progress, results, and achievements.
- b. Information about problems and opportunities is clear, accurate, and provided with an appropriate degree of urgency.
- c. Information and advice on matters within the given area of responsibility are sought from immediate manager as necessary.
- d. Clear proposals for action are presented at an appropriate time and with the right level of detail.
- e. Where proposals are not accepted, the reasons are considered and, where appropriate, alternative proposals are put forward.
- f. Where there are disagreements, efforts are made to avoid damaging the relationship with the immediate manager, using mediation when necessary.
- g. Ways of improving the relationship with the immediate manager are actively sought.
- h. Requirements of job role are satisfied.
- i. Activities are performed in a helpful and willing manner.

Range Statements

1. Communication: oral, written, formal, informal
2. Information and advice on: organizational policies, plans and procedures, legislation, personal and interpersonal issues, work and case methods, proposals concerning new courses of action

Evidence Requirements

The candidate should be able to demonstrate competence over a period of time across all the performance criteria and range statements. Competence is to be demonstrated in real work situations. The candidate should be able to explain the reasons for all his or her actions and cover "what if" scenarios. Candidates should also be able to answer oral or written questions covering items specified in the "Knowledge and Understanding" specification.

Knowledge and Understanding Specification

Principles, Methods, and Techniques Relating To …

- Principles of effective communication (a–f) (range 1 and 2)
- Own strengths and weaknesses (a–g) (range 1 and 2)
- Appeals procedure (f) (range 1)

Information and Data About …

- One's own and manager's job specification (c, f, h, and i)
- Manager's strengths and weaknesses (f and g)
- Communication channels (a–d) (range 1)

Assessment Guidance

Competence will be demonstrated during observations, by questioning, and by the compilation of a portfolio. Forms of evidence will include personal logs, reports, and witness testimony from colleagues.

UNIT RM5: CONTRIBUTE TO THE MAINTENANCE OF HEALTH AND SAFETY IN THE WORKPLACE

Element 5.1: Contribute to the Safety of the Workplace

The Standard

Performance Criteria

a. Relevant records are complete and accurate within individual's area of responsibility.
b. Safety problems and potentially unsafe features in the working environment are investigated, and immediate remedial action is taken within the individual's area of responsibility.
c. Safety problems and potentially unsafe features outside the individual's area of responsibility are reported promptly to the relevant person.
d. Health and safety standards are adhered to in accordance with current legislation.
e. Relevant ongoing training and instruction are accessed to enable the individual to perform his or her work safely and efficiently.

Range Statements

1. Records: accidents, incidents, equipment, instruments, case materials, operating instructions for equipment and instruments
2. Health and safety standards: operation of equipment, organizational policies and procedures, evacuation procedures
3. Safety problems and unsafe features: fabric of the workplace, operational equipment, case materials, personnel, chemicals

Evidence Requirements

The candidate should be able to demonstrate competence over a period of time across all the performance criteria and range statements. Competence is to be demonstrated in real work situations. The candidate should be able to explain the reasons for all his or her actions and cover "what if" scenarios. Candidates should also be able to answer oral or written questions covering items specified in the "Knowledge and Understanding" specification.

Knowledge and Understanding Specification

Principles, Methods, and Techniques Relating To …

- Methods of avoiding potential hazards in the workplace (b) (range 3)
- Implications of health and safety legislation (c) (range 2)
- Accessing training and instruction (d) (range 5)
- Investigating safety problems and unsafe features (b) (range 3)
- Taking remedial action in response to safety problems and unsafe features (b) (range 2 and 3)

Information and Data About …

- Types of records (a) (range 1)
- Organizational policies and procedures (c) (range 4)
- Potential hazards in the workplace (b) (range 3)
- Procedures to adopt when there are breaches of good practice (b and c) (range 3)
- Emergency procedures (b) (range 3)
- Legislation requirements: Health and Safety at Work Act and COSHH Regulations (c) (range 2)
- Availability of training and instruction (d) (range 5)

Assessment Guidance

Competence will be demonstrated during observations, by questioning, and by the compilation of a portfolio. Forms of evidence will include personal logs, reports, and witness testimony from colleagues.

UNIT RM5: CONTRIBUTE TO THE MAINTENANCE OF HEALTH AND SAFETY IN THE WORKPLACE

Element 5.2: Contribute to the Health and Safety of Personnel

The Standard

Performance Criteria

a. Cleaning standards and routines are undertaken in line with relevant legislation, relevant equipment manufacturer's requirements, and organizational requirements.
b. The working area is free from hazards, potentially hazardous work requirements are identified and minimized, and the relevant action is taken to carry out the work.

   c. Problems are identified and rectified within the individual's area of responsibility.

   d. Health, safety, and maintenance checks within the individual's area of responsibility are carried out regularly according to organizational requirements.

   e. Emergencies are dealt with, reported, and recorded accurately, completely, and legibly according to legal requirements.

   f. Manufacturer's instructions and legislative and organizational requirements relating to the safe use of equipment and instruments are followed.

Range Statement

1. Work requirements: case materials, operational equipment
2. Problems: personnel, equipment, instruments, fabric of the workplace, case requirements and materials
3. Health, safety, and maintenance checks of: work area, equipment, consumables, instruments, reagents, case materials
4. Personnel: colleagues, line manager, visitors
5. Emergencies: accidents, spillage of hazardous materials, volatile potential evidential material
6. Organizational requirements: procedures, instructions

Evidence Requirements

The candidate should be able to demonstrate competence over a period of time across all the performance criteria and range statements. Competence is to be demonstrated in real work situations. The candidate should be able to explain the reasons for all his or her actions and cover "what if" scenarios. Candidates should also be able to answer oral or written questions covering items specified in the "Knowledge and Understanding" specification.

Knowledge and Understanding Specification

Principles, Methods, and Techniques Relating To …

- Housekeeping methods, and how to carry them out (a, b, c, and d) (range 1 and 3)
- Methods of rectifying and minimizing hazards and potential hazards (b and c) (range 2)
- Using and handling equipment, instruments, and case materials safely (b and f) (range 3 and 4)
- Implications of health and safety legislation (a–f) (range 4)
- Carrying out health, safety, and maintenance checks (d) (range 3 and 5)
- Dealing with emergencies (e) (range 5)

Information and Data About …

- Housekeeping procedures and routines (a, b, c, and d) (range 1 and 3)
- Types of hazards (b, c, and e) (range 2)
- Emergency procedures (e) (range 4)
- Legislation requirements: Health and Safety at Work Act and COSHH Regulations (a–f) (range 6)
- Organizational policies and procedures (a, d, f) (range 5)

Assessment Guidance

Competence will be demonstrated during observations, by questioning, and by the compilation of a portfolio. Forms of evidence will include personal logs, reports, and witness testimony from colleagues.

ADDITIONAL UNIT

UNIT RM6: CARRY OUT PRIMARY ANALYSIS OF RECOVERED MATERIAL

Element 6.1: Prepare to Analyze Recovered Material

The Standard

Performance Criteria

   a. Tests and examinations to be carried out are agreed with the relevant personnel.

   b. Constraints which affect the way in which the tests and examinations can be carried out are identified, and a work plan is developed and confirmed with the relevant personnel.

   c. Quality assurance requirements are identified, agreed with the relevant personnel, and implemented.

   d. Continuity and integrity of items are maintained throughout the testing and examination preparation process.

   e. Equipment required is confirmed available, functional, and safe in accordance with manufacturer's instructions and health and safety requirements.

   f. Equipment faults are identified, and relevant remedial actions taken.

   g. Personal preparation requirements are carried out safely in accordance with statutory and operational requirements.

   h. Relevant information is accurately, legibly, and comprehensively recorded onto appropriate documentation.

Range Statements

   1. Constraints: nature of tests and examinations, size of potential evidence, amount of potential evidence, nature of potential evidence, time

   2. Relevant personnel: case supervisor, line manager, other specialists

   3. Equipment: electrical, optical, manual

   4. Personal preparation: use of personal protective equipment, hygiene

   5. Relevant remedial actions: report, record, replace

   6. Health and safety considerations: item type, condition of item, personal safety, safety of others

   7. Quality assurance requirements: equipment calibration, control samples, reference materials, avoidance of contamination, consideration of other possible examinations

Evidence Requirements

The candidate should be able to demonstrate competence over a period of time across all the performance criteria and range statements. Competence is to be demonstrated

in real work situations. Where opportunities for work-based assessments are not readily available, realistic simulations of the work activity may be used, although these should be set up and assessed in the normal working environment. The candidate should be able to explain the reasons for all his or her actions and cover "what if" scenarios. Candidates should also be able to answer oral or written questions covering items specified in the "Knowledge and Understanding" specification.

Knowledge and Understanding Specification

Principles, Methods, and Techniques Relating To …

- Quality assurance requirements (c) (range 5 and 7)
- Constraints on tests and examinations (b) (range 1 and 2)
- Determining and confirming a work plan (a and b) (range 1, 2, and 3)
- Continuity and integrity of items (d and h) (range 2)
- Operational effectiveness of equipment (e and f) (range 3, 5, and 6)
- Health and safety considerations (e, f, and g) (range 3, 4, 5, and 6)
- Recording information (d and h)
- Code of Ethics: the need for impartial judgments (a and b)

Information and Data About …

- Types of tests and examinations (a) (range 2)
- Work plan requirements (b) (range 1 and 2)
- Types of equipment (e, f) (range 3 and 5)
- Statutory requirements: Health and Safety at Work Act and COSHH Regulations (e, f, and g) (range 3, 4, 5, and 6)
- Information to be recorded (d and h)

Assessment Guidance

Competence will be demonstrated by a combination of observation in the work environment, oral questioning, and a review of the portfolio evidence produced by the candidate.

UNIT RM6: CARRY OUT PRIMARY ANALYSIS OF RECOVERED MATERIAL

Element 6.2: Perform Primary Analysis of Recovered Material

The Standard

Performance Criteria

a. Agreed tests and examinations are carried out safely and efficiently in a manner which enables the specified accuracy to be achieved.
b. Optimum relevant scientific information is derived from the tests and examinations performed.
c. Quality assurance requirements are maintained throughout the process.
d. Work procedures and practices are adapted as instructed to allow for different circumstances and conditions.
e. Results of tests and examinations are confirmed for accuracy, validity, and reliability.

f. Insufficient, inconclusive, and ambiguous data are identified, and relevant remedial actions are taken as agreed with the relevant personnel.

g. Continuity and integrity of items are maintained throughout the testing and examination process.

h. Information and data are recorded accurately, legibly, comprehensively, and contemporaneously onto appropriate documentation.

Range Statements

1. Circumstances and conditions: size of potential evidence, amount of potential evidence, condition of potential evidence, time constraints, priority

2. Information and data recording: written, sketches, photographic, diagrammatic

3. Quality assurance procedures: equipment calibration, peer checks, management checks, control samples, reference materials, avoidance of contamination, consideration of subsequent examinations and analyses

4. Health and safety considerations: item type, condition of item, personal safety, safety of others

5. Relevant personnel: case supervisor, line manager, other specialist

Evidence Requirements

The candidate should be able to demonstrate competence over a period of time across all the performance criteria and range statements. Competence is to be demonstrated in real work situations. Where opportunities for work-based assessments are not readily available, realistic simulations of the work activity may be used, although these should be set up and assessed in the normal working environment. The candidate should be able to explain the reasons for all his or her actions and cover "what if" scenarios. Candidates should also be able to answer oral or written questions covering items specified in the "Knowledge and Understanding" specification.

Knowledge and Understanding Specification

Principles, Methods, and Techniques Relating To …

- Health and safety considerations (a) (range 4)
- Carrying out tests and examinations to achieve specified accuracy (a)
- Obtaining optimum, relevant scientific information (b)
- Quality assurance requirements (c) (range 3)
- Adapting work procedures and practices to different circumstances and conditions (d) (range 1 and 3)
- Limitations of tests and examinations carried out (b, d, e, and f) (range 1 and 3)
- Identifying insufficient and inconclusive data (f) (range 1 and 3)
- Continuity and integrity of items (g and h) (range 2)
- Recording information and data (h) (range 2)
- Code of Ethics: the need for impartial judgments (a–h)

Information and Data About ...

- Types of tests and examinations (a, b, d, e, and f) (range 1)
- Types of scientific information (b, e, f, and h) (range 1)
- Quality assurance procedures (c) (range 3)
- Information and data to be recorded (g and h) (range 2)

Assessment Guidance

Competence will be demonstrated by a combination of observation in the work environment, oral questioning, and a review of the portfolio evidence produced by the candidate.

Appendix 3: Seventy-Eight Uses of Occupational Standards

RECRUITMENT AND SELECTION

1. Preparing recruitment specifications
2. Preparing job advertisements and details
3. A format for collecting information from referees
4. Identifying the required components of a current role or job
5. Identifying the required components of an anticipated or future role or job
6. An interview checklist for selectors
7. Advance information to job candidates and interviewees
8. Specifying induction and initial training

JOB DESIGN AND EVALUATION

9. Development of job and role specifications
10. Regular updating of job and role descriptions
11. Monitoring the pattern of job and role responsibilities in sections and organizations
12. Job design and redesign
13. Criteria for job evaluation
14. Criteria for the grading of staff
15. Criteria for payment and reward systems

ASSURANCE OF PRODUCT AND SERVICE DELIVERY

16. Quality specification for work processes and outcomes
17. Structuring and "loading" production systems
18. Monitoring of work processes
19. Guaranteeing customer service quality and standards by licensing job holders
20. Specification for contract tendering
21. Monitoring contract delivery and compliance
22. Evidence of competence for compliance with international standards (BS5750 and ISO9000)

LOCAL AND NATIONAL LABOR MARKET PLANNING

23. Analyzing and quantifying skill availability within local labor markets
24. Monitoring national and local skill supply shortages
25. Providing training and learning guarantees

IDENTIFYING INDIVIDUAL OR ORGANIZATIONAL TRAINING NEEDS

26. Specifying the skill or competence needs of an organization
27. Identifying individual learning needs
28. A format for individual action planning
29. Identifying group or organizational learning needs
30. Identifying previously acquired competence
31. Developing a strategic view of future learning requirements
32. Coordination of different Human Resource Development (HRD) processes

STRUCTURING LEARNING PROGRAMS

33. Linking training to business objectives
34. Linking training to national economic needs
35. Increasing the relevance and credibility of training and learning programs
36. Allowing new learners to see the "whole picture" in a simple and convenient format
37. Enabling learners to match the relevance of off-job training programs
38. Broadening the scope and relevance of traditional skills-based training
39. Identifying learning opportunities in the work environment
40. Coordination of on- and off-job provision
41. Development of learning contracts
42. Development of specific learning objectives
43. Development of knowledge content for learning programs
44. Specifying off-job content and learning processes
45. Specification of required outcomes and targets for external training providers
46. Monitoring external training providers
47. Evaluation and selection of learning resources against organizational requirements

DELIVERING AND EVALUATING LEARNING PROGRAMS

48. A format for structured learning in the work environment
49. Identifying progression routes for learners
50. Providing clear goals for learners
51. Highlighting opportunities for transfer between jobs or occupations
52. Evaluating individual and group training programs

CAREER GUIDANCE AND COUNSELING

53. A basis for information and advice for people entering a first career or job
54. A basis for information and advice for people changing to a new career or job
55. Assessing aptitude and potential for career or occupational areas
56. Identifying common and potentially transferable skills in different careers or occupations
57. Analysis of local and national career opportunities in outcome terms

ASSESSING ACHIEVEMENT

58. Identification of assessment opportunities
59. Specifying the methods and processes of assessment
60. A specification for formative assessment
61. A format for the collection of evidence for National Vocational Qualifications
62. A specification for summative assessment for public certification
63. A specification for internal assessment and appraisal
64. A format for joint review of learner progress
65. A format for individual review of progress and achievement
66. Criteria for the recording of achievement
67. A specification for self-assessment
68. A specification for peer or group assessment

DEVELOPMENT OF PUBLICLY FUNDED TRAINING PROGRAMS

69. Assessing requirements for national and local training provision
70. Assessing funding requirements for national training programs
71. Allocating funding for national training programs
72. Monitoring success of publicly funded programs
73. Providing coherence for national provision of qualifications
74. Development of formal assessment systems
75. Monitoring and assessing priorities for the development of new qualifications
76. Development of National and Scottish Vocational Qualifications (N/SVQs)
77. Updating of N/SVQs
78. Providing criteria for equivalence between national and international qualifications

Appendix 4: Professional Standards of Competence (National Occupational Standards in Forensic Science)

Science Technology and Mathematics Council

UNIT 1: PREPARE TO CARRY OUT EXAMINATIONS

Unit Summary

Unit 1 Prepare to carry out examinations

Prepare to carry out examinations This unit is about ensuring that adequate preparations are made prior to the examination of items and samples, originating from an incident that is subject to forensic investigation.

The unit divides into three distinct parts:

- Establishing the requirements of the case and the types of examinations that will meet them, and the development of an examination strategy
- Physical preparation of suitable equipment and work area(s) in order to maintain the integrity of the items and samples
- Initial inspection of the items and samples, and confirmation that the examination strategy is appropriate

The preparations that are made apply in all cases, irrespective of the environment in which the unit is conducted, for example at the scene of the incident or in a specialized environment such as a laboratory.

Scientific principles and practices must be adopted throughout this unit.

Health and safety of self and others and the preservation, integrity, and continuity of potential evidence are paramount throughout the unit.

This unit applies to any individual who prepares items and samples that will be subject to forensic examination. The individual may or may not go on to carry out the examinations him or herself.

The unit consists of three elements:

- 1.1. Determine case requirements
- 1.2. Establish the integrity of items and samples
- 1.3. Inspect items and samples submitted for examination

Performance Criteria

Element 1.1 Determine case requirements

You must ensure that you ...

1 Establish the circumstances of the incident, and consider these against exhibits received and examinations requested
2 Confirm that the items submitted are appropriate for the work to be undertaken
3 Establish the storage requirements of potential evidence, and make arrangements for safe, secure, and clean facilities
4 Agree and prioritize the sequence of the various aspects of work
5 Prepare equipment and work area(s) appropriate for the intended examinations
6 Identify and rectify nonconforming equipment
7 Record relevant information accurately, legibly, and comprehensively

Element 1.2 Establish the integrity of items and samples

You must ensure that you ...

1 Receive items safely and securely from storage facilities
2 Check items and samples against records, and identify any inaccuracies so that they can be rectified
3 Document details of storage, handling, transfer, and packaging of items and samples in a way which establishes continuity
4 Identify details of any packaging problems, and provide a resolution
5 Store and transfer items and samples in a way that avoids contamination, cross contamination, and loss of potential evidence

Element 1.3 Inspect items and samples submitted for examination

You must ensure that you ...

1 Safely remove items and samples from packaging in a manner that avoids contamination and cross contamination
2 Confirm the identity and identification of submitted items against documentation
3 Identify scientific evidence that can be derived from the items and samples
4 Select examination methods relevant to the items and samples submitted
5 Identify problems and potential problems, and consult others to resolve the matter
6 Identify and establish a sampling protocol for items to be examined
7 Maintain continuity of items throughout the inspection process
8 Record information accurately, comprehensively, and contemporaneously

---

Knowledge and Understanding

You need to know and understand ...

1   Why it is important to establish the details of the case, and how to do this
2   How to ensure that items and samples are safely and securely received
3   How to recognize relationships between the case and the items and samples received
4   Why it is important to assess the effect of potential evidence on other evidence types
5   How to select and prepare a range of equipment, consumables, and reagents that may be needed to locate, recover, and examine potential evidence
6   The extent and range of facilities available for examining items and samples
7   How to select the appropriate type of examination and work area
8   How to identify and rectify nonconforming equipment
9   The factors to consider when planning the storage and packaging of items and samples
10 How to store and transfer potential evidence, avoiding contamination, cross contamination, and loss of evidence

11   How to establish and maintain the integrity and continuity of potential evidence, and the importance of this
12   The legal requirements regarding the integrity and continuity of evidence, and the importance of satisfying them
13   What is meant by contamination and cross contamination, and how it can occur
14   How to identify and prevent contamination, cross contamination, and loss of evidence
15   How to avoid jeopardizing the integrity of potential evidence
16   Ways in which potential evidence may be lost, and how to avoid this
17   Why it is important to identify inaccuracies between items, samples, and records
18   The types of inaccuracies that might occur, and how to rectify them
19   The range, purpose, and limitations of different recovery methods
20   How to determine the most appropriate recovery and examination method(s) to suit different situations and different evidence types
21   The importance of identifying submitted items and samples
22   How to identify all relevant evidence types
23   How to sequence and prioritize the work, and the criteria to work to
24   How to assess the effect of examinations on other types of potential evidence
25   The principles of sampling
26   The problems which might occur when inspecting items and samples, and how to resolve them
27   The types of packaging problems that can occur and how to resolve them, including dealing with inappropriate labeling and packaging, inadequate seals, damaged packaging and seals, and contamination dangers
28   How to resolve problems associated with insufficient evidential material, inappropriate evidential material, additional evidence types, and contamination of evidential material
29   The type of advice to give clients, and how to provide advice
30   The importance of consultation
31   Who to clarify any discrepancies with concerning the items, samples, and records, and the importance of this
32   The roles and functions of the different organizations that may be involved in the forensic science process
33   What information is relevant, and how it should be recorded
34   Why it is important to record information in a format suitable for further use
35   How to identify the need for contemporaneous records and notes, and how to make them
36   What recording systems are available, and how to use them
37   Why it is important to record details of storage, handling, transfer, and packaging of items and samples

UNIT 2: EXAMINE ITEMS AND SAMPLES

Unit Summary

Unit 2 Examine items and samples

This unit is about identifying and recovering potential evidence from the items and samples submitted for examination.

The unit covers:

- Searching items and samples
- Recovering potential evidence, and its testing and comparison
- Recording the details of examinations and the collation of notes, including notes made by others

These activities may be carried out at the scene of the incident, in a specialized environment such as a laboratory, or at another suitable location. Scientific principles and practices must be adopted throughout this unit.

The methods used to recover and examine the scientific evidence will depend upon the type(s) of items and samples and the evidence type.

Health and safety of self and others and the preservation, integrity, and continuity of potential evidence are paramount throughout the unit.

This unit applies to any individual who examines items and samples that have been submitted for forensic examination.

The unit consists of five elements:

    2.1.   Monitor and maintain the integrity of items and samples
    2.2.   Identify and recover potential evidence
    2.3.   Determine examinations to be undertaken
    2.4.   Carry out examinations
    2.5.   Produce laboratory notes and records

Performance Criteria

Element 2.1 Monitor and maintain the integrity of items and samples

You must ensure that you ...

1 Handle items and samples in a way that prevents contamination, cross contamination, and loss of evidence
2 Uniquely label items and samples
3 Maintain the continuity of items and samples throughout the examination process
4 Record information accurately, comprehensively, and contemporaneously

Element 2.2 Identify and recover potential evidence

You must ensure that you ...

1 Carry out examinations in a sequence which ensures detection and optimum recovery of all types of potential evidence
2 Detect the existence of and identify the location of evidential material
3 Select and use recovery methods that optimize recovery
4 Identify any need for additional areas of expertise
5 Maintain the integrity and continuity of items, samples, and recovered material throughout the recovery process
6 Record relevant information accurately, comprehensively, and contemporaneously

Element 2.3 Determine examinations to be undertaken

You must ensure that you ...

1 Identify and select relevant examinations based on an accurate evaluation of the items and samples and the nature of the investigation
2 Plan and schedule examinations to enable reliable, fit-for-purpose results to be gathered
3 Seek expert advice in instances where additional specialist information is required relevant to the investigation
4 Record relevant information accurately, comprehensively, and contemporaneously

Element 2.4 Carry out examinations

You must ensure that you ...

1 Carry out relevant examinations safely and in a manner appropriate to the items and samples being examined
2 Adapt working procedures and practices appropriately to allow for different circumstances and conditions

3 Identify insufficient and inconclusive results, and take remedial action
4 Seek expert advice in instances where additional specialist information is required relevant to the examination
5 Record examination results and any adaptations to working procedures and practices accurately, comprehensively, and contemporaneously

Element 2.5 Produce examination notes and records

You must ensure that you ...

1 Make contemporaneous examination notes and records, ensuring they are fit for purpose, accurate, legible, clear, and unambiguous
2 Order notes and record information in a way that supports validation and interrogation
3 Uniquely classify records
4 File records securely in a manner which facilitates retrieval
5 Accurately collate examination notes on work carried out by others into the overall records

Knowledge and Understanding

You need to know and understand ...

1 The methods available to detect evidential material, and how to carry them out and achieve optimum recovery
2 The range, purpose, and limitations of different location and recovery methods
3 How to determine the most appropriate recovery method(s) to suit different situations and different evidence types
4 How to identify the location of evidential material
5 How the recovery methods selected optimize recovery, minimize loss, and avoid contamination
6 Why it is important to assess the effect of different location and recovery methods on different evidence types
7 The amount of time that each location and recovery method is likely to take
8 How to prepare yourself correctly to carry out the location, recovery, and examination of potential evidence
9 Current relevant health and safety legislation, and how it applies to your own work role
10 How to establish and maintain the integrity and continuity of potential evidence, and the importance of this
11 Why items and samples are uniquely identified
12 Ways in which potential evidential material may be lost, and how to avoid this
13 How to identify and prevent contamination and cross contamination
14 The range, purpose, and limitations of different examination methods
15 How to determine the most appropriate examination method to suit different situations and circumstances
16 The use and relevance of the examinations that are carried out
17 The operational and scientific factors to consider when determining the examinations to be undertaken
18 The criteria to work to in order to plan and schedule examinations
19 How to perform different examination methods effectively
20 The established scientific principles and practices to consider when carrying out different types of examinations
21 Why it is important to carry out the examinations in a particular sequence
22 Why it is important to assess the effect of different examination methods on different evidence types, and how to do this
23 The different circumstances and conditions you might be faced with when examining potential evidence
24 How to ensure that results are reliable and fit for purpose
25 How to recognize the limitations of your expertise and knowledge, and the importance of not exceeding these

26 The circumstances which might lead you to seek expert advice and/or additional expertise, and how to obtain this
27 How to recognize contamination, and the actions to take
28 How to adapt working practices and procedures to accommodate different circumstances such as size and condition of the potential evidence, location of the examination, time constraints, emergency, and risk of contamination
29 How to identify insufficient and inconclusive results from examinations, and how to rectify the problem
30 What recording systems are available, and how to use them
31 What information to record, and how it should be recorded
32 Why it is important to record information in a format suitable for further use
33 How to ensure that notes and records are fit for purpose, clear, and unambiguous
34 How to identify the need for contemporaneous records and notes, and how to make them
35 Who has the right of access to information held on record
36 How to keep records to protect the security of information
37 Who might wish to use the examination notes and records, and the ways in which they might be used
38 What the procedures and requirements are on the security and transmission of information
39 The classification systems used, and how they operate
40 How to collate and order notes and information, and the importance of this
41 How and where to record adaptations made to working practices and procedures, and why it is important to record these

UNIT 3: UNDERTAKE SPECIALIST SCENE EXAMINATIONS

Unit Summary

Unit 3 Undertake specialist scene examinations

This unit is about carrying out an in-depth scientific examination of a scene of incident.

The unit covers:

- Establishing the purpose and requirements of the scene examination
- The preparations required before the scene examination
- The scene examination

The purpose of a scene examination is to obtain information and to recover items and samples for subsequent examination in order to assist in determining what happened, the sequence in which it happened, and who might have been involved in the incident. This investigative phase will often be followed by an evaluation of the findings within the context of one or more hypotheses (Unit 4).

There is likely to be more than one organization represented at the scene, so good communication skills and collaborative approaches to work are therefore essential.

Locating, preserving, and gathering potential evidence are key skills within the unit. It is essential to take adequate precautions to prevent contamination and possible degradation of the evidence both at the scene and when submitting the evidence for forensic examination.

Health and safety of self and others and the preservation of potential evidence are paramount throughout the unit.

This unit applies to any individual who carries out forensic examination of a scene of incident.

The unit consists of three elements:

3.1. Establish the requirements of the investigation
3.2. Prepare to examine the scene of the incident
3.3. Examine the scene of the incident

Performance Criteria

Element 3.1 Establish the requirements of the investigation

You must ensure that you …

1 Ascertain the circumstances of the incident and the scene of the investigation from the relevant personnel and other sources
2 Determine the types of examinations to be carried out in accordance with the reported circumstances
3 Give due consideration to the possibility of linked scenes to ensure that relevant avenues of investigation are followed up
4 Determine the logistics of the operation, and resolve known problems with due regard to effectiveness, efficiency, and economy
5 Consider the safety of all personnel at the scene, and give advice to ensure relevant safety precautions are carried out
6 Identify equipment needed for the investigation, and make suitable arrangements to get it to the scene
7 Record relevant information accurately, comprehensively, and contemporaneously

Element 3.2 Prepare to examine the scene of the incident

You must ensure that you …

1 Establish effective working relationships with scene personnel in order to manage the scientific investigation of the scene
2 Assess, determine, and agree the types and sequence of necessary examinations with the relevant personnel in accordance with the circumstances of the incident
3 Identify the area of the scene, and delineate and protect it to preserve the scene
4 Agree and establish access to the scene, taking account of potential contamination and loss of evidence
5 Advise other personnel on the requirements for collecting data and recording notes
6 Record relevant information accurately, comprehensively, and contemporaneously

Element 3.3 Examine the scene of the incident

You must ensure that you …

1 Locate, identify, collect, and preserve potential evidential materials in a manner which ensures their integrity and reduces loss and degradation
2 Identify the need for additional areas of expertise and facilities, and employ and coordinate relevant personnel, where required
3 Collate preliminary investigations, and formulate initial hypotheses
4 Evaluate and interpret hypotheses, and undertake further action as necessary
5 Accurately report preliminary findings
6 Handle, package, seal, label, and record items in a way which prevents contamination and loss of evidence
7 Establish priority for the submission of items and samples to the laboratory
8 Make recommendations to relevant personnel to ensure that items and samples are securely packaged, stored, and transported
9 Record relevant information accurately, comprehensively, and contemporaneously

Knowledge and Understanding

You need to know and understand …

1 How to establish the details of the case, and the importance of this
2 The principles and methods involved in the investigative process
3 How to plan the logistics of the scene investigation

4   The use and relevance of the scientific investigative work that needs to be undertaken

5   How to determine the most appropriate examination methods to use

6   Why it is important to assess the effect of potential evidence on other evidence types

7   How to establish access to the scene

8   The information needed to plan the scientific investigative work

9   The operational and scientific factors to consider when planning the preservation, recovery, packaging, and transportation of items and samples

10 How to identify and preserve the scene(s) and the potential evidence

11 The extent and range of facilities and equipment available for preserving, recovering, and examining potential evidence

12 How to sequence and prioritize the scientific investigative work, and the criteria to work to

13 Why it is important to assess the effect of scientific investigative work of potential evidence on other evidence types

14 How to select, prepare, and use a range of equipment, consumables, and reagents that may be needed to preserve, recover, and examine potential evidence

15 How to apply dynamic assessment of risk at the scene(s) of incident

16 Current relevant health and safety legislation, and how it applies to your own work role

17 The types of safety precautions that may need to be taken to ensure the safety of all personnel at the scene

18 How to prepare yourself correctly to preserve and recover potential evidence and to carry out scientific investigative techniques

19 How to perform the scientific investigative work safely

20 The roles and functions of the different organizations and personnel that may be involved in investigating the scene(s) of incident

21 How your own role relates to that of others involved in the scene investigation

22 How to develop links and relationships with other personnel at the scene, and the protocols for doing this

23 The communication systems available, and how to make best use of them

24 The principles involved in giving advice on the interpretation of scene examination results

25 How to direct others to achieve common objectives

26 How to establish and maintain the integrity and continuity of potential evidence, and the importance of this

27 The legal requirements regarding the integrity and continuity of evidence, and the importance of satisfying them

28 How to avoid jeopardizing the integrity of potential evidence

29 How to identify contamination dangers, and how to avoid them

30 The established scientific principles and practices to consider when examining the scene(s)

31 How to determine the most appropriate recovery and examination method(s) to suit different situations and different evidence types

32 The operational and scientific factors to consider when performing different types of scientific investigative work

33 How to assess the effect of scientific investigations on other types of potential evidence

34 How to identify all relevant evidence types

35 How to preserve, recover, package, and transfer potential evidence, avoiding contamination, cross contamination, and loss of evidence

36 How to perform different preservation, recovery, and examination methods effectively

37 The amount of time which each preservation, recovery, and examination method is likely to take

38 How to establish valid and reliable information about the incident and to form an initial hypothesis

39 The information which would confirm or deny an initial hypothesis, and the reasons for this in particular cases

40 The importance of recognizing and taking account of any inconsistent information gained during the scene investigation

41 The principles and factors involved to process, evaluate, and interpret the results of the scene examinations

42 How to recognize and resolve problems during the scene investigation, including problems concerned with preservation of evidence, transportation, coordination with other scene personnel, welfare, time constraints, prevailing weather conditions, security, economics, safety, and risk of contamination

43 How to adapt working practices and procedures to accommodate different situations and circumstances and different evidence types

44 How to recognize the limitations of your expertise and knowledge, and the importance of not exceeding these

45 How to identify what information to record, and how it should be recorded

46 What recording systems are available, and how to use them

47 How to make contemporaneous records and notes, and the importance of this

48 Why it is important to record information in a format suitable for further use

49 The importance of and methods used to collate notes on work carried out, and the use to which the notes will be put

UNIT 4: INTERPRET FINDINGS

Unit Summary

Unit 4 Interpret findings

This unit is about summarizing and assessing the examinations, interpreting the results, and drawing conclusions prior to the preparation of a final report or statement.

The opinions drawn by the practitioner will be informed by databases, historical data, and/or personal experience. Rigorous quality assurance checks are of paramount importance throughout this unit.

The conclusions will address the case requirements as identified in Unit 1 and will do one of the following:

1. Provide support for a single hypothesis
2. Provide support for more than one hypothesis
3. Not support any particular hypothesis

This unit is relevant to any individual who is responsible for interpreting the findings of forensic examinations.

The unit consists of two elements:

4.1. Collate the results of the examinations
4.2. Interpret examination findings

Performance Criteria

Element 4.1 Collate the results of the examinations

You must ensure that you ...

1 Record and collate results accurately in a clear and unambiguous format
2 Complete an accurate evaluation of the examination results
3 Use sufficient results from specified examinations
4 Summarize results to meet the examination requirements
5 Present the results clearly in a structured format
6 Confirm that the evaluation, commentary, and support information is accurate and clearly presented

Element 4.2 Interpret examination findings

You must ensure that you …

1   Confirm that examination data are complete, comprehensive, and accurate
2   Base interpretations on the documented results and information provided about the incident
3   Consult relevant reliable sources of information at an appropriate time and in an appropriate way to assist the interpretation
4   Confirm results and data for accuracy, validity, and reliability
5   Draw opinions from the results and data clearly based on agreed criteria
6   Record relevant information accurately, comprehensively, and contemporaneously

Knowledge and Understanding

You need to know and understand …

1   The principles and factors involved in the examinations used
2   How to summarize results in relation to the examination requirements
3   How to collate and use results prepared by yourself and by others
4   The importance of and ways to establish the accuracy, validity, and reliability of examination methods
5   The range, purpose, and limitations of different methods available to present results
6   How to ensure that the presentation of results will meet the needs of the end user
7   How to ensure the accuracy of evaluation, commentary, and support information
8   How to present evaluation, commentary, and support information
9   The use and relevance of the different types of examinations
10 The scientific principles and practices on which interpretations are based
11 Why it is important to ensure the examination data are complete, comprehensive, and accurate
12 Why it is important to establish the accuracy, validity, and reliability of the examination results
13 The principles involved in processing, evaluating, and interpreting results
14 The criteria on which opinions are based, and how to record opinions
15 The sources of information available for consultation
16 How and when to access and consult sources of information
17 How the sources of information can be used to assist the interpretation
18 How to ensure that the sources of information are reliable, and the importance of reliability
19 What recording systems are available, and how to use them
20 What information is relevant, and when and how it should be recorded
21 Why it is important to record information in a format suitable for further use
22 How to identify the need for contemporaneous records and notes, and how to make them
23 How to keep records to protect the security of information
24 Who has the right of access to information held on record

UNIT 5: REPORT FINDINGS

Unit Summary

Unit 5 Report findings

This unit is about reporting the findings of the forensic examinations.

The unit covers:

- Production of reports on the examinations that have been carried out
- Participation in pretrial consultations, and presentation of oral evidence to courts and inquiries

Reports will be read by a wide range of individuals, most of whom will have little scientific knowledge. They will also be read aloud in courts of law. They must, therefore, be written as clearly and unambiguously as possible. In particular, care should be taken to ensure that the examinations conducted and the practices behind these examinations are described in language that ensures that they are understandable to nonscientists, such as a judge and jury.

Reports may provide factual information only. However, where an opinion is given, the report will:

- Outline the background to the incident, as understood by the practitioner
- Explain the requirement of the commissioning agency or customer
- Provide a description of the examinations conducted and their outcomes
- Make an assessment of the likelihood of the examination results given the hypotheses tested and the circumstances as understood by the practitioner

Pretrial consultation may be required in order to explain findings to the prosecution or defense barrister or solicitor. These consultations may occur well in advance of the trial or when the trial is underway. The practitioner will often be required to present the findings as an expert witness in court.

It is the responsibility of the practitioner to clearly explain the significance of the findings and to consider other hypotheses that may be proposed in pretrial consultations or when in court. The practitioner may also have to present evidence that has been established by others working under his or her instructions and supervision.

This unit is relevant to any individual who is responsible for reporting the findings of scientific examinations.

The unit consists of three elements:

5.1. Produce report
5.2. Participate in pretrial consultation
5.3. Present oral evidence to courts and inquiries

Performance Criteria

Element 5.1 Produce report

You must ensure that you ...

1 Establish the type, scope, and purpose of the report
2 Use information in the report which is current, relevant, and accurate
3 Report all results accurately, and clearly express the limitations of any tests used
4 Present a report that is logical, unbiased, accurate, and relevant and that meets the needs of the end user
5 Express conclusions and opinions within your area of expertise firmly based on the results and available information
6 Confirm that the report conforms to legal requirements and that you make appropriate reference to case notes and related materials
7 Submit the report for checking, and act upon any alternative explanations suggested in accordance with established scientific principles

Element 5.2 Participate in pretrial consultation

You must ensure that you ...

1 Provide advice based on established scientific principles which is balanced and realistic within the context of the case
2 Clearly explain your findings and their interpretation in the context of the case
3 Consider alternative explanations, test alternative hypotheses, and provide opinions
4 Identify, clarify, and summarize areas of agreement and disagreement
5 Seek feedback to determine whether those involved understand the outcomes of the consultations
6 Record relevant information accurately and comprehensively

Element 5.3 Present oral evidence to courts and inquiries

You must ensure that you ...

1 Conduct yourself in accordance with acceptable professional standards
2 Deliver your evidence in an audible and understandable manner
3 Give evidence consistent with the contents of the written report
4 Deal with questions truthfully, impartially, and flexibly in a language which is concise, unambiguous, and admissible
5 Identify and clarify any unclear questions before offering a response
6 Give explanations to specific questions in a manner that facilitates understanding by nonscientists
7 Consider and evaluate any additional information and alternative hypotheses presented to you, and express relevant opinions, taking into account the limitations on opinions which cannot be given without further examination and investigation
8 Clearly differentiate between fact and opinion
9 Express opinions within your area of expertise

Knowledge and Understanding

You need to know and understand ...

1 The different types, scopes, and purposes of reports
2 How to ensure that the information used is current, reliable, and accurate
3 How to structure the report and to present the results
4 Who the end users of reports are, and how they use the reports
5 Techniques to use to ensure that the report meets the needs of the end user(s)
6 The importance of expressing the limitations of any tests, examinations, and comparisons
7 How to use the results and other available information to support your opinions and conclusions
8 The use to which case notes and related materials are put, and how to reference them in the report
9 How to collate and use case notes
10 How to make balanced decisions and judgments
11 The established scientific principles and practices underpinning all conclusions and opinions
12 The importance of submitting the report for checking
13 The importance of investigating any alternative explanations offered, and the established scientific principles and practices involved
14 The legal requirements relating to scientific evidence, and the production and presentation of reports
15 The purpose of pretrial consultations
16 Court procedures, and the importance of following the procedures
17 Your role in the pretrial consultation
18 How to provide advice in pretrial consultations
19 The established scientific principles and practices involved in providing advice
20 How to ensure the advice you give is balanced and realistic
21 The ways available to explain your findings and to ensure that the explanation is clear
22 How to seek feedback to ensure that those involved understand the outcomes of the consultation
23 Your role in any court and inquiry procedures
24 How to address the different people involved in court and inquiry proceedings
25 The effect that your appearance and behavior can have on others
26 The importance of ensuring that evidence is consistent with the written report, statement, or other relevant document
27 How to present technical explanations to facilitate understanding by nonscientists
28 How to respond to questions
29 Why it is important to deal with questions using unambiguous language
30 How to clarify unclear questions before responding, and the importance of so doing
31 How to ensure that your evidence is audible and understandable
32 When and how to consider alternative hypotheses

33 How to test alternative hypotheses: when producing the report, suggested in pretrial consultation, or suggested in the court or inquiry proceedings

34 The established scientific principles and practices in responding to alternative explanations and hypotheses

35 The areas of disagreement that might arise, and how to handle them

36 The importance of clarifying areas of agreement and those of disagreement

37 How to recognize the limitations of your expertise and knowledge, and the importance of not exceeding these

38 How to assimilate differing opinions and propositions in order to formulate opinions within your area of expertise

39 How to identify what information to record, and how it should be recorded

40 The classification systems used, and how they operate

41 What recording systems are available, and how to use them

Appendix 5: Competency Assessment

Assess each case file against the criteria below.

Name of practitioner: _____

Reference: _____

Evidence types or area of work: _____

Criteria	Standard Met	Below Standard	No Evidence in File	Give Details of the Evidence Which Support Your Assessment Against the Criteria
1. The questions that the customer wants answered have been identified, and a suitable strategy has been devised to address them.				
2. The suitability of the items submitted to address the customer's questions has been assessed, and remedial action has been taken if necessary.				
3. The correct type of examination has been selected to address the case strategy and meet the customer requirements.				
4. The practitioner has carried out the various examinations satisfactorily and/or ensured that they have been carried out satisfactorily by others.				
5. The results of the examinations have been recorded appropriately and summarized where relevant.				
6. The results have been interpreted in accordance with established scientific principles using the CAI model.				

7.	The conclusions reached have been framed by consideration of at least two alternative hypotheses.			
8.	The report produced is based on the findings, is logical and easy to read, and answers the customer's questions.			
9.	The documentation contained in the file is fit for purpose.			

Assessor name: _____

Signature: _____

Date: _____

Appendix 6:
Functional Map

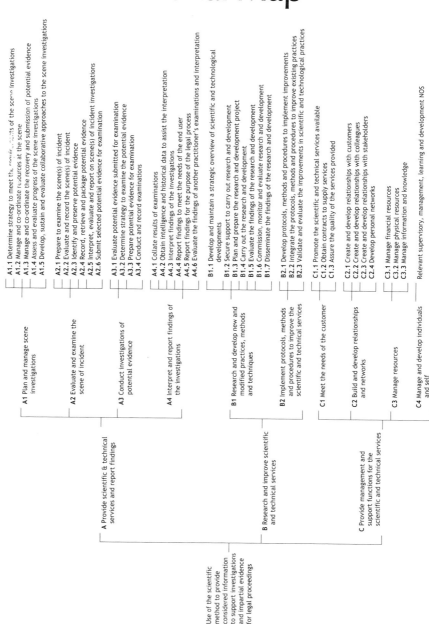

Use of the scientific method to provide considered information to support investigations and impartial evidence for legal proceedings

A Provide scientific & technical services and report findings

A1 Plan and manage scene investigations
- A1.1 Determine strategy to meet the requirements of the scene investigations
- A1.2 Manage and co-ordinate resources at the scene
- A1.3 Manage and co-ordinate the recovery and submission of potential evidence
- A1.4 Assess and evaluate progress of the scene investigations
- A1.5 Develop, sustain and evaluate collaborative approaches to the scene investigations

A2 Evaluate and examine the scene of incident
- A2.1 Prepare to examine the scene(s) of incident
- A2.2 Evaluate and record the scene(s) of incident
- A2.3 Identify and preserve potential evidence
- A2.4 Record, retrieve and package potential evidence
- A2.5 Interpret, evaluate and report on scene(s) of incident investigations
- A2.6 Submit selected potential evidence for examination

A3 Conduct investigations of potential evidence
- A3.1 Evaluate potential evidence submitted for examination
- A3.2 Determine strategy to examine the potential evidence
- A3.3 Prepare potential evidence for examination
- A3.4 Conduct and record examinations

A4 Interpret and report findings of the investigations
- A4.1 Collate results of examinations
- A4.2 Obtain intelligence and historical data to assist the interpretation
- A4.3 Interpret findings of the investigations
- A4.4 Report findings to meet the needs of the end user
- A4.5 Report findings for the purpose of the legal process
- A4.6 Evaluate the findings of another practitioner's examinations and interpretation

B Research and improve scientific and technical services

B1 Research and develop new and modified practices, methods and techniques
- B1.1 Develop and maintain a strategic overview of scientific and technological developments
- B1.2 Secure support to carry out research and development
- B1.3 Plan and prepare the research and development project
- B1.4 Carry out the research and development
- B1.5 Evaluate the findings of the research and development
- B1.6 Commission, monitor and evaluate research and development
- B1.7 Disseminate the findings of the research and development

B2 Implement protocols, methods and procedures to improve the scientific and technical services
- B2.1 Develop protocols, methods and procedures to implement improvements
- B2.2 Integrate the protocols, methods and procedures to improve existing practices
- B2.3 Validate and evaluate the improvements in scientific and technological practices

C Provide management and support functions for the scientific and technical services

C1 Meet the needs of the customer
- C1.1 Promote the scientific and technical services available
- C1.2 Obtain contracts to supply services
- C1.3 Assure the quality of the services provided

C2 Build and develop relationships and networks
- C2.1 Create and develop relationships with customers
- C2.2 Create and develop relationships with colleagues
- C2.3 Create and develop relationships with stakeholders
- C2.4 Develop personal networks

C3 Manage resources
- C3.1 Manage financial resources
- C3.2 Manage physical resources
- C3.3 Manage information and knowledge

C4 Manage and develop individuals and self
- Relevant supervisory, management, learning and development NOS

231

Index